PROPHECIES
AND
PROVIDENCE

✍ A Biblical Approach to Modern Jewish History

RABBI YEHOSHUA PFEFFER

DEVORA
PUBLISHING
NEW YORK ◆ JERUSALEM ◆ LONDON

Prophecies and Providence:
A Biblical Approach to Modern Jewish History
by Yehoshua Pfeffer

Copyright © 2015 by Yehoshua Pfeffer

Typeset by Ariel Walden

Printed in USA

First Edition

ISBN 978-1-934440-59-9

Devora Publications

Urim Publications
P.O. Box 52287, Jerusalem 91521 Israel

www.UrimPublications.com

*T*o the memory of my Grandmother MYRIAM bat Sarah,
whose life personified the chapters of this book.

In cherished memory of

Mr. MENACHEM YITZCHAK
(Manny) ORLINSKY

A true man of spirit

whose nobility and righteousness
live on after him

ת·נ·צ·ב·ה

BS"D

I have seen a copy of the outstanding book, *Prophecies and Providence*, which is authored by my dear, close and beloved disciple, Rabbi YEHOSHUA PFEFFER, *shlita*. RABBI PFEFFER is among the most prominent members of our *beis midrash*, and he has already written an excellent book that elucidates the subject of legal documents in Torah law.

Now his heart has moved him to turn his attention to the words of the prophets, and to show the manner in which their words have been fulfilled over the generations. The book is most outstanding, and there is a great need for it today, in demonstrating the truth of prophecy, and illustrating the constant providence of GOD over His world.

My blessing to my dear and beloved RABBI YEHOSHUA is that he should have the merit of magnifying and aggrandizing the Torah, and that the NAME OF HEAVEN should be sanctified though his work.

With great and deep love,

ASHER WEISS
Shevat 5769

Approbation of Rabbi Dovid Castle,
formerly Rosh Yeshiva of Yeshivat Itri, Jerusalem,
and author of *To Live Among Friends*
among many works

BS"D

Studying Jewish history is a unique endeavor, unlike studying the history of any other nation. It is not enough to collect accurate and voluminous data, to analyze events through the prism of multiple disciplines such as sociology, psychology, economics, anthropology or geography. As important as such information and analyses are in the context of the history of other nations, Jewish history cannot be understood on this basis. A fleeting glance is sufficient to reveal that Jewish history defies the laws and patterns of world history; yet historians and other scholars have still not internalized this basic and obvious truth.

The key to understanding Jewish history, as it is to all else, is Torah. Only when viewed through the lens of Torah, does Jewish history begin to offer up its true lessons. In his groundbreaking book *Prophecies and Providence*, RABBI PFEFFER begins to turn the key of Torah that can unlock the deeper meaning and significance in the events and experiences of the Jewish people over time. By approaching even modern Jewish history from a Torah perspective, RABBI PFEFFER is taking an important step into an area that has largely been neglected.

Like Torah study of any kind, opinions may differ. The reader may not agree with some of RABBI PFEFFER's interpretations or may wish to bring other sources to bear on the issues discussed. That is a legitimate and, for a work of this kind, welcome level of

[Note: The approbation was given to an earlier version of the work, which included two chapters on the Holocaust. These chapters have been omitted from the book.]

engagement. What's important is that it is understood that it is Torah, and only Torah, that will ultimately help us decipher the meaning of the events in Jewish history, past and present.

By venturing into such uncharted territory and offering Torah insights on even some of the most difficult chapters in our history, RABBI PFEFFER opens new avenues to understanding. Hopefully, this work will awaken the hearts of other Torah scholars to do the same. Only in this way will we be able to extract the true and deep teachings of our history and use them in furtherance of the purpose for which we, as a people, are here.

That GOD wants us to look to Jewish history as part of our holy service to Him is apparent in the fact that *Divrei HaYamim*, which for the most part recounts Jewish history, is one of the *sefarim* of *Tanach* – an integral part of Scripture. The sealing of *Tanach* with the end of the era of prophecy was not the end of HASHEM's communication with His People. There is an ongoing dialogue between HASHEM and the Jewish People which has never been, and will never be, even momentarily interrupted. Our experiences, as a nation and as individuals, are the medium of communication through which this dialogue occurs. It is therefore imperative that we think seriously about events, try our best to honestly interpret the messages from HASHEM hidden within them, and make every effort to learn the lessons we can extract from them.

May this work serve to create more awareness of HASHEM and the ways in which He is in ongoing communication with us, so that we may better fulfill His will, and merit full redemption with the coming of MASHIACH soon in our days.

Rabbi DOVID CASTLE
Nissan 5769

ISRAEL MEIR LAU
CHIEF RABBI
TEL-AVIV-JAFFA, ISRAEL

ישראל מאיר לאו
הרב הראשי
תל-אביב-יפו, ישראל

בס"ד, ב' סיון תשס"ט
25 מאי 2009

מכתב ברכה

הראני הרה"ג יקר יקרים רבי יהושע פפר שליט"א, עלים מספרו בשפה האנגלית בשם "נבואות והשגחה", אשר מטרתו להוכיח שכל דברי הנביאים אמת וצדק ודבר אחד מדבריהם אחור לא שב ריקם.

אין עתותי בידי לעבור על הספר, בשגם הוא בשפה האנגלית, אולם על המחבר ותורתו שמעתי גדולות ונצורות. עוד מצעירותו היה מבחירי הלומדים בישיבות הקדושות וראה ברכה מרובה בתלמודו.

לפני מספר שנים יצא לאור ספרו הראשון, ספר עיוני ויסודי בשם "בנין השטר", בו הראה רוב גבורתיה וחיליה באורייתא, אשר הללוהו ושבחוהו רבותיו גדולי התורה, כל זאת בצניעות ובאצילות נפש כיאה לבן עליה.

עתה חשקה נפשו להוכיח באותות ובמופתים אמיתות תורתנו הקדושה ודברי הנביאים, אשר המאורעות כולם, מבראשית ועד ימינו אנו, כולם רמוזים בדבריהם, וכיצד הבורא ברחמיו, מסובב כל הסיבות, משגיח על בניו, כנשר יעיר קנו על גוזליו ירחף. ניכר בין דפי הספר עמלו הרב של המחבר לאסוף את הדברים מספרי הנביאים, מדברי חז"ל ומבחינה היסטורית מדעית, להעמיד דברים על דיוקם, ולסדרם על מכונם, בסדר מופתי, דבר דבור על אופנו.

חזקה על איש טהור, אשר כל מעשיו לשם שמים, שלא תצא תקלה תחת ידו, דבריו יעשו פרי, ישפיעו וישעו רושם על לבבות הקוראים.

הנני לברך את המחבר החשוב שיראה ברכה בעמלו ויעזרהו ה' להגביר חילים לאורייתא מתוך מנוחת הנפש והרחבת הדעת וכל מילי דמיטב.

ביקרא דאורייתא,

הרב ישראל מאיר לאו

CONTENTS

ACKNOWLEDGMENTS

In a book whose primary focus is the Divine direction of world history, it is fitting that the Director be given the first and paramount acknowledgment. Through a vastly intricate maze of pathways, only a fraction of which are listed below, I found myself inspired to write this book, and able to achieve the final product placed before the reader. Contemplating the myriad elements of my own life, I bow my head in awe before the Master Craftsman, Who put them together and thereby made this book possible.

A prominent source of inspiration for this manuscript was a Hebrew book titled, *That Which is Coming Let Them Tell: Prophecies and their Fulfillment* (Jerusalem 2002), written by my close friend and colleague, Rabbi Shlomo Kushlevsky. Notwithstanding major differences in both style and content, Rabbi Kushlevsky's book, which dedicates several chapters to demonstrate the fulfillment of ancient prophecies in contemporary history, was instrumental not only as a source of inspiration, but also as a continual source of reference.

During the course of writing this book, my principal source of feedback has been my original editor and friend, Levi Bookin. It is perhaps by virtue of his working on a predominantly voluntary basis that I have merited the full scope of his critique, which has proven to be crucial in preparing the finished product. His broad knowledge of both European history and the Bible has also contributed much to the content of the book.

I must thank the Urim Publishing team, which has been a pleasure to work with, and in particular Sara Rosenbaum, whose meticulous editing was of the highest quality. Although he didn't ultimately publish the book, I should also thank Mr. Yaacov Peterseil for his keen interest in it, and for urging me toward publication.

At this opportunity, I would like to thank all those whose support and encouragement – in both financial and moral senses – enabled this work to come into being. Rabbi Asher Weiss, under whose auspices I continue to study the intricacies of Jewish monetary law, is a continual source of inspiration in all areas of Torah study and of life in general. Beyond his unique genius and erudition, his intellectual honesty and moral clarity have had a major impact on my own life.

My parents, who selflessly sacrificed so much for the sake of their children, have never ceased to extend us their gracious support, in all senses of the word. I sincerely hope that the constant search for truth that so characterized the upbringing I received has filtered through into the content of this book. My unbounded gratitude and love is the least I can return.

My parents-in-law, Rabbi Reuven and Mrs. Naomi Leuchter, have served as an ever-present beacon of light since the day of my wedding. The wisdom of my father-in-law is unique in more ways than one; his ability to assess the individual requirements of each disciple, guiding and teaching him on a fully personal level, is uncanny. I feel fortunate to have a place among this privileged group.

The spirit of the book is the spirit of my grandmother, Mrs. Myriam Pfeffer, who passed away on the eve of publication. Having encountered death in the Nazi camps and their aftermath, she found the inner strength to become the epitome of life, going on to enrich and enhance the lives of thousands of students – not least my own. Her perennial thirst for human depth and personal growth set a standard for the entire family, and for many others besides. The spirit she showed is the quintessential spirit of the Jewish People: a spirit that was cruelly battered for centuries, but which never died. My grandmother's generosity knew no bounds, and her desire to give played a significant role in my own personal growth. This book is dedicated to her memory.

In addition to the above, I would like to express my gratitude to all those who took the time to read the manuscript of this book, and to offer valuable comments and criticisms. These include my father and father-in-law; my brother, Nachum; Mrs. Shoshana Lesser; Dr. and Mrs. Reuven Packer; my close and cherished friends Osher Levene and Ranon Cortell; Rabbi Berel Wein; Prof. Yosef Mendelssohn; and Alex Porat. I owe a special debt of gratitude to Rabbi Dovid Castle, whose helpful comments and wise counsel were indispensable.

Finally, I must mention my wife – or as the sages prefer, my "home." Though my own roots were planted and nurtured by the labors of my antecedents, their final fruit, including this book and any other achievement that I have attained, are hers; without her, the tree would be barren. Hers is the warm light that accompanies a ship as she sets sail, secure in the knowledge of a welcoming shore. "Mine, and yours, are hers."

To all the above, and to the many individuals who remain unnamed, including friends, mentors and disciples to whom I owe much: Thank you.

PREFACE

It is inevitable that some readers will pick up this book and question the ideological background from which it emerged. Is the book a Zionist publication? Is it anti-Zionist?

I beg them to leave their questions aside. This book is essentially an apolitical work, and it has no inherent connection whatsoever with Zionism as a political movement. Although they may be mentioned in passing, the claims of both religious and secular factions against the Zionist movement, as well as the counterclaims of Zionist legitimacy, will not be treated.[1]

Instead, this book embraces a far broader outlook than the particular debate over the worthiness or otherwise of Zionism. The virulent brand of anti-Semitism recently embraced by Arab states, for instance, is not analyzed as a Zionist issue (is it primarily attributable to Zionist aggression, as some would have it, or not?) but, rather, as historical fact laden with theological meaning.

Because the intention is not to pass judgment or formulate political opinion, our study will not dwell on the actions of men and their motivations. Rather, it will engage specifically the *consequences* of these actions. Its aim is the placement of resultant Jewish history, a history as

---

1. See, however, Appendix D, where we have given a brief overview of the subject of the Three Oaths, one of the major religious issues confronting political Zionism.

contemporary today as it was sixty years ago, in a context of prophecy and providence.

Political Zionism came, and conquered; it no longer enjoys the popularity it once commanded, and time will tell what the future holds. Its achievements, however, of establishing a "Jewish State" in the Land of Israel and populating it with millions of Jews, are fundamentally distinct from its own existence as a political force. Whatever one's leanings concerning Zionism, the historical facts deserve serious consideration.[2]

In this connection, it is worth noting at the outset that the fulfillment of prophecies in the wake of the Zionist enterprise by no means implies the conferral of an elevated status on the State of Israel. The question of whether the State is the "pedestal of God's throne in this world," as Rabbi Avraham Yitzchak Kook (at least according to his son's interpretation) might have it, or a satanic manifestation as Rabbi Yoel Teitelbaum saw it, is not decided by the prophecy issue. The involvement of prophecy might make Rabbi Teitelbaum's position less tenable,[3] but it certainly falls short of bestowing the title of "Holy" on the Jewish State.

This matter will be discussed in greater detail in chapter six of this book.

*

Traditional Judaism (according to the great majority of its illustrious representatives) sees the attribution of the course of history to the hand of God as axiomatic.

With respect to Jewish history, the matter is deeper still. On its most superficial level, Scripture itself is a presentation of Jewish history

---

2. Even Rabbi Yoel Teitelbaum, who considered Zionism a direct manifestation of satanic forces, related its achievements to Divine providence. "We must thank and praise God for His great kindness of having mercy on our remnant, and saving our brothers in the Land of Israel from incarceration and the sword," he wrote. "But how much must we weep and cry over how our sins caused the salvation to come by such means" (*Al Hageulah ve'al Hatemurah*, section 42).

3. Rabbi Teitelbaum, clearly aware of this matter, sought to dismiss claims of prophetic fulfillment in the Zionist return and the establishment of the Jewish State.

– more specifically, Jewish history in the context of a relationship with God – from its first beginnings in the lives of the Patriarchs, and through to the Destruction of the Temple and the exile of the Jewish People. Shortly following the Destruction, prophecy was discontinued, and the history of the Jews was no longer committed to Holy Writ; nonetheless, Jewish history has not lost its elevated status. It remains a living embodiment of the word of God.[4]

Bereft of ongoing prophetic revelation, the reading of the Divine word latent in the course of history was drastically changed. Rather than the particular revelations of prophecy, this reading has for the most part been limited to a general faith in continual Divine guidance, with little insight into individual details.

Inspired by the colossal events of recent times, this volume makes a small attempt at concretization. Deprived still of new prophecies, it begs to find the meaning of ancient ones.

*

---

4. This concept emerges from a comment made by Rabbi Chaim Yosef David Azulai (*Chida, Kisei Rachamim*, Chap. 6).

Commenting on the Torah section of "When the Ark traveled" (Numbers, 10:35–36), which the Talmud considers (according to one opinion) as an entire book of Torah (see *Shabbat* 115b–116a), *Chida* cryptically states (citing from kabbalistic authorities) that although the smallest 'book of Torah' is, indeed, a 'small book,' it is one day destined to become a 'great volume.'

The journeying of the Ark with the Jewish People, which is the subject of the two verses in the aforementioned section of Torah, represents the identification of Jewish history (the journeys of the Jewish People) with Torah itself. Ultimately, the 'small book' that states the general principle will become a great volume, as the details of Jewish history and its dynamic relationship with God will be revealed.

A midrashic source suggests a similar idea. After mentioning the acts of several righteous individuals that were recorded in Scripture, the Midrash concludes by citing from Rabbi Levi: "In the past, a person would perform a mitzvah, and the prophet would record it. Today, who records a person's mitzvah? Eliyahu and the Messiah King write it, and Ha-Kadosh Baruch Hu signs upon it." Even after the annals of Israel are no longer written in Scripture, the record goes on.

I am indebted to my rabbi and mentor, Rabbi Moshe Shapira, for the first source, and to Avital Hazony for the second.

Without doubt, the meaning of Biblical prophecy is a matter of interpretation. There is virtually no text worthy of the name that can be understood without a degree of interpretation – the more so for ancient texts whose meaning is obscured by the tides of time. It is not my place to offer independent interpretations of Scripture, and I have relied exclusively on traditional commentaries and interpretations, sometimes mentioning more than one possibility where commentators differ over the textual meaning.

In this context, I should note the professedly non-academic nature of this volume. The work does not seek to describe how different thinkers approached the relevant issues, and certainly not to reveal the considerations and range of influences that caused them to adopt the positions they did, or to explain their choices of sources and style of interpretation. Though aware of other versions, this volume is concerned more with the Truth with a capital "T" than with a small one.

Because the work means to present a single worldview and endeavors to anchor it in prophecy, I have included little or no critical discussion of traditional positions and interpretations, and have not presented conflicting views beyond the scope of this work's *Weltanschauung*. At the very most, such views have been given passing mention in notes.[5]

Just as the work is non-academic, it is equally non-messianic. Although the concept of the future Messiah and Messianic Era are discussed within the theological structure of prophecy, and a significant section is even dedicated to the future war of Gog and Magog, the framework is not messianic or apocalyptic. The intention of the book is to demonstrate Divine guidance over history in the past, present, and future – and not to herald the coming of the Messiah, World War III, or some other event. I have tried to resist the urge to make apocalypse-like predictions pertaining to the near future, so many of which have failed (and continue to fail) the test of history; though I paint a fantastic

---

5. For instance, I have generally not mentioned the often radical opinions of Yeshayahu Leibowitz, and those of other thinkers that might dispute the very foundations on which this book is based. Though it might make for interesting reading, the profound debate that such deeply conflicting opinions can raise is not the focus of the present work, and the inclusion thereof would threaten its basic purpose.

picture, I have attempted to avoid the use of lurid colors. I hope I have succeeded in these endeavors.

In a similar vein, because of their special nature and place in rabbinic literature, I have not generally relied on works of Kabbalah. Although some works of Kabbalah include extensive material concerning the End-time, I have mentioned such sources only sporadically. Where they are mentioned, I have tried to ensure that other, classical sources are also given to back up the relevant argument.

*

Daniel is told to seal his messianic vision, "until the time of the End."[6] Malbim explains that the revelations of the End are not limited to the Messiah himself, who is destined to reveal the innermost secrets of Torah. Even as the End draws closer, the light of revelation will gradually shine brighter, radiating a glow of knowledge that was hitherto concealed. Malbim's idea is explicitly stated by the *Zohar*: "When the time of the Messiah is near, most of the people will know the End [*ketz*]."[7]

As of today, "most of the people" *do not* know the End, and taking the *Zohar*'s words at face value, we can deduce that the End *is not near*. Yet, it does draw closer, and we cannot know which revelations are included in the definition of Malbim, and which are not. A clear precondition for qualification, of course, is that they should involve some measure of Divine providence – for otherwise they would not be revelations at all.

It is in this direction – in reading historical events as revelations of Divine providence – that this book begs to make a small contribution.

Jerusalem

Sivan 5772 / June 2012

---

6. Daniel 12:4.
7. *Tikunei Zohar, tikun* 21.

INTRODUCTION

PROPHECIES AND PUZZLES

Most of the work ahead revolves around Biblical prophecies, extrapolated within the context of modern history. Before embarking on this historical-textual investigation, it is of value to introduce the essential criteria for defining true prophecy, and the general purposes for which prophecy – specifically, prophecy related to future events (in contrast to words of rebuke concerning the present) – was delivered by the prophets and recorded in Scripture.

Toward this goal, it is important to make a clear distinction between *prophecy*, which gives voice to the word of God, and *divination*, which employs mystical methods to predict the future.

In modern times, the practice of divination or soothsaying has been largely devalued; although they continue to exist, the Western world in particular is generally unprepared to place faith the supernatural. On the whole, the entire occupation with such matters is seen as mumbo jumbo. However, in pre-enlightenment times, the reading of palms and the like was not only commonplace, but enjoyed broad legitimacy as a kind of scientific method. If today we consider it normal to go to an investment analyst before investing our money in a financial scheme, in the past it would have been no less normal to attend a future-teller of one form or another.

The distinction between prophecy and divination will also serve to clarify the purpose of this book (as set out in the Preface), and introduce the themes I wish to highlight.

PROPHECY AND DIVINATION — PERFECT SCORES?

Maimonides, who remains the most renowned Jewish luminary since Moses,[1] clearly codified the essential difference between prophecy and divination:[2]

Yet surely the diviners and the sorcerers tell what will come in the future. What difference, then, is there between them and the prophet? But the words of diviners, sorcerers, and others of like kind, are partially fulfilled, and partially unfulfilled . . . and sometimes nothing of what they predict comes true, as the verse says, "frustrates the omens of the stargazers, and makes fools of the astrologers."[3] But the [true] prophet – all of his words are fulfilled, as it is written, "for nothing of the word of God shall fall to the earth."[4] And so it says, "The prophet that has a dream, let him tell a dream; and he that has My word, let him speak My word faithfully. 'What has the straw to do with the wheat?' says the Lord."[5]

True prophecy is indicated by results. The crown of prophecy can only be awarded to an individual whose prediction of future events is invariably correct. Whereas sorcerers, astrologers, and those who read the future in tea leaves and palms are essentially fallible, the word of God is forever true. God Himself lays down the challenge to match Him: "And who, as I, can proclaim – let him declare it. . . . And the things that are coming and that shall come to pass, let them declare."[6] In the mind and

---

1. Playing on a Biblical verse, admirers of Maimonides coined the epigram, "From Moses unto Moses, nobody like Moses has arisen" (Maimonides's name was also Moses).
2. *Laws of the Fundamentals of Torah*, Chap. 10.
3. Isaiah 44:25.
4. II Kings 10:10.
5. Jeremiah 23:28.
6. Isaiah 44:7.

word of mortal man, there is a guaranteed element of impurity; in the wheat of the word of God, there is no place for straw.

THE PURPOSE OF (FUTURE) PROPHECY

This fundamental difference is closely related to a further distinction between Divine prophecy and mere soothsaying: a difference of purpose.

Excepting such writers as Nostradamus, whose works borrowed much from Biblical sources (in conjunction with contemporary astrology), the conventional purpose of divination is personal gain. For instance, an investor may consult his astrologer for predictions of market trends, or a gambler may do so concerning the outcome of an impending event. Similarly, various types of diviners and seers are consulted about personal issues such as marital partnerships, children, success at work, and so on. The common denominator between these and similar issues, individual or national, is self-interest. Foretelling the future, if we assume a measure of success, is a useful tool to advance a human cause – whatever that cause may be. Few are the diviners and clairvoyants who devoted their energies to spiritual and non-material matters.

Because the purpose of non-prophetical prediction is generally limited to the worldly needs and functions of humanity, or those of particular sectors and individuals, it follows that a perfect score is not an absolute necessity. Even a sixty- or seventy-percent success rate would be sufficient to keep a fortune teller in business, for clients will overlook the thirty-percent failure rate for the net gain of success (which is how we hope investment analysts make their money). Moreover, even if the prediction of the diviner is not sufficiently conclusive to decide the action in question, it can nevertheless provide guidance – a worthy factor in weighing up the final course of action.[7]

---

7. Despite the fact that divination is not always reliable, it may still have a profound psychological effect on the client. The reliance of such hard-faced men as the Nazis on astrology, for instance, was remarkable. While Berlin was crashing about their ears, those in the Fuehrer-bunker were deriving comfort from the horoscopes of Hitler and Germany to convince themselves that salvation was at

The purpose of Biblical or Divine prophecy, however, is quite different. We do, occasionally, find prophetic revelations granted for personal purposes, such as Saul's search for his father's mules, when he turned to the prophet Samuel for Divine assistance.[8] Similarly, whenever David, Solomon, or subsequent kings of Judah contemplated a weighty decision (such as going to war), they would consult a seer or prophet, in order to obtain Divine guidance as to the correct course of action. In the absence of a full prophetic revelation, they would ask the High Priest to procure heavenly advice by consulting with the *urim vetumim*.[9]

Yet, the function of Divine prophecy, in contrast to the various forms of worldly soothsaying and divination, is profoundly deeper than aiding the narrow concerns of worldly life. In particular, prophecies that were delivered by God for recording in Scripture, which are of greater universal import than "personal prophecies," are clearly intended for some higher purpose. The famed medieval Biblical commentator Rabbi Don Isaac Abarbanel[10] suggested three such fundamental purposes of

---

hand. Ironically enough, President Roosevelt died at this stage – not that this made any practical difference to the war's outcome.

8. I Samuel 9:6.

9. The *urim vetumim* was a prophetic "device" by which Israel could consult with God before making crucial decisions, such as whether to go to war or not. See commentary of Malbim to the Book of Judges, 1:1.

10. 1437 (Lisbon)–1509 (Venice); Abarbanel (or Abarvanel, or Abravanel) was one of the few Biblical commentators whose teachings were revered by both Jewish and Christian scholars. Thanks to the overall excellence and exhaustiveness of his exegetical literature, and because he wrote lengthily regarding Messianic prophecies of Scripture, he was looked upon as a beacon for later Christian scholarship, which often included the tasks of translating and condensing his works. Although he generally rejected their Christological interpretations, he was clearly well versed in Christian exegesis and exegetes, and was unafraid to quote them when he felt them correct.

A leading scholar and politician of his time, he was appointed treasurer by several European kings, and used his social position to make penetrating comparisons between the social structure of society in Biblical times and that of the European society in his day (see, for instance, I Samuel 8, regarding the institution of the monarchy). As a historical scholar, Abarbanel was also able to contemporize the lessons of the historical eras described in Scripture, applying them successfully in his explanations of modern Jewish living. He was unflagging in his commitment

scriptural prophecies:[11]

- To teach us the truth of prophecy: To show that the Creator foresees events before they happen, and that He communicates His infinite knowledge to mankind through His faithful prophets.
- To convey to the individual, the nation, or the nations, advice and rebuke through the teachings of the prophets. Those who heed the warnings and instructions of the prophet – the word of God – will succeed and prosper. Those who do not will suffer dire consequences.
- To instill within mankind hope for the future, through belief in God's ultimate reward and His forthcoming salvation.

To a certain extent, the purposes suggested by Abarbanel can be demonstrated by verses in Scripture. Our current work, however, explores a fourth purpose of prophecy – one that Abarbanel may have intended to include in the first reason he proposed, yet of which he made no explicit mention.

THE SOURCE OF HISTORY

By means of prophecies that are borne out as history unfolds, Scripture serves to establish the fundamental principle of *Divine guidance over creation*. If the experience that man undergoes has been prophesied in advance, it is a sure indication that the events in question are not matters of chance and coincidence, but rather an integral part of a Divine plan – a link in the historical chain that leads the world from the advent of its creation to its final destiny.

Elsewhere,[12] Abarbanel does refer to this concept as being central to prophecy:

You have already learned . . . that God will not do anything without first revealing His secret to His servants the prophets, in order that men, both

---

toward using Scripture as a means of elucidating the status quo of his surrounding Jewish community, and was something of a pioneer in his method of historical, social, and political analysis, which he gracefully combined with classical literary method.

11. *Introduction to the Twelve* (Minor Prophets).
12. Commentary to Daniel (*Wellsprings of Redemption*) 9:2.

simple and elevated, should know that the things are guided by Him, and do not fall by chance.

Moreover, we find that Isaiah invokes this theme in the clearest of terms: "Who has wrought and done it? He called the generations from the beginning. I, the Lord, am the first, and with the last I am the same." (Isaiah 41:4). The verse implores us to realize that God, and no other, has wrought the events that take place before our eyes.

Faced with the tumultuous events of real life, political analysts and historians will seek to explain the motives of kings, presidents, and governors; psychologists will point at social trends and shifts in public opinion and reason; and philosophers will uncover underlying patterns of thought. The opinions of the experts may, of course, be quite correct. Yet prophecy reveals that there is a deeper factor, a causative layer unseen by human eyes. Behind the scenes lies a hidden hand that guides the world according to a Divine agenda.[13]

The following words, also from Isaiah, affirm the deep significance of this theme of prophecy. God Himself declares the purpose of prophetic revelation:

I have declared the former things from of old; from My mouth they have come forth, and I announced them. Suddenly, I did them, and they came about. Because I knew that you are obstinate, and your neck is an iron sinew and your brow brass – therefore I have declared it to you from of old. Before it came about, I announced it to you, lest you should say, "My idol has done them, and my graven image, and my molten image, has commanded them." (48:3–5)

"Former things," such as the exodus of the ancient Hebrews from Egypt, or the miraculous rescue of King Hezekiah and the city of Jerusalem from the legions of Sennacherib,[14] were foretold by prophecy in order

---

13. Malbim, in his superlative commentary to the Bible, also explains the verse in Isaiah in this light: We are instructed to know and to understand that the controlling forces of the world are not the powers of nature and chance, but rather the hand of God and His great power.

14. These two examples are given by Rashi, among the oldest and most universally accepted commentators on the Bible.

to render humankind unable to reasonably claim an alternative source for
their achievement.

The verse continues:

You have heard and seen all this; and you, will you not declare it? I have
announced to you new things from this time, even hidden things, which you
have not known. (Ibid., 48:6)

Just as events of the past were forecast by the prophets, so the events
of later generations were foretold, so that we should know their true
source. To fulfill the purpose of true prophecy – whether this purpose is
to declare the infinite knowledge of God, to give us hope for Divine salvation in the future, or to show us the constant guidance of the Divine
hand – "perfect scores" are a prerequisite. If some prophecies were to be
fulfilled while others would fail, there would be no reason to associate
the source of prophecy with the infinite perfection of the Divine. After
all, various forms of divination might also achieve a satisfactory record
of success, despite their reliance on already extant forces and not Divine
revelations. If prophecy is to indicate the hand of God in the destiny
of the world, thereby proving His knowledge and control or delivering
His message to mankind, it must bear the stamp of its Godly source.

RETROSPECTIVE UNDERSTANDING

With regard to the latter purpose of demonstrating God's control over
the universe, Divine prophecy does not necessarily presuppose clarity
on the part of the revelation. As long as ex post facto the connection
is made between the historic event and the scriptural prediction, the
purpose of prophecy is achieved. We learn to appreciate that the dom-
inant events of world history are not matters of chance, governed by
humanly assessable factors, but rather manifestations of the great master
plan of God.

Indeed, it is sometimes necessary to keep the future hidden, in spite
of prophetic revelation, so as not to interfere with the decisions that
men and women must make of their own accord.[15] Many prophecies

---

15. This idea touches on the known contradiction between human free will

are therefore difficult to interpret. Sometimes we find the words of Scripture clouded in obscurity, enveloped in a mist that is only dispelled after the foretold happening comes to pass.[16] After the event, however, it is crucial to apply our newly gained hindsight to Scripture, thus revealing the hand of God at work in shaping human history.

An example of this is found in the prophecy concerning the seventy-year exile of the Jews after the destruction of the First Temple. Although the prophecy was quite explicit, it was nonetheless ambiguous enough for several kings to miscalculate the due date of the foretold return.[17] Even Daniel, himself a prophet, miscalculated the time of the redemption, before realizing his mistake and arriving at the correct conclusion.[18] After King Cyrus permitted the return of Jews to the Land of Israel, and allowed them to rebuild the Temple, any lingering doubt concerning the calculation was dispelled.[19]

---

and the infinite knowledge of the Creator. How the two simultaneously coexist, on two distinct layers of existence, is not the current topic, and we shall not expound on it here. We may state, however, that the two layers – of man's free will and the infinity of Divine knowledge – meet in the very essence of prophecy. See also Appendix A.

16. An example of this can be found in the Book of Daniel (Chap. 7) in the prophecy of the Small Horn: "After this, I saw in the night visions, and behold, a fourth beast, dreadful and terrible, and strong exceedingly; and it had great iron teeth; it devoured and broke in pieces, and stamped the residue with its feet; and it was diverse from all the beasts that were before it; and it had ten horns. I considered the horns, and, behold, there came up among them another horn, a little one, before which three of the first horns were plucked up by the roots; and, behold, in this horn were eyes like the eyes of a man, and a mouth speaking great things." Although the meaning was clear to Daniel, this vision is quite glaringly ambiguous.

17. Jeremiah (29:10) prophesies that "After seventy years are accomplished for Babylon, I will remember you, and perform My good word toward you, in causing you to return to this place." From which starting point the seventy years must be calculated, however, is ambiguous. The Talmud (*Megillah* 11b) records that several kings met their downfall because of miscalculations based on this prophecy.

18. *Megillah* 12b.

19. The redemption, incidentally, remained incomplete chiefly because only a small fraction of the Jewish nation joined the four waves of return from Babylonia

PIECES OF THE PUZZLE

The work ahead relates mainly to the branch of prophecy that reveals the Hand of Providence through retrospective analysis of prophecies that have been fulfilled. As will be shown, Biblical prophecy is no less relevant today than it was at the time of the ancient Hebrews. Recent history has endowed us with such momentous events as the foundation of the State of Israel, and the tumultuous events prior to and in the wake of its foundation, many of which are foreseen by Biblical prophecy. Before such events occurred, the prophecies that relate to our time remained shrouded in obscurity. Only with the aid of hindsight, and through careful scrutiny of the verses, is the actual clarity of the prophecy revealed.

Furthermore, even a clear prophecy of *what* will happen does not necessarily describe *how* it will happen, the more so concerning prophecies that were recorded over two thousand years before the event occurred. Even given an explicit prophecy of what will come to pass, it remains difficult to envisage the manner in which the prophecy will actually be fulfilled.[20] For this reason, it may not be easy to relate Biblical

---

(led by Sheshbatzar, Joshua the High Priest, Zerubavel, Ezra, and Nehemiah). This provides a good illustration of the duality of God's infinite knowledge and the role of man's free will. Although the exile was prophesied to end after seventy years, the nature of the redemption remained dependent on the choices of man. It can be argued that hopes for the complete redemption of Israel, as prophesied by Jeremiah, Isaiah, Hosea, Amos, Ezekiel, Micah, Haggai, and Zachariah, could have been realized through the Second Temple, but were dashed by the indifference of the populace. Thus, the Talmud (*Yoma* 9b) describes how a sage from the Holy Land chastised his Babylonian contemporary for his antecedents' unwillingness to return with Ezra (see also *Seder Hadorot* 5,380, quoting from *Sema.*) In the second section of *Sefer Kuzari*, the Jewish sage admits his shame to the Khazar king as to the national sin, through which the destiny God had planned for the Second Temple remained unfulfilled. See also Appendix A, where we have dwelled on another aspect of this duality.

20. Had Biblical prophecies been expressed in modern terms, they would have been unintelligible at the time they were uttered. The converse question, which has been addressed by a number of Bible scholars in recent times, is the description of modernized methods, such as contemporary warfare, in ancient

prophecies to current affairs, despite the prophesied events taking place under our noses.

In the turbulent context of the modern age, it is both a challenge and a duty to point out the prophecies pertaining to a history that we have seen, and continue to see, with our own eyes. The Divine word is both present in Scripture and immanent in the course of history. By putting the two together, thereby seeking to achieve some degree of retrospective comprehension, we fulfill one of prophecy's fundamental functions: a Divine element is introduced into the confusing panorama of current affairs. This is the first purpose that this work is intended to achieve.

The second purpose, a purpose hidden between the lines rather than explicit in the text, is to present the reader with a jigsaw puzzle. A prevalent worldview is to see historical events as being essentially random. They draw, according to this Weltanschauung, from the erratic and unpredictable human psyche, from a being plagued by emotion and haunted by ambition. Seen through the prism of Biblical revelation, the same events become pieces in the colossal puzzle of universal destiny, sourced in a preplanned totality that always was and will always be.

Much as a child takes interest in fitting together a jigsaw puzzle, so we, sometimes as passive observers and occasionally as active participants, may seek to fit together the pieces formed by global events, until some semblance of a coherent picture is formed. A necessary prerequisite, however, is that the observer must be aware that a puzzle exists.

Biblical terms. Some scholars maintain that Biblical terms can be interpreted loosely as references to modern concepts. A horse, for instance, could be loosely interpreted as a "human transporter" (a modern vehicle of some description), and a bow and arrow as a rifle. Others have stated that any departure from an entirely literal version constitutes a desecration of prophecy. See Rabbi Moshe Yemini, *The Ways of Providence and Faith* [Hebrew] (1975, p. 153, note 13), who opposes the method of loose interpretation suggested by Rabbi Chayim Dov Rabinowitz in *Daat Sofrim* (p. 352). See also Rabbi Shlomo Kushlevsky's *Vaasher Tavonah Yagidu* (Jerusalem: 2004), pp. 178–191, for a lengthier discourse of this topic. Rabbi Kushlevsky espouses a "broadened literal interpretation," whereby Biblical terms can take on modern meanings, provided that such meanings do not involve a complete departure from the literal sense of the words.

Without necessarily dwelling on its subject (though at times it does), the current work aims to demonstrate the actual existence of the puzzle.

As in the case of a jigsaw, individual pieces often appear to possess little or no meaning. Only as they come together does recognition of a unified vision begin to dawn. As of today, the puzzle necessarily remains incomplete. Many prophetic revelations remain unfulfilled. Of certain events, we have only the vaguest inkling of *what* will happen, and even less as to *how* they will happen. The complete picture is seen only by the Creator, whose presence transcends the limits of space and time; mortal man is unable to see through the myopia of his worldly existence.

Nevertheless, if only we allow ourselves the openness of mind to consider it, perhaps we will find that the puzzle of global history, and in particular that which concerns Israel and the Middle East, has sufficiently taken shape for the pieces to impart profound meaning. Although some degree of interpretation is unavoidable, the meaning itself is not the principle focus of this book. For the purposes of this work, we are content, like many great men of past generations, with an awareness of the puzzle itself.

THE DIVINE LESSON

One further point remains to be made – an additional aspect of the general importance of prophetic revelation, and of the particular rationale for this book: historical insight.

In considering most historical events, a historian must take into account any number of intricately inter-related factors. These may include political trends, popular opinion, personal motivation, economic factors, ethnic and racial relations, and international pressures – among many others. Working one's way through the labyrinth to identify a single central theme, and thereby extract a serious lesson for the future, is no small task.

Modern analysis of World War II provides a classic example. To this day, there are tens, if not hundreds, of competing claims to "understanding" the War. To name but a handful, we might speak of the evils of nationalism, the psychopathic personality of Hitler, the decline of German political and social structures, or even of the illusionary "global

Jewish conspiracy." Naturally, all are claimed to be based on solid fact, with as little interpretation as possible. Are all true? Are any?

For instance, it would be no more true to state that Chamberlain's appeasement policy caused World War II than to say that the Japanese attack on Pearl Harbor caused the defeat of the Axis. Certainly, both were significant factors, yet they can only be judged within the context of hundreds of others, of which some may be no less significant.[21] Applying such analysis to new circumstances is no less complex a matter. When the Nixon administration pursued policies of détente vis-à-vis the Soviet Union, they were not deterred by the failure of Chamberlain's "appeasement."[22]

When history is viewed through the prism of Biblical prophecy, the complexity of numerous variables is simplified. The analyst is able to identify a single underlying issue, which provides a focal point for the many related themes and details involved. At times, this conceptual clarity will aid the historian, enabling him to place his finger on the event that truly decided the outcome. Conversely, the aspect of Divine intervention implied by prophesy may be a hindrance to the historian, who wishes to extract human lessons from an essentially human narrative.

For the honest truth-seeker, however, who prefers genuine truths to hypotheses and conjectures, prophetic revelation – when extracted expertly and honestly (no simple feat of course) – should not be ignored. Seen through the appropriate prophecy, the events of history are illuminated with a light of clarity. Although particular details may

---

21. Concerning Germany's loss of the war, we might mention such factors as the lost Battle of Britain, Hitler's muddled strategy during the invasion of Russia, the defeat of Rommel, the weakness of the Italians, and so on.

22. In fact, there would seem to be a clear difference between *détente* and appeasement. Whereas appeasement implies unilateral concessions made to a dangerous aggressor in the (remote) hope of assuaging his nationalist desires, *détente* is based on the interaction of two-state parties with a mutual interest in de-escalating an existing state of animosity and conflict. In the final analysis, however, the demarcation lines between the two are easily blurred, a fact underscored by the difference of opinion between policymakers.

remain unclear on a human plane, they become laden with meaning on the plane of Divine will and guidance.

The human lessons of history are of utmost importance. Applied with sagacity and discretion, they can offer indispensable counsel concerning the subtle craft of decision-making, and provide vital perspectives on such important issues as human identity, the workings of politics and society, the forces of good and evil, and so on. Yet sometimes – perhaps more often than not – the Divine lesson is more important even than the human one.

Chapter 1

LIGHT OUT OF DARKNESS

One of the most frequently recurring themes of Jewish theology is the emergence of light from darkness. True wisdom, the Talmud states, is only attained in the wake of an initial error (*Chagigah* 14a; *Gittin* 43a). Ultimate awareness of the unity of God, writes the great scholar and theologian Luzzato, is only achieved by the negation of the contrary – his first premise in explaining the purpose of evil in the world (*Daat Tevunot*, no. 38).

In its piercing and concise style, the Talmud sums up the issue: From the very inception of the world, night has always preceded day (*Shabbat* 74a). "There is no light," the *Zohar* teaches, "other than that which emerges from darkness" (1:32a).

Thus the Jewish calendar, in which each day is born with the fall of dusk at the end of the previous day,[1] extends the principle to the very fabric of the time continuum. Indeed, a cursory scan of the past reveals that Jewish history has closely adhered to the rule of "light from darkness." It is fair to say that no single achievement of the Jewish nation has come about without some period of darkness having first preceded it.

Thus, the very existence of Israel as a nation derived from long years

---

1. Unlike the solar calendar, in which night follows day, in the Jewish lunar calendar day follows night. Thus, whereas according to the solar calendar Friday night is part of the calendar day of Friday, according to Jewish law the Sabbath commences at nightfall on Friday.

of intense suffering at the hands of the ancient Egyptians;[2] the tablets of Torah finally received at Sinai were given only after the first set was smashed at the foot of the mount (Exodus 32:19); and the initial entry into the Holy Land could only be made after the entire generation that left Egypt perished in the wilderness (Numbers 32:13).

The same holds true for later times: The conquest of the Land by Joshua was only achieved after the failure at Ai (Joshua, Chap. 7); David's Kingdom was only established after the termination of Saul's; and the great "light" of the Oral Law, around which Jewish life has revolved throughout its years of exile, was preceded by the thick spiritual darkness of the Greek cultural revolution.[3] Of those who toil in the study of the Oral Law, the Midrash[4] applies the verse, "The nation that walked in darkness saw great light." (Isaiah 9:1).

In this manner, throughout their long and varied history, the highs of the Jewish People have always been preceded by marked lows.[5] "Hold

---

2. See Ezekiel 16:4, in which Israel's national redemption from Egypt is described in literal terms of childbirth. The unified "body of Israel" was born out of Egypt.

3. The Midrash writes that the word "darkness" of the verse "and the earth was unformed and void, and darkness was upon the surface of the deep" (Genesis 1:2), refers to the exile of Greece, in which the eyes of Israel were darkened. Commentaries explain that Greek wisdom is related to darkness in that it confines human awareness by the boundaries of his understanding. A Weltanschauung declaring that anything beyond the reach of human understanding does not exist denies the world Divine light. When the conquerors of the Greek Empire applied their cultural revolution even to the Jews and their Torah, a thick veil of spiritual darkness descended upon the world. Thus, the ninth day of Tevet, which is commemorated as the day on which the Torah was translated, is a Jewish Fast Day (*Shulchan Aruch, Orach Chayim* 580:2).

4. *Tanchuma*, Noah 3.

5. The same holds true for the patriarchal roots of the nation: Abraham, Sarah, Isaac, Rebecca, and Rachel were all initially barren before their prayers for children were answered. Abraham had to live through many trials and tribulations, including the Divine test that brought Isaac upon the sacrificial altar, before the patriarchal dynasty could finally be established. Both Isaac and, in particular, Jacob, lived difficult and testing lives. In Jacob's own words, "Few and bad have been the days of the years of my life, and they have not reached the life spans of my forefathers in the days of their sojourns" (Genesis 47:9).

tight in times of strife," declares the ancient Jewish conscience, "for there is light at the end of the tunnel." The glow of the Hanukah candles, lit annually in the winter darkness, brings the theme of "light from darkness" into our homes and personal lives. It is an eternal message of hope: Like that of Greece, the darkness of our exile will ultimately be dispelled, giving way to brilliant light.[6]

We should add that the Jewish attitude to suffering and evil is not confined to merely waiting for the coming light. Rather than engendering a passive or fatalistic approach, Judaism sees suffering as a call to repentance and spiritual elevation. The words, "On account of our sins we were exiled from our land" (mentioned in Sabbath and Festival prayers) are ever present on Jewish lips and in the Jewish conscience. Darkness indeed paves the path for future light, yet the revelation must somehow be drawn by human deeds, actions cleansed and refined by the hardships of the night. Such was the case of the light of Hanukah, which was brought into the world by the heroic efforts of the Hasmoneans. To the afflicted, suffering is thus not cause for theological speculation, but a summons to growth and repair.

Even a cursory reading of the Bible provides a sufficient demonstration that the fluctuating trail of Jewish history is not solely a matter of the Divine master-plan, but very much subject to human deed. Time and again, the invasion of the Land by hostile neighbors served as a call to repentance; after their ways were bettered, the people enjoyed periods of peace and tranquility. The two elements – human actions on the one hand and Divine providence on the other – are thus bound together on a single up-down path toward destiny.

---

6. The victory of the Hasmoneans over their Greek oppressors is seen as a spiritual victory of the light of Torah Judaism over the darkness of Greece; unlike other exilers, Greece forbade the Jews from occupying themselves with the Torah and its mitzvot (see Maimonides, *Mishnah Torah*, Laws of Chanukah 3:1). The miraculous victory over the Greeks was, therefore, a victory of the light of Torah over the darkness of its assailants.

BETTER TIMES

Although not without its particular problems,[7] the current period represents a peak in the history of the Jewish nation – at the very least in relation to its physical condition. By contrast with their condition over two millennia of exilic existence, Jews around the world are free to practice their religion as they please, encountering relatively little discrimination as a result of their chosen faith. Furthermore, while for two thousand years physical and political conditions prevented the Jews from residing in the Holy Land, today they are free to do so – as many millions actually do.

In the terms of the oscillating graph of Jewish history, it is rational that the more drastic the trough, the more radical the peak that comes in its wake. The mid-twentieth-century Holocaust of European Jewry, rapidly followed by the mass resettlement and reestablishment of Jewish sovereignty in the Land of Israel, is emblematic of this pattern.

David Graber, a youthful member of the "Oyneg Shabes" society that tirelessly documented Polish Jewish life under Nazi occupation, had been admitted to the society relatively late. News of the Final Solution was filtering through, and hopes for the survival of Polish Jewry had been all but extinguished. Nevertheless, he, and other members of the society, continued to write:

What we were unable to cry and shriek out to the world, we buried in the ground. . . . I would love to see the moment in which the great treasure will be dug up and scream the truth at the world. So the world may know all. So the ones who did not live through it may be glad, and we may feel like veterans with medals on our chest. We would be the fathers, the teachers and educators of the future. . . . But no, we shall certainly not live to see it, and therefore I write my last will. May the treasure fall into good hands, may it

---

7. This is true in a physical sense (danger to Jews, and certainly to the State of Israel, is not a thing of the past), and certainly in a spiritual sense, with assimilation and intermarriage posing grave threats to contemporary Judaism. These issues, however, were present well before the current period (post WWII) began, whereas the condition of Jews, both physically and spiritually, is much improved from pre-war times.

last into better times, may it alarm and alert the world to what happened . . . in the twentieth century.[8]

Finally, for those who survived to see them, "better times" arrived. They came, however, only in the wake of a horror without precedent – the most terrible period in the long annals of Jewish history.

FROM A TIME OF TROUBLE

The perennial hope of the Jewish People is redemption, of which the first phase is return to the Promised Land. Scripture has furnished ample evidence on which to base this hope:

For behold, days are coming – the word of the Lord – when I will return the captivity of My people Israel and Judah, said the Lord, and I will return them to the Land that I gave their forefathers, and they will possess it.[9]

The verses of Jeremiah continue to warn that the process of re-gathering will emerge from times of extreme hardship and strife:

For thus says the Lord: "Cries of horror have we heard – of fear, and not peace. Ask and see: Can a man bear children? Then why do I see that every man puts his hand upon his loins like a woman in childbirth, and all faces turn pallid? Woe! For that day will be momentous. None will be like it. It will be a time of trouble for Jacob; but he will be saved from it." (Jeremiah 30:5–7)

The Talmud (*Sanhedrin* 97a) quotes an additional verse to prove that harsh persecution at the hand of enemies is a sure sign of approaching redemption. "For before those days," the verse states, "those who travel back and forth had no peace because of the enemy." (Zechariah 8:10).

Over the centuries of their exilic experience, the Jewish People, who have had to travel "back and forth" from one host country to another,

---

8. Ringelblum Archive, part I, no. 132. Reprinted in Joseph Kermish, ed., *To Live with Honor and Die with Honor: Selected Docments from the Warsaw Ghetto Underground Archives Oyneg Shabbath* (Jerusalem: 1986), p. 66; cited in Samuel D. Kassow, *Who Will Write our History?* (Vintage Books, New York: 2009), p. 3.

9. Jeremiah 30:3–4.

have had precious little peace. In no period, however, have they been so deprived of the cherished commodity than during the years of the Holocaust.

Between the years 1939 and 1945 the Jewish People suffered indescribable agony. For a time, the threat of total extinction loomed over their heads; yet, their survival had long before been guaranteed. Even of the worst of times, God promises, that "I will chastise you with justice, but I will never eliminate you completely" (Jeremiah 30:11).

"They called you an outcast," continues Jeremiah. "She is Zion; there is none that cares about her" (30:17). In spite of the general apathy that characterized the world powers, which seemed to care little for the fate of the Jewish nation, the word of God proved true.

TOWARD REDEMPTION

The ensuing verses of Jeremiah envisage the Messianic times, when the throne of King David will be re-established – when Jacob will dwell in peace and tranquility and will fear none. Israel still awaits the coming of such times; she yearns for the era of peace and tranquility, which she has lacked throughout her long exile.

Yet, a process is underway. In miraculous fashion, following the calamity of the Holocaust, the Jewish People have returned – and continue to return – to their traditional homeland.

"For the day of their calamity is near," sings the verse, "and future events are rushing at them" (Deuteronomy 32:35). *Future events*, in the context of the Holocaust, were, indeed, just around the corner.

Rabbi Eliyahu Dessler, a leading Orthodox thinker who wrote with great fervor on the short years that bridged horrifying destruction and unparalleled (if far from complete) redemption, quoted from the *Zohar* (3:270a):

At the End of Days, God is destined to return Israel to the Holy Land, and to gather them from their exile. What is the 'End of Days'? It is that time, the end-time, during which Israel shall suffer greatly in exile. . . . "In your distress, when all these things will befall you, at the end of days" [Deuteronomy 4:30] . . . this is the Congregation of Israel.

The prediction of the *Zohar*, writes Rabbi Dessler, was fulfilled in the Holocaust, and in the quasi-redemption of the State of Israel that came in its wake.[10]

THE LONG JOURNEY

"Ultra-Orthodox and assimilated Jews would reunite tragically on the train to Auschwitz," writes Michael B. Oren, "the final destination on the 2,000-year-long path of Jewish powerlessness."[11] Unwittingly, perhaps, Oren thus relegates the "powerless" achievements of the 2,000-year exile – including of course survival itself, which is no slight feat for a small religious and ethnic group dispersed in hostile foreign lands – to the waste bin of history. In doing so he joins a well-chronicled Zionist tradition to return to the "normative Judaism" of the Bible, and make a gentle skip over more than two thousand years of Jewish culture and tradition.[12]

Yet, though it proved a terrible blow, the Nazi Holocaust did not symbolize the end of the two-thousand-year national journey through

---

10. Rabbi Eliyahu Dessler, *Michtav Me'Eliyahu*, vol. 5, p. 306. The nature of the State of Israel, and the "redemption" it brought, are discussed later in this book.

11. Michael B. Oren, "Ben-Gurion and the Return to Jewish Power," in David Hazony, Yoram Hazony, and Michael B. Oren, eds., *New Essays on Zionism* (Shalem Press, Jerusalem: 2006), p. 408.

12. Ben-Gurion, the first Prime Minister of Israel, was among the most renowned figures to speak of a return to the Bible, writing, "Biblical Judaism is the greatest of all human creations of its kind, and it alone is able to mend the world and to implement national and human justice" (Y. Beker, *Mishnato Shel David Ben-Gurion*, Tel Aviv 5719, p. 21). Yitzchak Tabenkin, a close associate of Ben-Gurion, was more elaborate: "The Bible influenced all generations of Judaism, not only with its religious value and content. The Bible is a spiritual reflection of the life of a nation of workers, of a people of conquerors, a nation of labor, a nation of 'life of this world.' The Land, the struggles of its conquest and life upon it, the development of the Hebrew character, the unity of tribes, the elementary relationship with the universe, with nature, with love and death and wisdom, their song and their gloom, social and national wars – all of these are reflected in the Bible with a genius of simplistic artistry" (Yitzchak Tebenkin, *The Conceptual Sources of the Second Aliah* [Hebrew], Devarim 2, Tel Aviv 1972, p. 24).

the exile of the nations; it does Jewish history a grave injustice to consider it so. It was, rather, in a terrible sense that we cannot begin to fathom, *part of the journey*. In spite of the aims of their perpetrators, the horrors of the Holocaust years remain a link in the long chain of Jewish history, which began with exile and heads toward redemption.

The Holocaust is broadly considered a unique event in the annals of Jewish history,[13] one that cannot be framed in terms of historic European anti-Semitism. With justification, the Holocaust has been labeled the "Third Destruction of World Jewry,"[14] an event that changed the face of Jewry in proportions similar to those of the destructions of the first and second Temple.

Yet, just as the destructions of the Temple and the subsequent exiles did not imply a break in Jewish history – but, as Scripture makes clear, were part of an historic progression, forming a cycle of exile and redemption – so the Holocaust may not be viewed as a "gap" in Jewish history, a hole that separates one era from another.

If anything, it would be more correct to view it as a "bridge."

THE DRESSING AND THE WOUND

Israel Lichtenstein, who was appointed physical guardian of the Oyneg Shabes archives, buried the first cache of documents in 1942. A secular Jew plunged into the Nazi inferno, Lichtenstein remained well aware of the eternity of the Jewish People. He concluded his testament with the following words:

We are the redeeming sacrifice for the Jewish People. I believe that the nation will survive. We, the Jews of Eastern Europe, are the redeemers of the People of Israel.[15]

---

13. The uniqueness or otherwise of the Holocaust has been discussed by many Jewish thinkers, including Emil Fackenheim, Eliezer Berkowitz, David Weiss, and others; see Oliver Leaman, *Evil and Suffering in Jewish Philosophy* (Cambridge University Press 1995), p. 191. As far as the conscience of the Jewish People is concerned, however, it is hard to see it as simply "another expression of everyday anti-Semitism."

14. The term is used by Jacob Lestschinsky, *Crisis, Catastrophe and Survival.*

15. Ringelblum Archive, part I, no. 1190. Reprinted in Kermish, *To Live*

Similar sentiments were recorded by "Szlamek" (his real name was Shlomo Fajner or Bajner), a religious Jew who had escaped from Chelmo:

Each of us wanted to survive to see the liberation but, more than that, our greatest desire was for the survival of the Jewish People [*klal Yisrael*]. Each one of us would have given up his life with the greatest of pleasure if only that would guarantee the future of our people.[16]

One cannot but feel that the sentiments were well-placed. The nation survived, and began to thrive once more, in the merit of the generation that was lost.[17]

The traditional *Selichot* prayers, which merge historical calamity with confessions of sin and entreaties for forgiveness, include a particularly evocative praise of God: "From the wound itself, You fashion the dressing."[18] Day evolves out of night. The "dressing" of the State of Israel and the current condition of Jewry was formed out of the "wound" of the Holocaust.

Rabbi Elchanan Wasserman, just hours before his murder at the Ninth Fort, expressed the idea of light emerging from darkness even as the Nazi cloud descended upon his own community. He did so by quoting the prayer of mourning for Jerusalem: "For You, God, with fire You consumed her, and with fire You will rebuild her." Rabbi Wasserman enjoined his disciples to repent, and to realize the value of their sacrifice: "The very fire that will consume our bodies is destined to reestablish the House of Israel."[19]

The fulfillment of his prophecy continues to unfold.

---

with *Honor and Die with Honor*, pp. 58–59; cited in Kassow, *Who Will Write our History?*, p. 388.

16. Ringelblum Archive, cited in Kassow, *Who Will Write our History?*, pp. 289–90.

17. The concept of the Jewish People's revival being founded on the martyrdom of Jews in the Holocaust has been expounded on by Rabbi Shalom Noach Berezovski, *Haharuga Alecha*.

18. *Selichot* for the First Monday of Monday-Thursday-Monday sequence.

19. Rabbi Shlomo Lorentz, *Bimchitzatam* [Hebrew] (Jerusalem: 2008), vol. 2, p. 99. Rabbi Wasserman's final address was witnessed and recorded by Rabbi Ephraim Ashri.

MODERN JEWISH HISTORY

Modern Jewish history, which is strongly associated with the State of Israel, did not begin with the establishment of the Jewish state. If the Jewish day begins with the preceding nightfall, modern Jewish history began with the darkness of the Holocaust.

In making this statement I do not mean to engage the complexities of Holocaust theology. Though we detect a pattern of day and night, of light that follows darkness, we might remain far from finding a justification for the night. Debate of such justification – if the word can be spoken in the context of the Holocaust – is beyond the scope of this work.[20] My objective, rather is only to note that the period of the Holocaust, and the entire exile of which it was the terrible climax, was not an aberration in Jewish history, an anomaly in the relationship of love between God and Israel. Though his face was hidden, God was there with us; He suffered the suffering of his nation – "I am with him in strife" (Psalms 91:15) – and ensured that it ultimately survived.

Hitler's rhetoric before and during the war indicates that his campaign against the Jews was the principle manifestation of a greater war, against religion and against God. The "Heil Hitler!" greeting, which compulsorily replaced such humane expressions as "good morning" and "good afternoon," was symptomatic of a desire to supplant traditional religion with a new idol. In November 1938, on the eve of the infamous *Kristallnacht*, Hitler declared this:

We must be clear that in the next ten years, we will certainly encounter un-heard-of critical conflicts. . . . [I]t is the ideological struggle of the entire Jewry, freemasonry, Marxism, and churches of the world. These forces – of which I presume the Jews to be the driving spirit, the origin of all the negatives – are clear that if Germany and Italy are not annihilated, they will be annihilated.[21]

The Jewish People were not annihilated. The victory of their national spirit is the victory of God.

---

20. See Leaman, *Evil and Suffering in Jewish Philosophy*, pp. 185–219.

21. Briefing of SS leaders; quoted in Ian Kershaw, *Hitler: A Biography* (W. W. Norton & Co., N.Y.–London: 2008), p. 448.

Though the hidden ways of God's providence are beyond human comprehension, it seems that the same spiritual power that oversaw the return of the Jewish People to their ancestral homeland was somehow active even as the forces of evil struck the unspeakable blows of the Holocaust. The verse that declares, "I am with him in strife" concludes with the words, "I will release him and I will bring him honor" (Psalms 91:15). Tragedy and survival, both so glaringly supernatural, were, and continue to be, parts of the same Covenant.

The constructions of the First and Second Temple were both preceded by victory over the evil of Amalek,[22] the Biblical arch-enemy of Israel[23]; we live in hope that the painful victory over what was perhaps Amalek's latest manifestation will be revealed as the precursor to the construction of the Third.[24] According to Rabbi Joseph B. Solovcichik, the "devil of doubt and destruction" that ruled the night of the Holocaust – a certain reference to the evil of Amalek[25] – ushered in the Beloved of Israel:

Eight years ago, in the midst of a night of the terrors of Majdanek, Treblinka, and Buchenwald; in a night of gas chambers and crematoria; in a night of total divine self-concealment; in a night ruled by the devil of doubt and destruction who sought to sweep the Lover from her own tent into the Catholic Church; in a night of continuous searching for the Beloved – on that very night the Beloved appeared. The Almighty, who was hiding in His splendid *sanctum*, suddenly appeared and began to beckon at the tent of the Lover, who tossed

---

22. The First Temple, founded by David and build by Solomon, was built after Saul's defeat of Amalek (see I Samuel, Chap. 15). The Second Temple was constructed after the victory over Haman, descended from Amalek (see Esther 3:1), as described in the Scroll of Esther. Even the initial construction of the Tabernacle in the wilderness followed the defeat of Amalek by Moses and Joshua (see Exodus, Chap. 17). See also, in this connection, *Shem MiShmuel, Motzaei Yom Kippur*, 5681.

23. See Exodus 17:14, Deuteronomy 25:17–19.

24. On the connection between Amalek and the Nazis, see Rabbi Yoel Schwartz, *Yemei HaPurim*, and Rabbi Zalman Sorotzkin, *HaDeah VehaDibbur*, among many modern commentaries.

25. The *gematria* (numerical value) of the word *Amalek* is equal to that of the word *safek*, doubt. Amalek is described as the "devil of doubt," a power of evil that undermines faith in God.

and turned on her bed beset by convulsions and the agonies of hell. Because of the beating and knocking at the door of the mournful Lover, the State of Israel was born.[26]

Finally, into the depths of darkness shone a ray of eternal hope. Daylight broke.

CHOSEN PEOPLE

In *The Jewish Century*, historian Yuri Slezkine writes that "From being God's Chosen People, the Jews had become the Nazis' chosen people, and by becoming the Nazis' chosen people, they became the Chosen People of the postwar Western world."[27] The statement is true and well put, yet it lacks a fundamental insight that cannot be overstated. The continuous chosenness of the Jewish People, by the world and even by the Nazis, did not *replace* their being God's Chosen People. Though it is hard to say, and impossible to comprehend, *it was a factor of it.*[28]

It is with this in mind that we turn our eye to the events of daytime: the return to Jews to the Land of Israel.

---

26. Rabbi Joseph B. Soloveitchik, *Kol Dodi Dofek: Listen – My Beloved Knocks* (translated by David Z. Gordon, Yeshiva University, 2006), p. 31. The allegory is based on the fifth chapter of the Song of Songs.

27. Yuri Slezkine, *The Jewish Century* (Princeton University Press, Princeton: 2004), p. 366.

28. Many have grappled with the question of covenant theory in light of the Holocaust, and arrived at radically different conclusions. In an earlier version of this volume, I expounded on the writings of different Jewish thinkers on the subject, and tried to place the Holocaust itself within the framework of prophecy. On second thoughts, I decided that the subject matter was too delicate, and the discussion itself too involved, for inclusion in this volume; perhaps the material will one day see the light in some other format and time.

✑ *Chapter 2*

THE PEOPLE AND THEIR LAND

For two thousand years, the political condition of the Jewish nation was entirely anomalous. Whereas the British dwelt in Britain, the French in France, and the Afghans in Afghanistan, the nation of Israel was scattered all over the world.

Aside from its physical implication, the exile of the Jews from their Biblical homeland carries deep spiritual meaning – for the ultimate purpose of the Jewish nation is intimately related with the Land of Israel. Only regathered to the Land can the Jewish People fulfill its quintessential, preordained task.

Scripture reveals that the Jewish nation was formed for the sake of glorifying God. Isaiah delineates the concept quite brusquely: "This nation I have fashioned for Myself, that they should declare My glory" (Isaiah 43:21). In the first half of the same chapter, the task of glorification is closely associated with the final gathering of the nation:

Do not fear, for I am with you; from the East I shall bring your seed, and from the West I shall gather you; I will say to the North: "Give them over!" and to the South: "Do not withhold! Bring My sons from afar, and My daughters from the ends of the earth, everyone who is called by My Name and for My glory have I have created him; I have formed him; even I have made him." (43:5–7)

The words of Isaiah, which clearly integrate the theme of God's glorification with Israel's re-gathering, are unfolding before our eyes.

"Do not fear," God tells His people, "for I am with you." Throughout the horrors that overcame them, inhuman suffering that no voice can speak, God remained with His people. The process of ingathering, whose foundations had previously been laid, gained momentum. One by one, the countries around the globe began to "give over" their Jews, and, from all the corners of the earth, the People of Israel began to return to their Land.

SETTLEMENT AND CONQUEST

Rabbi Dr. Chaim Zimmerman has made an incisive observation that highlights the significance of the current ingathering.[1]

When the Jewish People made their original entry into the Promised Land, territorial conquest preceded the division and settlement of the Land. This fulfilled many Biblical predictions that promised that the nation would "conquer the Land, and settle it"[2] – specifically in that order. In the current ingathering, however, the order was reversed: the settlement of the Land by Jewish immigrants, whose presence in Mandatory Palestine catalyzed the establishment of the Jewish State, *preceded* the defensive military campaign against the indigenous Arab population.

Predictably, almost all references to the conquest and settlement of the Land occur in the Pentateuch and the Book of Joshua. Past the Book of Joshua, the conquest and settlement had already become historical fact. Only in one instance does Scripture make further mention of the duality of conquest and settlement, placing the events in a future context. Remarkably, this passage is also singular in its reversal of the order of conquest and settlement.

"Save me, O Lord," begins the chapter of Psalms, "for the waters have reached until the soul!" (69:2). The greater part of the chapter is devoted to a stirring description of hardships, combined with longing

---

1. Dr. Chaim Zimmerman, *Torah and Existence* (Jerusalem-New York: 1986), pp. 74–75.
2. See, for instance, Numbers 33:53; Deuteronomy 11:14, 17:14, 26:1; and Joshua 19:47 – among many other sources.

for redemption: "I am sunk in the mire of the shadowy depths, and there is no foothold. . . . I am wearied by my outcry, my throat is parched; my eyes pined, waiting for my God" (69:3, 5). Finally, the chapter moves on to Divine salvation:

Your salvation, O God, shall raise me high . . . For the Lord hearkens to the destitute, and has not despised His prisoners . . . For God shall save Zion and build the cities of Judah, *and they shall settle there and possess it.* (69:30, 34, 36)

Rabbi Zimmerman is well justified in introducing the passage as "astonishing and incredible." Some three thousand years before the event, King David recorded how God will save Zion, raising them out of bottomless depths to their Land. In a marked departure from countless verses that speak of "conquest and settlement," the chapter of Psalms reverses the order, precisely reflecting the events of the current return.

TWO STAGES OF RETURN

The process of ingathering and redemption will eventually culminate in the blissful existence depicted by Isaiah:

The wolf shall dwell with the lamb, and the leopard shall lie down with the kid. . . . They shall not hurt nor destroy in all My holy mountain; for the earth shall be full of the knowledge of the Lord, as the waters cover the sea. . . . It shall come to pass on that day, that the Lord will set His hand again, the second time, to recover the remnant of His people, that shall remain from Assyria, and from Egypt, and from Pathros, and from Cush, and from Elam, and from Shinar, and from Hamath, and from the islands of the sea. (43:6, 9, 11)

Elsewhere, the verse makes clear that this glorious state of affairs will be achieved only through the "Root of Jesse" (1:1, 10). The final gathering of the people, as Maimonides codifies in his *Mishnah Torah*, will be conducted by the long-awaited Messiah (Laws of Kings 12:3).

Yet, the central role of the Messiah in eschatological events poses no theological contradiction to the re-gathering that we have witnessed in recent years. According to many leading Jewish luminaries, including

Rabbi David Kimchi (1160–1235),[3] Rabbi Moshe Sofer (1762–1839),[4] and Rabbi Meir Aldabi (c. 1310–c. 1360),[5] the Messiah will be revealed only *after* the people will be gathered to Jerusalem.[6] The order of Jewish prayers, which consistently places the ingathering before the advent of the Messiah, supports this position.[7] Although the full wonder of the ingathering and the glory of the latter days await the leadership of the Messiah, the first stage of the return is independent of the Messiah King.

Two distinct stages of ingathering are virtually explicit in the words of the Prophet: "The word of my Lord, God, Who gathers in the dispersed of Israel: 'I will gather others to him, added to those of him that are gathered.'"[8] The ingathered, the verse tells us, will be *added to those already gathered.*

Furthermore, we may glimpse the two phases of return – one prior to the Messiah, and one following his arrival – in the words of Jeremiah:

"Return, faithless children," says the Lord, "for I am your husband, and I will take you – one from a city, and two from a clan." . . . And it shall be, when

---

3. *Commentary to Bible*, Hoshea 2:2 (1:11). Usually known as *Radak*, which is an acronym for his name, Rabbi Kimchi lived in the south of France in the twelfth and thirteenth centuries. Because his commentary was translated into Latin, it played an important role in compiling the renowned King-James-I-authorized translation of the Bible.

4. Commonly known as the *Chatam Sofer* (after his seminal talmudic works), Rabbi Moshe Sofer was the leading authority of his generation in areas of Jewish law and erudition. His rulings are respected across the spectrum of Orthodox Judaism, and his writings on Torah thought and philosophy have been influential in molding the outlook of Orthodoxy in subsequent generations.

5. *Shevilei Emunah, netiv* 10, Chap. 1. Rabbi Aldabo was a grandson of Rabbeinu Asher ben Yechiel (1250–1327), one of the foremost medieval authorities, whose rulings form the foundation of modern Jewish Law.

6. Rabbi Sofer deduces this from the wording of Maimonides' *Commentary to the Mishnah*, Sanhedrin 1:3.

7. This is true of the benedictions of the Weekday Amidah (the central prayer), and of the requests made at the end of *Birkat HaMazon* (Grace after Meals). See Talmud, *Megillah* 17b, which explains the chronological progression of the Amidah benedictions.

8. Isaiah 56:8.

you are multiplied and increased in the Land . . . they shall call Jerusalem the throne of the Lord; and all the nations shall be gathered unto it, to the name of the Lord, to Jerusalem. (3:14–17)

The verse describes the return to Zion as "one from a city and two from a clan." This, indeed, was the prevailing picture of those who escaped the European catastrophe.[9] Many of those who reached the Holy Land were alone, without family or acquaintance[10]; their coming, and the coming of those who preceded them, was the first step in the return of the Jews.

Of this first stage, which is readily associated with the current ingathering, we may apply the words of a later chapter in Jeremiah: "Behold, I shall bring them from the land of the North and gather them from the ends of the earth. . . . With weeping they will come, and through supplications I shall bring them" (31:7–8). As Abarbanel explains, the gathered people will weep over the extreme hardships and tribulations that befell them in exile.

The second stage, however, is described by Jeremiah as a "multiplication"; no longer will the nation be composed of lonely individuals. Although Jeremiah does not mention it, the coming of the Messiah must be interjected at some point. After his coming, the last part of the prophecy will be readied for its glorious fulfillment. In the words of Isaiah, the final gathering will be a "second redemption" (11:11). Like the first time, when the Children of Israel were redeemed from Egypt with wondrous miracles, so shall the final redemption be in glory and exultation, in joy and jubilation.[11]

---

9. Although a trickling of Jews had begun to settle in Palestine from the end of the nineteenth century, mass immigration only began in the period between the two World Wars. Typically, youth would break away from their families to make the journey alone. After the Holocaust, these immigrants, together with other survivors who had made their way to Palestine, found that they were bereaved of many, if not all, family members.

10. It is interesting that verse 18 mentions the gathering from the land of the north, which implies the European lands from which the first immigrants to Palestine (of the nineteenth- and twentieth-century *aliyah*) arrived.

11. A Jewish prayer, recited at the spiritual zenith of the week (in the Sabbath

FUTURE AND PRESENT RETURNS

Although the present return to Jerusalem is clearly significant, and occupies a considerable presence in scriptural prophecy (as will be demonstrated below), there are clear prophecies of ingathering that cannot be reasonably applied to recent events. For instance, chapter 29 of Deuteronomy extends the Admonition of the previous chapter, proclaiming how the full brunt of the curses shall befall the wayward nation:

Therefore the anger of the Lord flared against that Land . . . and the Lord removed them from their soil with anger, with wrath, and with great fury, and cast them to another land, as this very day. (Deuteronomy 29:26–27)[12]

Following this warning, which was clearly and emphatically fulfilled in the First Destruction and its subsequent exile, the verses continue to console Israel with brighter prospects for the future:

It shall be, when all these things come upon you – the blessing and the curse, which I have presented before you – then you will take it to your heart. . . . And you shall return unto the Lord your God, and hearken to His voice, according to everything that I command you today. . . . Then the Lord your God will bring back your captivity, and have mercy upon you. . . . The Lord your God will bring you to the Land that your fathers possessed, and you shall possess it; He will do you good, and make you more numerous than your forefathers. (Deuteronomy 30:1–5)

The verses imply that the re-gathering of the exile will be preceded by the spiritual return of the people, who will hearken to the voice of God, and fulfill His commands. This has not been the case in the present ingathering to Israel. Moreover, the promise of Israel's being more numerous than were their forefathers has not yet been fulfilled.

Mussaf prayer), expounds on this theme: "He shall bring us salvation, and redeem us for the second time; and proclaim once again, in His mercy, before the eyes of all living creatures: 'Lo, I have redeemed you, in the latter just as the former, to be a Lord unto you.'"

12. Deuteronomy 29:26–27 (27–28).

During the Holocaust, the population of Jews in the world shrunk by a third; their numbers have not recovered.[13] Clearly, the verse refers to a future ingathering of the people, whose numbers might be bolstered by millions of Jews who are unaware even of their own identity: "those who are lost in the land of Assyria and those cast away in the land of Egypt" (Isaiah 27:13).

One of the verses of the passage, however, implies that the return will be split into two parts:

Then the Lord your God will bring back your captivity, and have mercy upon you, and will return and gather you from among all the peoples, whither the Lord, your God, has scattered you. (Deuteronomy 30:3)

Rabbi Meir Simcha of Dvinsk (1843–1926), who wrote his renowned commentary to the Torah (*Meshech Chochmah*) before the turn of the twentieth century, noted the double expression of return (commenting on Deuteronomy 30:3):

The Jews that are in captivity, and who wish to escape from the Diaspora like [a prisoner from] the dungeon of captivity, will be returned first. *He will return and gather you*. . . . these are the Jews who find comfort in a foreign land, and do not desire the Land of Israel. They, too, will later be gathered, and returned.

This is very much the current situation in the State of Israel. Those who wished to make their way to the Holy Land – the determined few who came before the State arose, and the masses that immigrated after the foundation of the State (including some 250,000 immigrants from Western Europe and the Americas) – have done so.[14] Those who have chosen not to, for reasons of economy, physical or social comfort,[15]

---

13. In 1939, there were 17 million Jews in the world, and by 1945 only 11 million. While in the 13 years following the Holocaust the Jewish population grew by one million, it took another 38 years for it to grow another million. Today, as births are offset by assimilation and intermarriage, the Jewish population is increasing by a tiny 0.3 percent per annum.

14. Precise figures are available (also online) from the Central Bureau of Statistics (Israel).

15. This does not mean to criticize those Jews who do not make the return to

religious ideology, or ignorance of their heritage, will ultimately be gathered in.[16]

THE PEOPLE AND THEIR LAND

The significance of the current return is emphatically highlighted by the physical condition of the Land. Over the course of the Jewish exile, the Land of Israel languished in its desolation. Even in the millennia that preceded the Crusaders, the earth of the Holy Land was almost entirely bereft of both inhabitants and produce. After the Crusades of the eleventh and twelfth centuries, the condition of the Land deteriorated even more. As Solomon Grayzel put it: "The actual state of Palestine had somehow come to stand for the miserable state of the Jewish People. Both were desolate; both were in hostile hands; both awaited God's redemption."[17] One pilgrim, at the end of the fifteenth century, reported that a mere four thousand families lived in Jerusalem. Of these, only seventy were Jewish, and they, "of the poorest class, lacking even the commonest necessities."[18]

For the Bible student, this desolation comes as no surprise. Ezekiel clearly announces that the Land would not give her abode and her fruit to any nation but Israel:

Now you, son of man, prophesy to the mountains of Israel, and say, "Mountains of Israel: Hear the word of the Lord. Thus said the Lord God: 'Because the

---

Israel because of such reasons. In fact, we find in the Jerusalem Talmud *(Berachot* 18b) that one of the sages instructed a fellow sage to reside outside the Holy Land, for reasons of physical conditions.

16. The spiritual return of the people is also split into two parts. The first verses of the passage refer to the repentance of the people, who shall return to their God with a full heart and soul. Only later, however, will the spiritual elevation be complete, when God will "circumcise your heart and the heart of your offspring, to love the Lord your God, with all your heart and with all your soul, that you may live." The first part of the people's repentance may come in conjunction with the first part of the return; as we will mention later, it can be argued that this repentance has already commenced.

17. Solomon Grayzel, *A History of the Jews* (Philadelphia, The Jewish Publication Society of America, 1947), p. 465.

18. Ibid., p. 464.

enemy has said against you, "Hurrah! The heights of the world have become an inheritance for us . . ."' Thus said the Lord God to the mountains and to the hills, to the streams and to the valleys, to the desolate ruins and to the forlorn cities, which have become a scorn and a derision for the remaining nations all around. '. . . I have lifted up My hand – surely the nations that surround you shall bear their shame, but you, O mountains of Israel, you shall shoot forth your branches and yield your fruit to My people Israel, for they are soon to come. For, behold, I am with you, and I will turn to you, and you shall be tilled and sown. I will make people numerous upon you – the entire House of Israel, all of it; the cities shall be inhabited, and the ruins shall be rebuilt.'" (36:1–10)

More briefly, we find the same prophetic idea in the admonition of Leviticus. Amidst the plagues that God promises to inflict upon the nation should it turn to sin, He declares, "I will make the Land desolate; and your foes that dwell upon it will be desolate" (Leviticus 26:32). The sages state that although it forms a part of the admonition, this particular verse harbors a great blessing.[19] Nachmanides,[20] in commenting on the verse, makes the point forcefully:

That which is written, "your foes who dwell upon it will be desolate," is a good tiding, foretelling that throughout the exile, the Land will not accept our enemies. This, too, is a great proof and promise for our people, for you will not find amid the entire settlement soil that is good and prosperous . . . for since we departed from the Land, it has accepted no people and tongue; all of them seek to settle it, but they are unable to do so.

---

19. *Midrash Torat Kohanim*; cited by commentary of Rashi, on Leviticus 26:32.

20. Nachmanides (1194–1270), or Rabbi Moshe ben Nachman (Ramban), was one of the greatest Jewish leaders of the Middle Ages. His commentary to the Torah has become a classic work among all Bible students, and the *halachic* (practical) decisions that emerge from his commentary to the Talmud carry much weight. It was probably through the influence of Nachmanides, who was involved on several occasions in disputes with neighboring Christians (Nachmanides lived in Spain for most of his life) over religious and theological issues, that the Christian Church introduced its four methods of Scriptural interpretation: *quattuor sensus scripturae*. The four methods – literal, allegorical, exegesis, and mystical – are mentioned and expounded on by Nachmanides in many instances.

History has borne out Nachmanides' words with pinpoint accuracy. Since the Jews departed the Land, it has remained desolate. Although the Land of Israel attracted the nations of the world like a magnet, the conquering nations – Christian and Muslim alike – failed in their efforts to settle and inhabit the Land. Even in modern times, in centuries of European empires that spanned the globe, the Land of Israel remained desolate, in a more primitive state even than its Arab neighbors of Egypt, Syria, and Lebanon.

Had the Land been settled by an industrious and cultured people, populated and developed by a foreign nation, the Jewish attachment to their ancient homeland would have been sorely eroded. In the face of a flourishing occupation two thousand years old, our historical claim to the Land would have been rendered meaningless, our rights to it null and void. The Land, however, was loyal to the Jewish People; it waited anxiously for their return.

Since this return commenced, the Land, as if by miracle, has begun to flourish once again. As long ago as the first present-day *aliyah* of the early nineteenth century, well before the official establishment of the State, returning Jews had begun to orchestrate the agricultural re-settlement of the Land.[21] More land was purchased at the close of the century, and waves of immigration at the start of the twentieth century were accompanied by major agricultural progress, achieved by draining swamps and by widespread afforestation, and fueled by the determination of the settling pioneers to realize their dreams. By the time the State was founded, an agricultural infrastructure was already in place; the soil was ready for the massive expansion of recent decades, which has made the small state a prominent exporter of fruit and vegetables.[22]

---

21. The first agricultural settlement, Petach Tikvah, was founded by members of the old Yishuv in 1878. All the founding members were Orthodox Jews. Even before the establishment of the State, in 1937, it was awarded the status of a city. Despite the wide chasm that separated their religious beliefs, David Ben-Gurion would later recall the initiative and foresight of these pioneering settlers with great admiration.

22. Relative to land size, Israel would be among the leading exporters in the world. In practice, Israel is the sixteenth largest exporter of fresh vegetables, and the thirtieth largest exporter of fresh fruit.

MOUNTAINS OF ISRAEL

We return to the prophecy in Ezekiel (chap. 36), as mentioned above:

And you, Mountains of Israel, shall shoot forth your branches and yield your fruit to My people Israel, for they are soon to come. For, behold, I am with you, and I will turn to you, and you shall be tilled and sown. I will make people numerous upon you – the entire House of Israel, all of it; the cities shall be inhabited, and the ruins shall be rebuilt.

A talmudic passage relies on this prophecy to place the agricultural recovery of the Land in the broader context of Divine Providence. The Jewish weekday prayer (the weekday *Amidah*), which is traditionally recited thrice daily, presents an order of nineteen benedictions. The Talmud (*Megillah* 17b) notes that the prayer, which was instituted by the Men of the Great Assembly (a body that included Ezra and Zerubavel as well as other prophets and national leaders), outlines a sequential time line.

Among the thirteen central benedictions that comprise the mainstay of the prayer (the first and last three are more associated with praise than prayer), the sixth relates to the blessing of the Land, whereas the seventh concerns the ingathering of the people therein. The Talmud explains the proximity of the two benedictions by quoting the aforementioned verse in Ezekiel (36:8): "But you, O mountains of Israel, you shall shoot forth your branches and yield your fruit to My people Israel, for they are soon to come." The renowned medieval commentator Rabbi Shlomo Yitzchaki (Rashi) explains that the future ingathering of the people will take place *in conjunction* with the blessing of the Land. This is precisely what we have witnessed over the course of the past century.

THE MOST REVEALED END

Another talmudic passage confirms the deep significance of the renewed fertility of the Land, and brings to light an important implication of the current return. A gathering-in-sin (see the next chapter of this work), it would appear, was predestined to come simultaneously with the blooming of the Land.

The Talmud (*Sanhedrin* 97b) cites at length a dispute of two sages concerning the redemption of Israel in the latter times. Rabbi Eliezer maintained that the redemption will come only after the people repent for their sins, citing many verses that seemed to uphold his position. Rabbi Yehoshua, however, maintained that the people would ultimately be redeemed, even in a sinful state, likewise reinforcing his position with several verses. The final verse cited by Rabbi Yehoshua, which seems to have decided the dispute, is a verse at the end of the Book of Daniel.

Addressing the man clothed in linen, who had appeared to Daniel in a prophetic vision, Daniel asked the question of all questions: "How long until the concealed[23] End?" (Daniel 12:6). The question, of course, was not concerning the return of Ezra, which Daniel knew would come shortly; the reference was to the "concealed" End of latter days. Daniel describes the response:

I heard the man clothed in linen, who was above the waters of the river, as he lifted his right hand and his left hand to the heavens and swore by the Life of the Worlds that after a period, periods, and a half, upon the completion of the fragmenting of the hand of the holy people, all these would be finished. (12:7)

The words of the verse seal the talmudic debate. Rabbi Eliezer remained silent.

We may not know how to compute the period referred to in the verse: Daniel, himself, states that he did not comprehend that which he heard, and, upon inquiring, was told that the matter would be obscured "until the time of the End" (12:9). Yet, implicit in the vision is that there is a set time, a period after which Israel will be redeemed. No longer would the people be fragmented; regardless of their spiritual condition, they would be reunified in their homeland.

Immediately following this discourse, the Talmud records an additional teaching: "Rabbi Abba taught, no *ketz* (End) is more revealed than the verse, 'And you, Mountains of Israel, shall shoot forth your branches and yield your fruit to My people Israel, for they are soon

---

23. The word "*pelaot*" is interpreted by Metzudot Zion (an early commentator on the Bible, and an expert in Hebrew grammar) to mean "concealed."

to come.'" Of all signs, the most definite indication of imminent redemption is the rebirth of the Land, which yields her fruit to Israel. This prophetic insight, which is today fulfilled, follows the foregoing talmudic conclusion which has likewise been accomplished in the current return: *the ingathering of the people even in a state of sin.* Implicit in the juxtaposition of the talmudic dicta is their simultaneous fulfillment: the agricultural recovery of the Land will be accompanied by a return of the people in unbelief.

We will return to the gathering of the people in unbelief in the next chapter. Meanwhile, a pause for reflection is perhaps in order. In spite of the dangers and hardships the world (and the Jewish People, in particular) continues to know, it is no small privilege to be alive in the current period, thereby to witness the continual unfolding of great events. The End has not yet come, yet the signs are visible. As you read these words, the restoration of people and Land continue to unfold together, just as the prophets foretold.

THE FIRST AND SECOND RETURNS

It is fascinating, in the context of the Land and its people, to compare the current return to its Biblical predecessor, when the Persian King Cyrus gave his consent for the Jews to return to their Land. Concerning the latter, we find the following prophecy in chapter nine of Jeremiah, which relates to the desolation of the Land in the time of the Destruction:

For the mountains I will raise [My voice] in weeping and wailing, and for the pastures of the wilderness a dirge, for they are parched, without a person passing by; and they will not hear the sound of cattle; from bird of heaven to animal, they have wandered off and gone. I shall make Jerusalem heaps of rubble, a serpent's lair; the cities of Judah I shall make a wasteland, without inhabitant. (Jeremiah 9:9–10)

We have already seen, both from Biblical and historical perspectives, how the desolation of the Land was a central aspect of Jewish exile. In the first instance, the Talmud (*Shabbat* 145b) explains that the desolation was to endure for fifty-two years, in keeping with the numerical equivalent of the word *animal* (*behemah*). Indeed, after fifty-two years of exile, Cyrus permitted the nation to return to its homeland, and Jews began to repopulate the Land. Eighteen years later, in the second year of the reign of Darius, the seventy years of exile had terminated, and the construction of the Second Temple was completed.

Yet, despite the end of the years of desolation, the return of the nation from Babylon was not a complete redemption. Contrary to the hopes of leaders such as Ezra and Nehemiah, a large and influential proportion of the Jews elected to remain in the lands of their exile.[24] Those who did return to the Land, moreover, failed to re-establish the glory of the First Temple era. The monarchy of the House of David was absent from the nation's helm; instead, the people went through many stages of political turmoil, and were generally at the mercy of foreign powers. The revealed miracles that imbued the First Temple with a Divine aura were absent in the case of the Second. The single indication that redemption had come to pass was the condition of the Land: from a state of total desolation, it responded to the Jewish return.

The parallels that can be drawn between the state of affairs at the time of the First Return and that of modern-day Israel are unmistakable.

Like the First Return, the current ingathering was made possible by the grace of the nations – first through the initiative of the United Kingdom, and later through the support of the United States and the consent of the United Nations. Indeed, President Harry S. Truman, who hurried to issue an official statement recognizing the provisional Jewish government as de facto authority of the new Jewish state – and thereby angering U.S. delegates to the UN and top-ranking State Department officials who were not notified of the decision – cited his childhood dream of repeating the benevolence of Cyrus as the background for his decision.[25] The unsettled internal politics of the State of Israel, its

24. The Talmud (*Yoma* 9b) records that Reish Lakish, a talmudic Master whose ancestors had returned to the Land of Israel in the First Return, refused to shake the hand of Rabba, son of Bar Chana, whose family had declined to return from the Babylonian exile. "We hate you," exclaimed Reish Lakish, which Rashi explains referred to all the Babylonians, whose apathy toward the return had caused the redemption to remain incomplete.

25. This was stated in a private conversation with Rabbi Shlomo Lorentz, in

heavy dependence on the foreign policies of international powers, and their influence (in particular that of the United States) even in Israel's internal affairs, closely parallel the condition of the Jewish settlers in the First Return. Significantly, the sign of redemption shared by the two returns is that the physical desolation of the Land, both then and now, was remedied.

Furthermore, we find that even after Cyrus gave his permission for the Jews to return to the Land, the Jews' trouble and hardships had by no means ended. On the contrary, soon afterward, the Jews of the Persian Empire found themselves under threat of total annihilation at the hands of Haman. Their salvation is celebrated to this day in the annual festival and feast of Purim. Similarly, after the British had granted the Jews the right of return to their homeland, world Jewry was once again threatened with extermination: Haman's seat was filled by Hitler, the architect of the genocide of the Jewish people. As in the precedent of the Persian Empire, the Jews ultimately survived.[26]

---

explaining why the U.S. rushed to recognize the State of Israel notwithstanding State interests contrary to the decision. Truman added that in the new age of nuclear confrontation, he expected the Jewish People to be a "beacon unto the nations," just as they had been three thousand years ago [Rabbi Shlomo Lorentz, *Bimchitzatam* (Jerusalem: 2008), vol. 2, p. 262].

26. Some modern interpreters have made far-reaching and detailed comparisons between the Purim saga and the Holocaust. The hanging of the ten Nazis at the close of the Nuremburg trials, for instance, has been linked to the hanging of the ten sons of the wicked Haman. The hanging of the war criminals, according to this interpretation, fulfilled the otherwise puzzling request of Esther that the ten sons of Haman be hung again (Esther 9:13).

Going beyond the superficial comparisons, the obsession of Hitler and Nazi Germany with the Jews, and their ultimate desire to murder the entire Jewish population of Europe, is perhaps an indication of the presence of Amalek, the traditional archenemy of the Jews and of their God (see Exodus Chap. 17, Deuteronomy Chap. 25, and I Samuel Chap. 15). The sages reveal that Haman was a descendent of Amalek, which explains his burning desire to cleanse the world of all Jews. As is explained in chapter seven of this work, Germany is dubbed by the Talmud as "Germamia of Edom" – Edom (Esau) was Amalek's paternal grandfather – which, while not implying that all Germans are of the evil nation, does lend credence to the association of Nazi Germany with Amalek.

Assuming the validity of the link, it was with some insight – far more than he

An additional point to note is the spiritual level of the returnees. The religiosity, or lack thereof, of the pioneering Zionists is no secret: The secularism of today's State of Israel was established by its Labor-Zionist founders. Less well known, perhaps, is the lowly religious level of those who made the First Return from Babylon with Ezra and Nehemiah. The verses of the Book of Ezra describe how Ezra had to coerce the people into separating from the Gentile wives they had taken;[27] Radak adds that they were not particular in observance of the Sabbath, and in other matters of Jewish Law (commentary to Malachi 1:1). Yet, from modest beginnings, the First Return progressed until the Land of Israel became home once more to a vibrant Jewish community, the central focus of Jewish life worldwide. The same has happened today.

The similarities we have pointed out are not matters of chance. They are alluded to in Scripture itself (Isaiah 44:25–28):

> Thus said the Lord . . . I am the Lord . . .
> Who frustrates the omens of the stargazers,
> And makes fools of the astrologers;
> Who makes wise men retreat,
> And makes their knowledge foolish;
> Who confirms the words of His servant,
> And fulfills the counsel of His messengers;
> Who says of Jerusalem, "It shall be settled,"
> And of the cities of Judah, "They shall be built up,
> And I will rebuild its ruins;" . . .
> Who says of Cyrus, "He is My shepherd,

---

could have been consciously aware of – that Hitler declared total war against the Jews, proclaiming the conflict with the Jews a matter of "them or us," and preaching Germany's need to "recognize the most dangerous enemy and strike at him with all its concentrated power" (*Mein Kampf*). Of all the nations of the world, there is only one that the Torah (and hence Jewish Law) appropriates for utter destruction: Amalek. In the context of the Israel-Amalek confrontation, Hitler's inability to coexist with Jews – even with converted Jews, or Jews whose claim to Judaism was limited to one Jewish grandparent – is understandable. The two nations are, indeed, mutually exclusive. The ultimate fall of Nazi Germany, and the survival of the Jews, presages which of the two will finally emerge victorious.

27. See Ezra, Chap. 10.

He will fulfill all My desires,"
To say of Jerusalem, "It shall be built,"
And of the Temple, "It shall be established."

Maimonides explains that the verses refer primarily to the final redemption. The stargazers and the astrologers promise that Israel will never emerge from their state of lowly exile; they are eternally damned, a people forever punished and forsaken. In confirming the words of His prophets, God makes of them fools: Jerusalem will once more be settled, the cities of Judah rebuilt. Yet, immediately after the eschatological prophecy of the End-time, the verses are directed at Cyrus, the Gentile king who was God's emissary in initiating the return from Babylon. The implication, as Rabbi Yissachar Shlomo Teichtel has pointed out, is that the final redemption will come by similar means: Israel will be permitted to return to their Land by a modern-day Cyrus – by the grace of foreign nations.

REMEMBRANCE AND REDEMPTION: THE GRACE
OF FOREIGN NATIONS

Although the comparison between the two returns has only surfaced in recent years, the idea of such a correlation has been recorded in Jewish sources long before the current waves of *aliyah* began. In the Book of Jeremiah, the prophet foretells the return of seventy years: "After seventy years for Babylon have been completed, I will remember you and I will fulfill for you My favorable promise, to return you to this place" (29:10). The word *efkod* (remember), whose Hebrew root is the word *pakad*, does not imply a full-scale redemption,[28] but rather the first stage of the process.

The Vilna Gaon[29] taught that the final redemption will likewise

---

28. The Hebrew word for redemption is *"geulah"*; see, for instance, Exodus 6:6 concerning the redemption from Egypt, and Isaiah 41:14 concerning the final redemption.

29. Known as the Vilna Gaon (the Genius of Vilna), Rabbi Eliyahu Kremer

incorporate a first stage of *pekidah*, a *remembrance* before the complete redemption is revealed. Of this phase the prophet envisages a return of "one from a city and two from a clan" (Jeremiah 3:14), an ingathering that remains restrained and limited, like the gathering of the time of Cyrus. Ultimately, however, God promises that "With great mercy I shall gather you" (Isaiah 54:7), implying a revealed outpouring of Divine kindness, uninhibited by moderation and restraint.[30]

In the light of this distinction, the profound role played by the nations of the world in the current return takes on still deeper meaning. The complete redemption implies the return of God to his people; when that time comes, Israel will not require the assistance of any Gentile nation. In the remembrance stage, however, the aid of foreign powers was essential to the rebuilding of the Jewish People and the resettlement of their land.

We have already mentioned the verse in Deuteronomy that splits the Jewish return into two parts: "Then the Lord your God will bring back your captivity . . . and will return and gather you from among all the peoples" (30:3). Commenting on the verse, Nachmanides explains that the First Return will be by the grace of the nations; only the second will come through overt Divine intervention.[31] The idea that the final redemption will begin with the clemency of global powers is also expressed by Rabbeinu Saadya Gaon (882–942),[32] Rabbeinu Bachya (died c. 1050),[33] Radak (1160–1235),[34] Abarbanel (1437–1508),[35] and other prominent ancient authorities.

In this sense, the current period can thus be understood as one of

---

(1720–1797) was the undisputed leader of the traditional faction of world Jewry. His commentaries and annotations are venerated by virtually all sectors of Jewry, and many treat his every word as authoritative.

30. Annotations to *Tikkunei Zohar Chadash*, p. 27a; the first stage of the redemption is compared to the action of the weaker left hand, while the final stage is compared to the action of the right.

31. *Commentary to Song of Songs* 8:12.

32. *Emunot U'Deot, maamar* 8, Chap. 5.

33. *Commentary to Bible*, Leviticus 11:4–7.

34. *Commentary to Psalms* 146:3.

35. *Commentary to Psalms* 147:2.

pekidah: a stage of remembrance that precedes the final redemption. In fact, the word *pakad* (remembered) is also used in specific reference to *impregnation*. When Sarah miraculously became pregnant with Isaac, the verse uses an identical form: "The Lord remembered Sarah as He had said" (Genesis 21:1).[36] The final redemption, however, is described by the prophet as a *birth*: "Has a nation ever been born at one time, as Zion went through her labor and gave birth to her children?" (Isaiah 66:8). The first stage, which must pre-empt the final birth, is a stage of *impregnation*.

Much as in the course of a pregnancy, the ultimate joy of birth is preceded by pain and suffering;[37] we can but hope that this phase is already behind us. In the First Return, the course of redemption proceeded no further than this first stage; in the current return, we await the final birth.

THE FLOURISHING SHARON

A midrashic source notes the sequential order implied by the prophecy of Isaiah:

The wilderness and the wasteland will rejoice over them; the desert will be glad and blossom like a lily. It will blossom abundantly and will rejoice, with joyousness and glad song; the glory of Lebanon has been given to her, the majesty of the Carmel and the Sharon; they will see the glory of the Lord, the majesty of our God. (35:1–2)

"This comes to teach you," writes the Midrash, "that when the Lord shall reveal His Presence upon Israel, He shall not reveal Himself at once, but rather in stages." The verses present a chronological sequence. The wilderness will rejoice,; then the desert and will bloom abundantly, then the majesty of the Lebanon will be restored. Finally, "they shall

---

36. See also Talmud, *Rosh Hashanah* 10b.

37. Vilna Gaon, ibid. He extracts this from a comparison of the future redemption to the Biblical redemption from Egypt; the first result of Moses' appearance to Pharaoh, as is written in the verse, was the harshening of the Jews' working conditions.

see the glory of the Lord."[38] We are living through the first stages of the prophecy.

We have discussed the prophecy of Ezekiel, which was directed toward the mountains of the Holy Land. A further prophecy of Isaiah serves to complement his vision:

Thus said the Lord: "Just as when the wine is found in a cluster, one says, 'Do not destroy it, for there is blessing in it,' so will I do for My servants, not to destroy everything. I will bring forth seed from Jacob, and out of Judah the heir of My mountains; My chosen ones shall inherit it, and My servants shall dwell there. The Sharon shall be a fold of flocks, and the valley of Achor a place for herds to lie down in, for My people that have sought Me." (65:8–10)

Before the return of Jews to the Land, the area of the Sharon, which is located in central Israel, consisted of little more than swampy wasteland. After the swamps were drained by the early Zionist immigrants, the area began to bloom once more, heralding a return to its ancient beauty.

Notably, the benedictions of the Amidah follow a similar pattern to that which pervades the verses of Isaiah. Following the theme of ingathering, the weekday prayer moves forwards to the glory of future times: the restoration of true judges, the fall of the wicked, the reward of the righteous, the rebuilding of Jerusalem (the Temple), and the establishment of the House of David (the Messiah). Having described the rebirth of the Sharon, the verses of Isaiah move on to depict an altogether golden future. The world will witness the creation of *new heavens and a new earth*; weeping and sadness will be replaced by perpetual joy and celebration, as God rejoices over Jerusalem and exults with His people (65:17–19).

NEXT YEAR IN YERUSHALAYIM

The last of the twelve central benedictions of the Amidah prayer relates to the concept of prayer itself: We pray that God should hear our prayers, and we bless His merciful attribute of doing so. The previously mentioned chapter of Isaiah may well have been among the sources

---

38. *Midrash Tanchuma*, Deuteronomy 1.

used to determine the weekday prayer, and ends on a similar note: "It shall be that before they call, I will answer; while they yet speak, I will hear" (65:24).

Significantly, this verse is added to the Amidah prayer during fast days, most of which were instituted as days of mourning and prayer over the Destruction. Following the last of the twelve central benedictions, the Jewish prayer proceeds to the final Restoration: "Who returns His Shechinah [Holy Presence] to Zion." The prayers and the pleas, the yearning and the tears – even the hopeful declaration, "Next year in Jerusalem!" that Jews have proclaimed at the holiest moments of the year for two millennia[39] – will ultimately bear their fruit.

Despite his description of the utopian existence of future times, the prophet returns to a familiar theme: "They will build houses and inhabit, they will plant vineyards and eat their fruit" (Isaiah 65:21). In those days, the fulfillment of the prophecy will be complete. No longer will disputes rage over possession of the Holy Land: "The Lord your God will bring you to the Land that your forefathers possessed – and you shall possess it" (Deuteronomy 30:5). No longer will people live in fear of wars and terror, of disengagement and evacuation.

Those days are not yet come; yet the process that leads toward them – a progression that has been extant since the first instant of the world's existence – is becoming apparent.

---

39. The declaration is made twice a year – at the close of Yom Kippur, and at the end of the Passover Seder.

⌀ Chapter 3

INGATHERING IN UNBELIEF

SETTLED IN UNBELIEF

One of the hallmarks of the current ingathering is the predominantly secular nature of returnees, and the correspondingly secular nature of the Jewish State.

Many leaders and members of the Orthodox community, and in particular its Haredi[1] branch, have felt acute distress at the sight of the Jewish State (and its Zionist founders) trampling underfoot the religious values and practices so central to Orthodox Judaism. Among Zionist leaders themselves, some saw the movement as being antithetical to traditional religious praxis, believing that the Zionism means to "sanctify life in place of sanctifying God,"[2] or that the concept of Jewish nationalism is wholly incompatible with traditional notions of passivity in relation to matters of redemption and the Land of Israel.[3] It is true that the great majority of Zionist leaders distanced themselves from ex-

---

1. The most theologically conservative form of Orthodox Judaism, whose members closely adhere to the minutiae of Torah law and tradition, and oppose cultural integration into modern society. Although unclear demarcation lines between Orthodox denominations makes their populations difficult to determine, Haredi populations may be as large as 800,000–1,000,000 in Israel, and 500,000 in the Diaspora (principally U.S. and Europe).

2. Ben-Zion Dinur, *BeMifneh HaDorot* (Jerusalem 5714), p. 9.

3. Baruch Kimerling, "Religion, Nationalism and Democracy in Israel," in *Zemanim* 50–51 (1994), p. 116 [Hebrew].

treme positions of Zionism's ideological incompatibility with religious values and observance (such as those expressed by Chaim Brenner),[4] yet it remains clear that if Zionism was not a secular movement, it was certainly a movement that had a concrete effect of secularization on its followers.[5] Rabbi Eliezer Gordon could thus state of Zionism that "more than it purifies the defiled, it defiles the pure," adding that he does not wish to contaminate his own "pure ones."[6]

The secular and secularizing nature of the movement that brought about the establishment of the State has provided elements of the Orthodox community with reason enough to play down (or entirely ignore) the historic and theological significance of the State of Israel, and of the massive Jewish return to the Land of Israel associated with it. The harsh reality of the fulfillment of Biblical prophecies in a context of extreme secularism represents a theological paradox that has proven hard to swallow.

As is well known, the most vociferous criticism of the State and its leaders was made by the venerable Rabbi of Satmar, Rabbi Yoel Teitelbaum, who did not mince words in censuring the State:

For if we took all the breaches [of law] of this generation and the numerous sins committed all over the world and placed them on one side of the scales, and the Zionist State on the other, it would tip the scales, because it is the root of all evil, the ultimate source of defilement, the prime cause of injury in all the world – and it is they who defile the entire world.[7]

Rather than the fulfilment of prophecy, Satmar continues to perceive the State as no less that a satanic manifestation – "the root of all evil" and "the ultimate source of defilement." Most Orthodox Jews feel uncomfortable with this definition, and as will be detailed below in chapter 6, prefer to leave the State's theological status undefined. All

---

4. See Yosef Salmon, *Do Not Provoke Providence: Orthodoxy in the Grip of Nationalism* (Jerusalem 2004), pp. 317–326 [Hebrew].

5. Salmon, p. 14.

6. Ze'ev Aryeh Raviner, *HaGaon Rabbi Eliezer Gordon* (Tel Aviv 5728), p. 134.

7. Rabbi Y. Teitelbaum, *Vayoel Moshe* (Brooklyn, N.Y.: 1956), p. 11.

of Orthodox Jewry, however, expresses the strongest disapproval of the State's sometimes fervent secularism.

In itself, however, the irreligious nature of returnees should not be perceived as detracting from the theological significance of the return. As demonstrated in the previous chapter, the Jewish resettlement of the Land and its flourishing agriculture constitute sure signs of great things afoot.

Moreover, several sources indicate the virtue of Jewish occupation of the Land, notwithstanding highly irreligious behavior on the part of some settlers. Concerning one sinful generation, God tells Ezekiel, "The House of Israel dwell on their land and they have contaminated it with their way and with their acts" (36:17). Based on this verse, the Midrash offers a powerful insight: "God said, 'Would that the children of My people should dwell in the Land of Israel, even if they contaminate it.'"[8] The settlement of the Land is thus presented as a worthy objective irrespective of the spiritual level of the settlers.[9]

In a similar vein, we find in the Talmud that Omri, a king of Israel and father of the notorious Achav, was awarded kingship over Israel[10] as reward for his having established a city – the city of Shomron – in the Holy Land (*Sanhedrin* 102b). Despite his being singled out in Scripture as being more corrupt even than all the evil kings who preceded him (I Kings 16:25), Omri was rewarded for settling the Land. His deed was considered worthy in spite of his selfish intentions,[11] and notwithstanding his extreme wickedness.

---

8. *Yalkut Shimoni*, Lamentations Chap. 3, no. 1038.

9. This teaching of the sages is somewhat surprising. Twice in Leviticus we find the verse warning Israel lest they stray from the statutes of God, which will cause the Land to "disgorge them" (Leviticus 18:28, 20:22). How, then, does God wish the people to remain upon the Land even in a state of iniquity? See Teichtel, *Eim Habanim Semeichah* (p. 203), who suggests an approach to resolve this contradiction. It may be suggested that the nature of the Land, which is to disgorge its sinful inhabitants, can be overruled by Divine intervention, thus enabling the people to dwell in the Land even in a sinful state.

10. Both his son and his grandson ruled over Israel.

11. Omri built the city to rival the city of Jerusalem (*Yalkut Shimoni*, I Kings, Chap. 16).

The belittlement of the current return through reference to the secular nature of modern returnees is particularly strained in view of the low religious level of the returnees from Babylon, who returned from exile to resettle the Land and rebuild the Temple. In accordance with several prophecies of redemption, and despite their iniquities (which we have already outlined in the previous chapter), the Babylonian returnees went on to rebuild the ruined Temple.

Although the comparison between the returnees from Babylon and those of modern times cannot be precise, the Midrash does state of them that they were "pleasant in their deeds" (*Genesis Rabba* 71:3). Nothing pleasant is found in Scripture about their deeds,[12] apart from their willingness, in contrast to other elements of the nation, to return to the Land of their fathers.[13] The same, it would appear, can be said about the current returnees: Despite their distance from Jewish tradition, their return to the Land is *pleasant* before God.

Original opponents of Zionism applied the words of Psalms to the nascent movement: "Unless the Lord builds the house, its builders labor in vain on it" (127:1). Such, for instance, were the words of Rabbi M. N. Kahane-Shapira of Kishunez:

Heaven forbid that we walk in the way of these sinful people, who strive for natural redemption. This striving is forbidden. . . . The act of *teshuvah* [repentence] alone is a legitimate means to hasten the End, but acts of ingathering [the exiles] and of bringing [Israel to their land] depend solely upon the hand of God: Unless the Lord builds the house, its builders labor in vain on it; unless the Lord watches over the city, the watchman keeps vigil in vain.[14]

---

12. Although the people ultimately repented from their wayward deeds (see Ezra, Chap. 10), the "pleasant deeds" of the Midrash refers to the resettlement of the Land and the rebuilding of the Temple, which took place before the later penitence.

13. This point is made at length by Rabbi Yissachar Teichtel, *Eim Habanim Semeichah*, pp. 106–109.

14. A. B. Steinberg, *Daat HaRabanim* (Warsaw: 1902), p. 39; cited in Ravitzky, *Messianism, Zionism, and Orthodox Radicalism*, p. 18.

It appears that this verse served as the inspiration that convinced the Rebbe of the Lubavitch Hassidism, Rabbi Shalom Dov Baer Schneersohn, that the Zionist dream would never be realized:

Their presumptuous goal of gathering [the exiles] together on their own will never come to pass, and all their strength and their many stratagems and efforts will be of no avail against the will of the Lord. They will try one idea after another, like garments, but it is the counsel of the Lord that will prevail.[15]

Several decades earlier, the same verse had already been quoted in criticizing the disciples of the Vilna Gaon, who were the first to actively pursue a course of political ambition in settling the Land.[16] Yet, if we accept as axiomatic that no building can be built without Divine assistance (the more so in the Land of Israel), we are forced to conclude that the current return in the form of the State of Israel, which has become an established fact of the modern world in spite of the dangers it continues to face, was indeed built with the help of God.

This argument, which has been taken up in a modern context by Rabbi Dr. Chaim Zimmerman,[17] was put forward by the disciples of the Vilna Gaon themselves: "For had it not been that God desired us, He would not have shown us all of these, to bring us to our resting-place and our heritage."[18] Indeed, a number of Torah luminaries commented on the Divine providence manifest in the rebuilding and resettlement of the Land, in spite of their great distance from political Zionism and its secular leaders.[19]

---

15. Shalom Dov Baer Schneersohn, *Iggerot Kodesh*, secs. 130, 309–310.

16. See Arie Morgenstern, *Natural Redemption: The Disciples of the Vilna Gaon in Israel 1800–1840* [Hebrew] (Maor, Jerusalem: 1997), p. 17.

17. Rabbi Dr. Chaim Zimmerman, *Torah and Existence* (Jerusalem – New York: 1986), p. 67.

18. P. Greivsky, *Miginzei Yerushalayim*, book 2, p. 3; cited in Morgenstern, *Natural Redemption: The Disciples of the Vilna Gaon in Eretz Israel*, p. 89. The quote is part of a text that was used for fundraising purposes. It concludes, "It is a sign of the Commencement of the redemption [*atchalta degeulah*]."

19. For instance, Rabbi Yosef Chaim Sonnenfeld commented, "How can one fail to see God's hand in all this? We must work to settle the Land, with faith in God, Who gave us His Torah" (*HaIsh Al HaChoma*, vol. II, p. 57). Likewise, see

Even secular leaders – at least some of them – were aware that they were part of a historic progression whose significance went far beyond the nationalist project of other nation states. Years before his dream materialized, the Zionist leader Ze'ev (Vladimir) Jabotinsky placed more confidence in Divine assistance than he did in Zionist compatriots. Expressing his fear that the Old Zionist Organization [as opposed to Jabotinsky's Revisionists] would preclude the Jews from playing the role of *sage-femme* [midwife] in the exodus of European Jews to Palestine, Jabotinsky – certainly no saint in terms of religious practice – concluded: "But the march of events is so ordained by God Himself that it will end in the *Judenstaad* independently of what we Jews do or do not do."[20]

Having said this, the very fact that the current return consisted of mainly secular returnees, children of the European Enlightenment, and products of the revolutionary culture of the early twentieth century, is highly noteworthy. What is the meaning, from a theological perspective, of this striking feature of the recent ingathering?

THE ETERNAL DREAM

To reach a possible understanding of the issues involved, we first introduce some historical background.

The concept of the Jews returning to their Biblical homeland, though it remained dormant for many years, is of course no invention of the twentieth century. The Jewish People, for whom Biblical prophecy remained eternally contemporary, and who faithfully transmitted their ancient heritage from generation to generation, have always lived in hope of the coming return. Indeed, the word of God to Jeremiah emphasizes the importance of bequeathing this theme to posterity:

---

the comment made by the *Chafetz Chaim*, as cited in chapter six of this work, p. 149.

20. Joseph B. Shechtman, *Fighter and Prophet: The Life and Times of Vladimir Jabotinsky* (Eshel Books, Silver Spring), p. 352; some might treat the statement with skepticism, though Jabotinsky's biographer clearly did not.

The Lord, the God of Israel, said, "Write down in a book all these words that I am telling you. For, behold, days are coming," declares the Lord, "when I will return the captivity of My people Israel and Judah," says the Lord, "and I will return them to the land that I gave their forefathers, and they will possess it." (Jeremiah 30:3–4)

In the *Amidah* prayer,[21] which we have already mentioned in the previous chapter, the subjects of six of the twelve central benedictions are somehow related to the ingathering of Israel.[22] The entire prayer forms an order, leading the Jewish People toward final redemption, ingathering, and the glorious times of the Messianic Kingdom. Excepting the anomaly of the German Reform Movement and some contemporary derivatives, the concepts of Jerusalem and Zion have remained central in Jewish hearts throughout the ages. The Jewish nation has forever hoped for, prayed for, and lived in anticipation of being ingathered *en masse* to *Eretz Yisrael*.

Yet, though they never ceased to hope, the Jews' enduring faith in future redemption was, until the late nineteenth century, seldom accompanied by practical action aimed at realizing the ancient dream. The traditional attitude – an attitude prevalent until the present day among more conservative segments of Orthodox Jewry – was that such fundamental matters as redemption and ingathering were entirely in the hands of God. Man is required to partner with God through prayer, and through performing the ordinances of the Torah,[23] but this obligation

---

21. Traditionally known as the *Amidah* because it is recited while standing, or the *Shemoneh Esrei* (after its original eighteen benedictions).

22. Although only one of these benedictions makes explicit mention of it, all six are closely linked to the return of the people to their homeland. These are: the redemption, the ingathering of the nation to its land, the return of the judges, the rebuilding of Jerusalem, the salvation that will come through the offspring of King David, and the return of the Divine Presence to Zion

23. The Torah, and, by way of extension, the Oral Law (recorded predominantly in the Talmud), in which the conduct expected of a Jew is recorded. The Law includes principles of social interaction, religious ritual, and directives that govern day-to-day life.

falls short of actively seeking to realize the Jewish dream by political or military means.

In the Jewish tradition, the path toward destiny is seen to be paved with bricks of mitzvot (Torah precepts) and prayers – and not with force or political guile.[24] In fact, taking up the sword, or, according to some, even forming a political agenda, infringes upon the law of the Three Oaths,[25] which binds the Jewish People to their exilic status until they are released from it by God.[26] According to the Targum, the instruction to be wary of "pressing the End" was issued as long ago as in the time of Joseph in ancient Egypt.[27] The End is to be anticipated, but not forced.

In later times, when the possibility of settling the Holy Land by means of diplomacy and political processes began to surface, the theological stance objecting to such an agenda was radically sharpened. For virulent anti-Zionists such as the Munkaczer (Rabbi Chaim Elazar

---

24. According to Jewish tradition, the Torah existed long before the world was created, and served as the heavenly tool with which the world was fashioned. (See Proverbs 8:30, which is traditionally interpreted as referring to Torah; see also Talmud, *Pesachim* p. 54a; *Zohar*, vol. 1, 5b.) It includes, in a concealed and esoteric sense, everything the world contains, and every historical event that has taken place and is destined to take place. The destiny of the world is therefore inextricably bound to Torah. When the Jewish People, who were given the Torah at Sinai, fulfill its precepts, they manifest the hidden layers of Torah in a tangible, physical sense, thus partnering God in leading the world to its predetermined destiny.

25. Indeed, the anti-Zionist stance of many religious leaders was founded on the prohibition of the Three Oaths. *Vayoel Moshe*, the vehemently anti-Zionist book authored by Rabbi Yoel Teitelbaum, is based entirely on the proscription of the Oaths; see also the letter of Rabbi Yaakov Loberbaum (the renowned *Netivot HaMishpat*) to his disciple Rabbi Z. H. Kalisher, in which the former sharply criticizes the attitudes adopted by the latter toward settlement of the Land of Israel, invoking (among other concerns) the prohibition of the Oaths to require the maintenance of the exilic status quo.

26. See Appendix D, in which we have briefly treated the subject of the Three Oaths.

27. Targum Yonatan b. Uziel, Genesis 50:25. According to Targum, when Joseph adjured his brothers to ensure that his bones would be taken from Egypt, he added an oath that they should not press the *ketz*.

Shapira) and Satmar (Rabbi Yoel Teitelbaum) Rebbes, the harsh for-
mulation of Rabbi Yehonatan Eybeschutz (eighteenth century) became
a standard norm:

The congregation of Israel shouted out their vow. . . . For even if the whole
people of Israel is prepared to go to Jerusalem, and even if all the nations
consent, it is absolutely forbidden to go there. Because the End is unknown
and perhaps this is the wrong time. [Indeed,] tomorrow or the next day they
might sin, and will yet again need to go into exile, heaven forbid, and the latter
[exile] will be harsher than the former.[28]

In addition, although many (and perhaps most) authorities over the
generations have ruled that there is a Biblical mitzvah (directive) to live
in the Holy Land, a mainstream ideology among European Jewry underscored a certain danger in living a "mundane" life enveloped in the
holy aura of the Land. The twelfth-century Maharam of Rothenberg,
perhaps the leading authority of his time, warned his fellow Jews of
living in the Land of Israel:

Let him be abstinent in the Land and beware of any transgression, for if he
sins there, he will be punished most severely. For God supervises the land and
watches over its inhabitants. He who rebels against the kingdom from within
the king's palace is not the same as he who rebels outside it.[29]

Anti-Zionist leaders such as the Munkaczer Rebbe stressed the holiness
of the Land and the danger of its defilement by improper settlement;[30]
the Munkaczer himself added that life in the Holy Land should only be
contemplated by those willing to devote their lives to the pure study of
Torah and worship of God. In his words, "the evil forces have become
stronger in our Holy Land and they undermine its very foundation
through their plowshares and agricultural colonies."[31] With respect to
the Holy Land, the Munkaczer saw materialism as a manifestation of

---

28. Rabbi Yehonatan Eybeschutz, *Ahavat Yehonatan* (Warsaw: 1872), p. 74a.

29. *Shut Maharam* (Berlin: 1891), pp. 14–15.

30. See *Minchat Elazer*, vol. 5, sec. 16.

31. *Shaar Yissachar* 2:373; quoted in Aviezer Ravitzky, *Messianism, Zionism,
and Jewish Religious Radicalism*, Translated by Michael Swirsky and Jonathan
Chipman (University of Chicago Press: 1996), p. 47.

evil forces; indeed, the presence of evil in the Holy Land was a theme on which the Munkaczer elaborated, often warning of the "external forces" that cling to sources of holiness. The choice of the Land by the Zionist movement was itself adequate demonstration that "the adversary himself chose his dwelling in Jerusalem."[32] This perspective is, of course, radical, and its extreme tones were generally not found among contemporaries. Yet, the position could only sprout from a certain background of mainstream reluctance toward immigration to the Holy Land.[33]

Doubtless, the origins of this reluctance are not rooted in *halachic* (legal) theory alone. Practical considerations are no less central in understanding the traditional tendency toward passivity and submissiveness with respect to immigration to the Holy Land.

Replying to the proposal of a certain "man of rank," who suggested the establishment of a Jewish state in Palestine, Moses Mendelssohn responded by praising the courage of the individual and lauding the "bold project." However, he went on to reject the "great idea," citing the nature of the Jewish people as the primary obstacle to its realization:

The greatest obstacle in the way of this proposal is the character of my people. It is not ready to attempt anything so great. The pressure under which we have lived for centuries has removed all vigor from our spirit . . . the natural impulse for freedom has ceased its activity within us. It has been changed into a monkish piety, manifested in prayer and suffering, not in activity.[34]

Loyalty to Germany may also have been a factor in Mendelssohn's negative reply to the proposition; the statement concerning the generally passive nature of the people, however, was quite true (and was considered a virtue by later anti-Zionist rabbis). Although Mendelssohn's

---

32. *Divrei Torah*, vol. 6, sec. 25; quoted in Ravitzky, *Messianism, Zionism, and Jewish Religious Radicalism*, p. 47.

33. Concerning the obligation to live in the Holy Land, the Munkaczer Rebbe asserted that the mitzvah applied only during the time of the first Jewish conquest, and felt that this was why Maimonides did not include the mitzvah in his list of the 613 Commandments.

34. Moses Mendelssohn, *Gesammelte Schriften*, ed. G. B. Meldelssohn (Leipzig: 1843–45), 5:493–494; quoted in Ravitzky, *Messianism, Zionism, and Jewish Religious Radicalism*, p. 11.

statement was made in a particular time, place, and context, it remains indicative of the general nature of the Jewish People in its exilic condition, where active political measures were considered an expression of faithlessness in future Divine redemption.[35]

Even given the desire and willpower to do so, this exilic condition generally implied that the Jewish People lacked the social and material requisites necessary for generating a return to Zion. Scattered across many countries and several continents, the Jews had to focus their energies on ensuring their spiritual and material well-being, often amidst unwelcoming hosts. Their leaders were fully occupied with the organization and maintenance of traditional Jewish communal life, and could devote little attention and energy to nationalistic ideals. The dreams of redemption and ingathering remained dreams.

One of the rare occasions on which some practical attempt was made to restore a Jewish Palestine was seen in the efforts of Joseph Nasi, an influential Portuguese Jew, whose faith forced him to escape his homeland, eventually bringing him to Istanbul. By various twists of fate, Nasi gained the favor of the Sultan, whose empire included the Holy Land. In 1561, he used his influence to establish a Jewish settlement in Tiberias and one in Safed. Subject to the sovereignty of the Sultan, Nasi was granted the authority to rule locally. He rebuilt the town and its walls, and attempted to establish it as a textile center by planting mulberry trees, and by encouraging craftsmen to move there. The plan was abandoned when the Ottomans and the Republic of Venice went to war, which shifted the Sultan's preoccupations to more pressing needs.[36]

On other occasions, the proclamation of a false messiah raised the spirits of the people, before leaving them dejected sevenfold after his exposure as a fraud,[37] and it is not surprising that representatives of the

---

35. See Shlomo Zalman Landau and Yosef Rabinowitz, *Or LaYesharim* (Warsaw, 1900), p. 5; in their polemic tract, which the authors claim was endorsed by many leading rabbinic figures, Landau and Rabinowitz write that the Zionist notices urging people to act on their own behalf in the context of exile and redemption was a heresy, "publicly denying our faith in the Divine redemption."

36. See Sol Scharfstein, *Chronicle of Jewish History* (Ktav Publishing House, 1997), p. 167.

37. The most prominent of these, Shabbetai Zvi on the seventeenth century

traditional (Haredi) sector of Orthodox Judaism equated the Zionist concept of the Jeiwsh State with past hopes of false messiahs:

People like Herzl and Nordau declare their intention to found a state of Jews in the Land of Israel with permission from the governments, and in spite of this being entirely impossible in any sense of the natural order, still they find fervent believers who follow them with the same zeal as false messiahs of old. . . . Even were entry to the Land of Israel permitted to us, can it be believed that a land holy unto the two religions that rule over the entire world . . . over which rivers of blood have been spilled in wars over its conquest . . . [will be given over to us]? Somebody in possession of right mind will not even dream of a state of Jews, for dreams are but an extension of waking thought, and a wise heart will never conceive of so implausible an idea.[38]

The treatise continues to explain that the gathering of Israel to its homeland cannot happen before the advent of Elijah the prophet, and points to previous failures as clear precedents for the current endeavor. Aside from short-lived arousals, and with the exception of the disciples of the Vilna Gaon,[39] the traditional Jew thus continued to quietly hope, pray, and dream.

CHRISTIAN PRAGMATISM

Yet, while the reality of a Jewish homeland remained all too distant for the Jew, the significance of the Jews and their Biblical homeland had found a voice in an altogether unexpected source. After the translation of the Bible into English in the early seventeenth century (under the auspices of King James I of England), a school of thought emerged believing firmly in the literal realization of the many prophecies that foretold the return of Israel to their Land.

---

and Jacob Frank on the eighteenth, arose to lay claim to the title of Messiah. Ultimately, they were exposed as frauds: Frank converted to Christianity, and Shabbetai Zvi to Islam. Jewish morale was struck a heavy blow by these events, which played a major role in the rise of the Hassidic Movement that swept across Europe in the eighteenth century.

38. Landau and Rabinowitz, *Or LaYesharim*, p. 21.
39. See below, p. 214.

In 1585, Francis Kett, a Fellow of Corpus Christi, Cambridge, was brave enough to articulate these views in his tract, "The glorious and beautiful Garland of Man's Glorification containing the godly misterie of heavenly Jerusalem." Two years later, his "heresy" was punished by burning at the stake. Yet, in spite of the severe reaction, the concept of a Jewish return to Palestine had taken root. In 1607, Thomas Brightman published a book in Basel called *Revelation of the Revelation*, in which he wrote, "What, shall they return to Jerusalem again? There is nothing more certain; the prophets do everywhere confirm it." Other prominent individuals of the same period began to express similar beliefs, and the idea gained considerable momentum.[40] Isaac de la Peyrere, who was the

---

40. In 1621, Sir Henry Finch published The *Restauration of the Jews*, which predicted the restoration of the people of Israel in her homeland, and how "all the gentiles shall bring their glory into thy empire." The book provoked strong opposition from both Church and state, and King James I, who saw the book as a personal libel, arrested Sir Henry and the publishers. They were released shortly after, but the episode served as a caution for others. Nevertheless, the idea had taken root, and continually gained momentum, although it shared the Jews' disappointment at the 1666 exposure of Shabbetai Zvi.

Sir Isaac Newton was less public about his theological beliefs, partly because of their heresy (for one, he did not believe in the Trinity), and partly because he was content to submit his insights to writing, and to teach them to a small group of disciples. In addition, and unlike contemporaries such as Finch, Mede, William Lloyd, and even his protégé Whiston, who saw a certain apocalyptic urgency in the Jews' restoration, all of them making predictions of major events during the seventeenth or eighteenth centuries, Newton felt no such urgency, and predicted the restoration to be at least three centuries away. Naturally, this would not have enhanced the popularity of his theology.

In fact, the bulk of Newton's theological manuscripts were not given public exposure until 1991; when they were disclosed, they added much to Newton's *Observations* in revealing the author as a fervent believer in the return of the Jews, which he perceived as being a central theme of Biblical prophecy. Of the Christians who fail to appreciate the secret behind the "Restoration of all things," Newton writes (I have modernized old words): "For they understand not that the final return of the Jews' captivity and their conquering the nations [of the four Monarchies] and setting up a righteous and flourishing Kingdom at the day of judgment is this mystery. Did they understand this they would find it in all the old Prophets who write of the last times, as in the last chapters of Isaiah where the

French Ambassador to Denmark during the mid-seventeenth century, could even write a book wherein he bravely argued for a restoration of the Jews to Israel *without conversion to Christianity*. He was made to suffer for his beliefs, but was not burnt at the stake.[41]

By the eighteenth century, the Restoration Movement, which later evolved into the Christian Zionist Movement, included a distinguished list of theologians, writers, and politicians.[42] Ironically, much of the drive for the Jewish homeland between the sixteenth and nineteenth centuries thus came from Christians rather than Jews. One example of this phenomenon is seen in the actions of Charles Henry Churchill, a British resident of Damascus, who zealously propagated the idea of creating a Jewish State in Palestine. In 1841 he wrote a letter to the Jewish philanthropist Moses Montefiore, in which he stated, "I consider the object to be perfectly obtainable. But, two things are indispensably necessary. Firstly, that the Jews will themselves take up the matter unanimously. Secondly, that the European powers will aid them in their views."[43]

Some decades later, another Churchill, the great statesman and British Prime Minister, Winston, would do much for the cause of the

---

Prophet conjoins the new heaven and earth with the ruin of the Jews' captivity and their setting up a flourishing and everlasting Kingdom" (Jewish National and University Library [Jerusalem] Yahuda MS 6, f. 12r).

41. See Ira Robinson, *Isaac de la Peyrère and the Recall of the Jews*, Jewish Social Studies; Spring 1978, vol. 40, issue 2, pp. 117–130.

42. Noteworthy was Thomas Newton (1704–1782), the Bishop of Bristol, whose *Dissertation of the Prophecies* was an important text for the movement. In the book, he writes, "Our Savior's words are very memorable: 'Jerusalem shall be trodden down of the Gentiles, until the times of the Gentiles be fulfilled.' It is still trodden down by the Gentiles, and consequently the times of the Gentiles are not yet fulfilled. When 'the times of the Gentiles' shall be 'fulfilled,' then the expression implies that the Jews shall be restored: And for what reason, can we believe, that though they are dispersed among all nations, yet, by a constant miracle, they are kept distinct from all, but for the farther manifestation of God's purposes toward them?"

43. Another popular figure in the Restoration Movement of the same period was George Gawler (1796–1869). He wrote a book in 1845, in which he stated that the Jews were to replenish the deserted towns and fields of Palestine.

Jews and their desire for statehood. A self-declared Zionist, Churchill did everything in his power to further the cause of the Jews' returning to Palestine. During his period in office as Colonial Secretary, it was his vision alone that prevented the allocation of Palestine to King Abdullah Hussein, whose domain was thus limited to Transjordan.[44] And it was Churchill's determination as Prime Minister that denied the Palestinian Arabs self-government,[45] which threatened to dash all Jewish hopes of mass immigration and the establishment of a Jewish majority.

In 1878, Sir Lawrence Oliphant, who was a fervent supporter of the Restoration, set out with great zeal to secure the ancient homeland for European Jewry. He obtained the endorsement of Lord Salisbury and of Benjamin Disraeli (Lord Beaconsfield),[46] and his mission was encouraged even by the Prince of Wales – the future King Edward VII. Yet, by the time Oliphant set off for Constantinople in 1880 to see the Sultan, Disraeli had fallen from power, and British foreign policy no longer supported such an agreement with the Turks.

---

44. Churchill achieved this in a number of meetings on his 1921 visit to Palestine and the colonies.

45. Churchill did a great service to the Zionist cause by failing to implement the 1939 White Paper, which promised Palestinian Arabs autonomous government after five years – a decision that Churchill regarded with much disdain. Fortunately for Churchill and the Zionists, the majority of the Arabs had certainly not aided the Allied effort during WWII, and many of them had, in fact, supported the enemy. This diverted attention from the promise contained in the White Paper. Had an Arab government been appointed, the State of Israel would not exist today. Throughout his political career, Churchill's commitment to the implementation of the Balfour Declaration was unfailing, and was undoubtedly a crucial factor in preparing the ground for the future Jewish State.

46. Disraeli was a Jew by birth, but a Christian by faith. Together with many prominent contemporaries, such as the Earl of Shaftesbury (Anthony Ashley Cooper, who noted in his diaries that the signs were right for the return of the Jews to Palestine), Lord Palmerstone, Robert Browning, George Eliot, John Adams, and others, he firmly embraced the concept of a restored Jewish State.

THE CHRISTIAN-ZIONIST ALLIANCE

While Christians were debating and deliberating the issue of the Jews' return to their homeland, the matter remained fairly dormant on the Jewish scene. Although settling the Holy Land was traditionally viewed as a lofty ideal,[47] few dared to convert the ideal into actual emigration. Prominent exceptions were the *aliyot* of two groups, whose messianic fervor drove them to settle the Land despite the hardships involved.

In 1777, a group of early Hassidim, disciples of Rabbi Yisrael Baal Shem Tov[48] and of his chief disciple, the Maggid of Mezritz, made their way to Palestine and founded a settlement in Tiberias. Thirty-one years later, a group of disciples of Rabbi Eliyahu of Vilna[49] followed in three waves of immigration. They initially made their settlement in Safed, where they established the community of *Perushim*,[50] and began to integrate into their new surroundings. Eventually they succeeded in founding an Ashkenazi community in Jerusalem that would provide the Orthodox community with a foothold for social influence in the future.[51] These European immigrants joined sporadic waves of immigrants over the centuries from Muslim lands such as Morocco, Turkey, Iraq, and Yemen.

Despite these exceptions, the prevailing attitude throughout was that those who braved the harsh living conditions of Eretz Yisrael did so as individuals, or as small communities, with no real nationalist ambitions.

---

47. Prominent medieval Jewish sources explain that performance of Torah law outside the Holy Land is incomparable to its performance in Eretz Yisrael (see *Commentary of Nachmanides to Torah*, Leviticus 18:25). Additionally, there are several laws that relate to the Land and its crop, which can only be performed within the Biblical boundaries of the Holy Land.

48. Literally "the Possessor of a Good Name." Commonly known as The Besht, an acronym of his name, the Baal Shem Tov founded the Hassidic movement, which swept across Europe in the late eighteenth and nineteenth centuries.

49. See above, p. 62, note 29.

50. Literally "detached ones," implying detachment from worldly affairs, in favor of total dedication to Torah study and commitment to fulfilling its precepts.

51. For an in-depth account of the early years of this settlement, and its repercussions for future years, see mainly Arie Morgenstern, *Hastening Redemption* (Oxford University Press, NY: 2006).

Even Sir Moses Montefiore (1784–1885), who took a great interest in the Jewish community in Palestine, focused his resources and influence on developing settlements and aiding the settlers, but not on nationalistic aspirations. He believed, as did the vast majority of Jews, that Jewish nationalism would only be founded by the Messiah. Personal immigration to the Holy Land, an act marking a deep expression of yearning for the Land and its inherent holiness, was seen (at most) as a powerful prayer, which might even serve to hasten the redemption. It surely had no perceived connection with the redemption itself.

The Haskalah Movement of Jewish Enlightenment was no more inclined toward nationalism than their traditional brethren. On the contrary, the outspoken aim of its early members was to integrate into the Gentile societies in which they lived, and they preached undivided loyalty and devotion to their host countries. Thus, when Theodor Herzl set out his Zionist ideal in *Der Judenstaat* (*The Jewish State*, 1896), the idea was met with ridicule from a wide spectrum of Jewish leaders.[52] Herzl, however, refused to give up.

In his role as an Austro-Hungarian journalist, Herzl witnessed the Dreyfus Affair firsthand, in which a French general was wrongfully convicted of treason and imprisoned, against a background of deep and vociferous anti-Semitism.[53] Herzl concluded that the essence of the Jewish problem was not individual, but national. The only way to improve the lowly standing of Jews was by ending their long condition of national anomaly. The Jewish question, in his view, was a matter of international politics. Such views had been aired before, in particular in the *Chibat Zion* and *Chovavei Zion* organizations – the precursors to Zionism – and by Rabbi Shmuel Mohilever who led them.[54] Herzl,

---

52. Ironically, the issue of Herzl's Zionism was one of the few issues on which Orthodox and Reform rabbis were united: both entirely rejected the idea.

53. The scene that most aroused the spirit of Herzl was a crowd of incensed "enlightened" citizens chanting, "Death to the Jews."

54. These organizations, formed toward the end of the nineteenth century, espoused principles similar to those of modern Zionism, though often from a religious perspective. Most of them were formed spontaneously by groups of Eastern European Jews, after they realized that assimilation was not having the desired impact on the anti-Semitic culture of their host countries. The groups,

though crediting Rabbi Mohilever with the title of the first political Zionist, decided to take matters into his own hands.

Yet, however much he believed in the ideal, Herzl needed help. His request for financial assistance from wealthy Jews such as Baron Moritz de Hirsch and Baron Edmond de Rothschild were in vain. For such a grand political plan, he also needed friends in high places. Who could lend him this crucial assistance?

Herzl found the answer in the Christian Restoration Movement – specifically, in William H. Hechler (1845–1931), then chaplain of the British Embassy in Vienna. The son of a Hebrew scholar, Hechler's Bible studies convinced him that the restoration of the Jewish State was imminent. Inspired by *Der Judenstaat* to believe that the Biblical visions could become a tangible reality, he placed himself entirely at Herzl's disposal to assist in bringing the vision to reality.[55] Herzl accepted the offer, and utilized Hechler's impressive connections to arrange a meeting with Grand Duke Frederic of Baden (who approved Herzl's plans), making further use of his influence to arrange meetings with Kaiser Wilhelm II. Ultimately, these meetings came to nothing, and Germany rejected the Zionist plan. Yet Herzl, chiefly because of his partnership with Hechler, had succeeded in establishing widespread legitimacy for his fledgling movement.[56] With the support of British Restorationists, the Herzl-Hechler alliance would meet with its greatest success in London, where the World Zionist Congress was held in 1900, amidst the rallying cry of "Palestine for the Jews!" Herzl died of pneumonia in 1904; on his death bed, he told Hechler (who was the last non-family

---

typically named "Lovers of Zion," "Love of Zion," "Children of Zion," and so on, achieved some degree of *aliyah* (immigration to Palestine), and raised some funds for the purchase of lands, including Rabbi Mohilever's important achievement of recruiting Baron de Rothschild to fund the project of settling the Land of Israel – yet lacked professional organization as well as political clout.

55. More on Hechler's life and achievements can be found in "The Meeting that Changed the World," *Christians for Israel Today*, fall 1996. The article is available online at www.c4israel.org/articles/english/e-u-00-1-pile-meetchangworl.htm.

56. The first World Zionist Congress convened in Basel in 1897 (Hechler was present). The meeting with the Kaiser took place in 1898.

member to see him), "Greet Palestine for me. I gave my life's blood for my people."

THE HAND OF PROVIDENCE

Suspending the historical reel at this juncture, we should note the hand of providence at work behind the scenes. Herzl was not a religious man; in fact, he was so deeply assimilated that he failed to circumcise his son,[57] and could even conceive of a grandiose solution to the "Jewish problem" by means of mass conversion to Catholicism.[58] It is hardly surprising that Hans Herzl converted to Christianity, before he and the remainder of Herzl's family ultimately met tragic ends.[59] From a religious perspective, an individual so far removed from his Jewish roots as Theodor Herzl appears to be a strange choice for the person to lay such vital foundations for the historic return to the Jewish homeland.

We will return to this question in greater depth at the end of this chapter. From a pragmatic perspective, however, the decidedly Western

---

57. Responding to the Zionist leadership, Hans wrote of his father, "Even as he was becoming the leader of the Jewish People, he refused, at the advice of his confidants, to bring me into the covenant of faith and circumcise me. And it surely has not escaped you that every year my father lit a Christmas tree and continued to do this even in his final year. My father told our nannies that they should recite the Christian prayers with us every morning and every night" (Joseph Nadba, p. 69).

58. Herzl writes of this plan in his diary entries between 1893 and 1895: "I desired to solve the 'Jewish problem.' With the assistance of the Roman Catholic Church, we will create a major movement among the Jews to openly and proudly convert to Christianity. . . . The conversion to Christianity will take place in the cathedral by the light of day, after a festive parade and a ringing of the church bells. We shall do it with pride; we have no need to hide it" (Diaries, p. 14). Ultimately, Herzl abandoned the idea, and made no mention of it in later political activities.

59. Herzl's only son shot himself dead at the funeral of his sister Pauline, who was a drug addict and died supposedly of a morphine overdose. Herzl had a third daughter, who married and had a son before perishing at the hands of the Germans. The son was transported to safety, but killed himself after the war, when the fate of his family and Jewish brethren became known to him.

and secular nature of its founders was clearly much to the benefit of Zionism. The words of Rabbi Yekutiel Yehudah Halberstam, speaking in London on the first leg of his 1955 journey to Israel, are instructive in this respect. In a sermon he gave before an audience of Chassidim, the Rebbe of Zanz-Kloisenberg stressed the importance of going to live in Israel and making the desert bloom. One of the other Chassidic rabbis present commented that perhaps the tone of his words had been "too Zionist." The Rebbe replied with characteristic incisiveness:

However, we – the religious ones – busy ourselves only with criticizing, while they – the freethinkers . . . busy themselves with practical action and creating facts. . . . I, too, used to believe, in the past, that this was our task. . . . I used to curse the heretics with great intensity . . . but in vain. I have realized that they are becoming stronger. I therefore said to myself: "Would it not be better that we exchange roles – that is, I will build *Eretz Yisrael*, and let them, the secular people, be the ones to curse me."[60]

Rabbi Halberstam's witty response expresses criticism of his own previous position, which assumed the general stance of passivity adopted by the religious leaders of Europe. For the Rebbe, the success of the Zionist enterprise led to an ideological turnabout: Rather than praying and criticizing, the new role of Orthodox Jewry was building and doing. In his eyes, historical fact had proven that God favored practical action over the traditional course of passive inaction. For the pioneering Zionists, however, the initiative to build and to do did not emerge from religious contemplation, but rather from the Western cultures in which they were bred.

Were it not for this cultural background of Zionist leaders, the movement would probably never have come into being; certainly, it would not have realized the dream of creating a Jewish State. Theodor Herzl, Max Nordau, and Ze'ev Jabotinsky, considered by many to be the (unholy) "trinity" of political Zionism, were all of pure Western breed. Their significant contribution to the national redemption of Jewry was not extracted, as Joseph B. Shechtman has written, from the

---

60. Yechezkel Frankel, *Lapid HaEsh* (Bnei Brak, 1997), vol. 2, p. 483.

mines of the Jewish mode of life, but rather from wholesale assimilation and integration with the outside world.[61]

It is fascinating to contrast the leadership of Chaim Weizmann, who grew up in the small shtetl (hamlet) of Motele, deep in the Jewish Pale of Settlement, with that of Jabotinsky. Jabotinsky's Zionism, just as Herzl's and Nordau's before him, was built on modern ideas of national normalcy. Its strength derived not from traditional Jewish values, but from a virile, instinctive self-assertion in the face of a hostile and provocative non-Jewish world. Weizmann, whose policies of placating the British at every opportunity reflected the mentality of his traditional upbringing, stated in his *Trial and Error* that "Jabotinsky, the passionate Zionist, was utterly un-Jewish in manner, approach, and deportment" (p. 63). He reproached Herzl for the same reason, and was indubitably right in both cases. Yet he fails to note that many great advances of political Zionism were forged out of the deep ideological cleavage between himself and the "un-Jewish" Zionists he criticizes.

In addition to their European mentality, the alliance with Christian Zionists, whose influence upon statesmen and men of power culminated in the Balfour Declaration of 1917,[62] could only have come into being by virtue of the overt secularism embraced by Herzl and his followers. Centuries of bitter experience with the Church and its mission had brought the Jews expulsions, persecution, massacre, and forced conversion – all in the name of God. Traditional Orthodox Jewry would have been too suspicious to accept a partnership with the Christian Zionists, however ostensibly pure their intentions.[63] The assistance volunteered

---

61. Joseph B. Shechtman, *Fighter and Prophet: The Life and Times of Vladimir Jabotinsky* (Eshel Books, Silver Spring), p. 553.

62. Arthur Balfour, who encouraged and finally made the historic Balfour declaration, was a professed Restorationist. It is interesting to note that Balfour was no friend of the Jews in a general sense, and even sponsored the 1905 Aliens Act to restrict Jewish immigration to the United Kingdom. This emphasizes that the Christian Restoration was a Christian ideal, with Christian motives, and did not necessarily imply personal sympathy with the Jews.

63. A notable exception to this rule was the alliance formed by Rabbi Menachem Mendel of Shklov with British evangelicals in Jerusalem. The venerable leader of the Perushim community considered the alliance essential for

by the fervent Christian Zionist Orde Wingate,[64] for instance, whose trainees included such future military leaders as Yigal Allon and Moshe Dayan, was crucial in the general development of what was to become the Israel Defense Forces. The secular nature of the returnees permitted the formation of an environment – political, military, and social – that could foster the emergence of the Jewish State.

Observing the broader historical picture, it is striking that the United Kingdom, which in 1917 took over governmental power over the Land of Israel from the Turks, was the country with the strongest heritage of Christian Zionism. This heritage was among the critical factors that combined to set up the political conditions from which the Jewish State could emerge. Other factors relating to the U.K. include the timely favor shown by important statesmen such as Winston Churchill toward Jewish and Zionist causes, along with the providential influence of Chaim Weizmann[65] and other prominent Jewish figures. Although the relationship between Zionism and British officialdom later turned sour, the process had been initiated.

We have already commented on the involvement of Gentile nations in the ingathering of Israel in the previous chapter. To the comparison

---

his efforts to establish an Ashkenazi community in Jerusalem. The Christian missionaries were only too pleased to reciprocate, and soon reported their unprecedented achievement of befriending one of the leading rabbis and Torah scholars of the generation. The Diaspora community was predictably disturbed by the association with missionaries, and the friendship did not continue into future generations (see Arie Morgenstern, *Natural Redemption: the Disciples of the Vilna Gaon in the Land of Israel, 1800–1840* [Hebrew], pp. 135–157).

64. For a balanced and comprehensive biography of this controversial figure, see John Bierman and Colin Smith's *Fire in the Night: Wingate of Burma, Ethiopia, and Zion.*

65. Winston Churchill, then First Lord of the Admiralty, asked Dr. Weizmann, then a teacher of chemistry at Manchester University, if he could produce 30,000 tons of synthetic acetone, which was urgently required for the war effort. Weizmann's important contribution was one of the influences that prompted the Balfour Declaration, in which it was stated that "His Majesty's Government views with favor the establishment in Palestine of a national home for the Jewish People."

with the First Return sanctioned by Cyrus, we might add the following prophecy:

I will say to the North, "Give them over!" and to the South, "Do not with-hold!" Bring My sons from afar and My daughters from the ends of the earth. (Isaiah 43:6)

This prediction has been widely realized in the mass immigrations of Jews to the State of Israel, and most recently in the long-awaited arrival of Jews released from their imprisonment in the former Soviet Union. The foundation of the Jewish State, in which the Gentile nations were much involved, may also be considered part of this prophecy's fulfillment.

Rabbi Joseph B. Soloveichik has described the fateful session of the United Nations that approved the plan to partition Palestine (and es-tablish the Jewish State) in the following words:

I do not know who the representatives of the press, with their human eyes, saw to be the chairman . . . but he who looked carefully with his spiritual eye saw the true Chairman Who conducted the proceedings. (*Kol Dodi Dofek*, p. 32)

In the Scroll of Esther, when we read that "On that night, the king could not sleep" (6:1), the Talmud informs us that the deeper reference is not to Ahasuerus, but to the *King of the Universe* (*Megillah* 15b). The awakening of Ahasuerus was merely an earthly reflection of the Divine awakening to the plight of the Jewish People. Here, too, the nations gave their permission – but the true permission was granted by the King of nations.

RETURN IN UNBELIEF

The secularism of Herzl and his followers is even an integral facet of Biblical prophecy.

The state that Herzl envisaged, upon which he based his 1902 uto-pian novel *Altneuland* ("Old-New Land"), was liberal, enlightened, and profoundly secular. The book inspired many Jews of that period to take steps toward the realization of Herzl's vision. The conclusion of the book, "If you will it, it is no fairytale," which highlights the centrality of human deed while pushing Divine direction out of the picture, became the unofficial motto of the Zionist Movement. Eventually, the State was founded in the spirit of Herzl's vision: on secular foundations, by secular Jews, and with secular principles. God is notably absent from the national anthem, "*HaTikvah*" ("The Hope"), which poetically embodies the everlasting hope of the Jew. This, as we will see below, was no chance occurrence. The Declaration of Independence narrowly escaped a similar fate when an intentionally obscure reference to the Rock of Israel was inserted at the last moment.

In terms of Biblical prophecy, the clearest reference to a return to the Land in a state of sin is found in Ezekiel:

Thus said the Lord God: "It is not for your sake that I act, O House of Israel, but for My holy Name that you have desecrated among the nations where you came . . . I will take you from among the nations and gather you from all the lands, and I will bring you to your own soil. Then I will sprinkle pure water upon you, that you may become cleansed; I will cleanse you from your contamination and from all your idols. I will give you a new heart and put a new spirit within you; I will remove the heart of stone from your flesh and give you a heart of flesh. I will put My spirit within you, and I will make it so that you will follow my decrees and guard My ordinances and fulfill them" (Ezekiel 36:22–27).

Although the word *then* of the verse, "Then I will sprinkle pure water upon you," does not occur in all translations, the actual order of the verses implies that the gathering to the Land will precede God's purification of the people. Clearly, this process did not occur in the gathering of Ezra and Nehemiah, who returned to the Land after seventy years of exile. The leaders who led the return were all faithful to God and His Law, and were obviously distant from the "desecration of the Name" that the verse refers to. Although the leaders did chastise the people, and purged wayward deeds from their midst, this hardly resonates with the great spiritual elevation (from deep sinfulness to transcendent purity) implied by the verse.

In the recent ingathering, however, the nature of the immigrants – leaders and followers alike – was predominantly secular. Following the lead of the founder and subsequent leaders of the Zionist Movement, secularism was made an official policy of the new State. The Old Yishuv (settlement) of traditional Jews was shunned, and immigrants from Orthodox backgrounds were secularized, sometimes forcibly. The most renowned example of this is was the treatment of Yemenite children during the first years of the State. Children were separated from their parents, to be educated with a brand of atheism in which the only elevated principle was Zionism. They were coerced into desecrating the Sabbath, and the secular culture of the new Israel was instilled in them, entirely devaluing sacred traditions of millennia. In some camps, no kosher food was available. Torah, they were taught, and its "rigid" system of law and belief, was valid only in Yemen.[66] The first kibbutzim,[67] to which immigrants of all backgrounds were sent, were bastions of aggressive, intolerant secularism.

Fitting the word of the prophet, this phase of the return began in rampant unbelief. The people were not brought to the Land *because* of their deeds, but rather *in spite* of their deeds. "It is not for your sake that I act, O House of Israel, but for My holy Name that you have desecrated among the nations." Although the people were undeserving, God's plan, and the word He had spoken to the prophet, directed them back to the Holy Land.

REBUILT AND REJUVENATED

We still await the fulfillment of the ensuing verses, in which God infuses the nation with a new spirit, and returns them to His word. But though remaining far from complete, the first signs of the new age can already be discerned.

The secularism of the original settlers was to some extent a by-product of their Zionist idealism. Eliezer Berkovits has written:

---

66. Such regretful episodes have been widely chronicled in recent years. See especially Moshe Shonfeld's *Genocide of the Holy Land* (Brooklyn, N.Y., 1980).

67. The kibbutzim were populated predominantly by members of the *HaShomer HaZa'ir* (Young Guard) movement, which was actively, and at times militantly secularist.

To achieve what has been achieved in such circumstances was made possible only by a fanatical will, fanatically concentrated on that one aim, to build. . . . There was only one way open: To concentrate all available energy, physical as well as spiritual, on the task at hand. Everything had to be subordinated to the one aim of returning to the land. . . . The "fanatics" had neither time nor energy to spend on the very intricate problem of fitting traditional Judaism into the new framework they were creating.[68]

As Berkovits himself writes, the glowing ideal of return has lost its sparkle: "Zionism is good for the exile; it is bad for Zion."[69] Second- and third-generation Israelis are realizing the emptiness of return only for the sake of return, and are turning to tradition to fill the void.

Thus, in contrast to the secular atmosphere in which the State was founded, the outlook of the population of Israel has continued to shift significantly toward mainstream Judaism. Against all the odds, the national religion has flourished, reversing the trends of pre-State times. Although still outnumbered by the secular population, the number of observant Jews living in Israel (who abide by the dictums of the Torah) has grown exponentially, reaching approximately one million Jews. Moreover, a general thirst for meaning can be discerned (in particular among youth), so that whereas in past generations a return from secularism to Orthodoxy was socially untenable, today the path is well-trodden, and continues to widen.

Rabbi Shalom Noach Berezovski, who led the Hassidic court of Slonim from 1981 until his death in 2000, has expressed great wonder at the rebuilt world of Jewish Orthodoxy:

With our own eyes we have witnessed revelations that no dreamer would have dared to imagine just a generation ago. Suddenly, a wonderful generation arose, a generation of Torah and careful observance of mitzvot; a generation in which tents of Torah flourish, and in which the standard of Torah study is extremely high. Together with this, the Hassidic courts are blossoming in full splendor, and a remarkable *teshuvah* movement, entirely unheard of

---

68. Eliezer Berkovits, *Essential Essays on Judaism*, ed. David Hazony (Shalem Press, Jerusalem 2002), p. 165.

69. Berkovits, *Essential Essays on Judaism*, p. 173.

in generations past, has arisen. . . . Without a doubt, there is no natural explanation for all of this; God Himself . . . has cherished and cultivated this generation.[70]

A long way remains until the words of the prophet can be literally applied. Although much progress has been made, we cannot say that we have yet received a new "heart of flesh." Yet, verse 33 of the same chapter implies that there is not long to wait:

Thus said the Lord God: "On the day when I cleanse you from all your iniquities, I will cause the cities to be inhabited; and the ruins will be built. The desolated land will be tilled, instead of having been desolate in the eyes of every passerby. People will say, 'This very land, which had been desolate, has become like the Garden of Eden; and the ruined, desolate, and demolished cities have been fortified, inhabited!'" (Ezekiel 36:33–35)

The expression "on the day" does not imply the same twenty-four hour period. It does, however, mean that the two prophetic ideas mentioned in the verse will be fulfilled in the same era. Although there are large portions of the Land that have yet to be rebuilt, in particular those that remain in Arab hands, the fulfillment of the prophecy is certainly under way. The State of Israel may still not resemble the Garden of Eden – but, as we have already seen in the previous chapter, it has made considerable progress after centuries of total devastation.

God promises that together with the rejuvenation of the Land, the Jewish People will be "cleansed of their iniquities." The fact that Israel remains far from being clean of iniquity reflects the incomplete state of the rebuilding; the unprecedented settlement and development of the Land, however, which has been achieved in recent times, indicates that the process of cleansing has also begun.[71]

---

70. *Kuntress Haharugah Alecha*, p. 28.

71. In chapter four of this book we have defined the current stage of the redemptive process as Evening-Morning, as found in the Book of Daniel. This term, which implies the eve before the dawn of the redemption, appears more descriptive of the current condition than the *atchalta degeulah* (beginning of the redemption) common in Religious Zionist circles. The specific religious definition and status of the State of Israel is discussed further in chapter six.

BORN AT ONE TIME

The closing chapter of Isaiah describes how God is destined to return to Jerusalem, how His glory will spread among the nations, and tells of the ultimate downfall of the wicked. Near the beginning of the chapter, Isaiah addresses a specific element of the nation:

Listen to the word of the Lord, you who fear his word: "Your brethren, who hate you and shun you say: 'the Lord is glorified because of my reputation.' But we shall see your gladness, while they will be shamed. . . .[72] Before she even feels her labor pains, she will give birth; before any travail comes to her, she will deliver a son! Who has heard such as this? Who has seen such as these? Has a land ever gone through its labor in one day? Has a nation ever been born at one time, as Zion went through her labor and gave birth to her children?" (Isaiah 66:5–8)

One eyewitness to the 1948 establishment of the State of Israel was certain he had seen the fulfillment of this prophecy:

That was exactly what I had been permitted to see with my own eyes! On one day – May 14, 1948 – Israel was born as a complete nation, with its own government, armed forces, and necessary administrative functions. True, everything had been improvised hastily and on a small scale. Yet all the necessary ingredients were there to make Israel a sovereign nation within its own borders. So far as I knew, such an event was without parallel in human history. [73]

Bearing in mind the many millions of Zion's children who have yet to return to their homeland, the assessment of the prophecy's fulfillment appears premature. Nevertheless, it appears that the return catalyzed by the establishment of the State of Israel does represent a partial fulfillment – perhaps a microcosm of the prophecy's full eventual realization.

---

72. The last words of this verse have been translated in several ways. The translation given follows the Artscroll Chumash (Stone Edition), which follows the commentary of Rashi. The differences in translation do not make a significant impact on the overall lesson extracted from the passage.

73. Derek Prince, *Promised Land: The Future of Israel Revealed in Prophecy* (Chosen Books, 2005), p. 46.

The numbers of returnees, and the pace at which they returned, are most impressive: Between the two world wars, some 375,000 Jews immigrated, a number that was more than doubled in the three years following the establishment of the State (684,000 Jews arrived in the Land between 1948 and 1951). Before long, the Jewish population had risen to four million, gathered in from some hundred different countries around the globe, before receiving a further boost by the great influx of Jews from the former Soviet Union.[74]

It is likely that these events are included in the prophecy of Zion's "giving birth to her children." The prophecy, as we have mentioned, is certainly not a reference to the redemption of Ezra, which never reached a degree to which "who has seen such as these?" could be written in wonderment. Of course, many more Jews may yet be born to Zion;[75] but the number of Jews living today in the Holy Land is certainly substantial. Bearing in mind the great presence of Jews today, the future presence of Jews on the Land is unlikely to be considered so marvelous a wonder (though of this we cannot be certain). Although its completion remains ahead, it therefore appears that the current gathering of the Jews in Israel is included in the words of Isaiah.[76]

---

74. Between 1990 and 1994, the Israeli population increased by 12 percent due to the freedom of emigration granted to Soviet Jewry.

75. Anyone born of a Jewish mother, even if the father is non-Jewish, is considered a Jew according to Jewish law. Therefore, many individuals who identify themselves as non-Jews are, in fact, Jewish. The return of the Ten Tribes of Israel (See Appendix C) would also add a large number of people who are actually Jewish, yet might not know it. Nevertheless, the verse does state that the Jews are numerically the smallest among the nations: "Not because you are more numerous than all the peoples did the Lord desire you and choose you, for you are the fewest of all the peoples" (Deuteronomy 7:7).

76. As noted in the text, we cannot say that this logical proof is absolute. The ways of God can surprise even the surest reasoning, and even another exile of the Jewish nation remains a theoretical possibility, only to be "born" at a future time. Yet, in a scriptural sense, it does not appear that such an exile is destined to take place. We find no reference in Scripture to a third exile of the Jews. On the contrary, the verse promises, "I will plant them upon their Land, and they shall no more be plucked up out of their Land, which I have given them" (Amos 9:15).

CHILDREN OF THE LIVING GOD

Returning to Isaiah's prophecy, we find that the prophet addresses the righteous of the generation:

Listen to the word of the Lord, you who fear his word: "Your brethren, who hate you and shun you, say, 'The Lord is glorified because of my reputation.' But we shall see your gladness, while they will be shamed." (Isaiah 66:5)

In rapid succession, the verse mentions three distinct terms: "your brothers," "[those] who hate you," and "[those who] shun you." The Talmud interprets each of these terms as referring to groups opposed to the faithful minority who abide by the Divine Law.[77] The "brothers" are *Masters of Scripture*, who respect only the written word of the verses, but ignore the Oral Tradition of how they should be interpreted.[78] "Those who hate you" are *Masters of the Mishnah*, who fail to appreciate the depth and intricacies of the Law. "Those who shun you" are the ignoramuses, the lowest segment of the people, who have no knowledge at all of the Divine word (*Bava Metzia* 33b).

The time of ingathering, Isaiah foresees, will not be for the righteous alone. The righteous will take their part, yet they will be joined by Jewish groups who oppose them. Rabbi David Kimchi (*Radak*), without mentioning the talmudic teaching, similarly explains that when Israel will be gathered to their homeland, there will remain groups who hate the righteous. It would seem that this prophecy was brought to fulfillment (at least partially) through the secular nature of the Jewish State, which was a direct consequence of the views of its founding fathers.

According to Rabbi Kimchi, we find an additional prophecy that presents a precise reflection of this state of affairs. In the light of his

---

77. Interestingly, the Talmud interprets those who fear His word as *talmidei chachamim* – scholars of Torah Law. Those who truly fear the word of God will set themselves squarely at the task of implementing every nuance of the Divine word; the only way to achieve this is to reach a high level of scholarship. A high level of righteousness and subtle erudition of the Law go hand in hand.

78. See Maharal, *Chiddushei Aggadot*, for an explanation of why this group is called Brothers, a title that hides their opposition to the righteous.

interpretation, the following words of Hosea refer to an ingathering that will take place *before the advent of the Messiah*:

Yet the number of the Children of Israel shall be like the sand of the sea, which can neither be measured nor counted; and it shall come to pass that instead of that which was said to them, "you are not My people," it will be said to them, "Children of the living God." And the children of Judah and Israel shall be gathered together, and they shall appoint themselves one head, and ascend from the land, for great shall be the day of Jezreel.[79]

The prophecy is certainly referring to the ingathering of Israel in the latter days, and not of the limited return that took place in the times of Ezra and Nehemiah. As the commentators point out, the return that culminated in the building of the Second Temple was only a partial return of Judah and Benjamin, and cannot be called a gathering of Judah and Israel.

Some commentators understand that the "appointment of one head" – the Messiah – will take place before the ascent to the Holy Land.[80] Radak, however, explains that the reverse will be true: The ingathering will precede the appointment of the Messiah.

Rabbi Shlomo Yitzchaki (Rashi), the great medieval commentator, seems to agree with the assertion. In his commentary to Psalms (70:1), Rashi compares the prayer of David to a king, who, in a burst of fury, banished both his sheep and his shepherd, and shattered the pen. After some time, the king mended the pen, and returned the sheep, but did not recall the shepherd – at which time, the shepherd prayed for his own return. David, from whose descendants the Messiah will arise, thus prays: The pen is built and the sheep are returned, but the shepherd has not been recalled. The Messiah, by implication, will come *following* the return of Jews to their rebuilt homeland.[81]

It is interesting that Rabbi Kimchi, in contrast to Rashi's commentary

---

79. Hosea 2:1–2.

80. This is the opinion of Nachmanides (*Commentary to Torah*, Exodus 1:10), and of Malbim.

81. The proof from Rashi is brought (in the name of "a great contemporary rabbi") by Teichtel, *Eim Habanim Semeichah* (Kol Mevaser, Jerusalem, 1998), p. 102.

to Psalms, does not give any source or explanation for his assumption concerning the order of events. We might suggest that he derived it from the fact of the initial return in a state of sin, which precludes the nation's appointment of the Messiah to lead them. On the face of it, history is proving him right. The Messiah has not come, but the nation has begun its historic return to the Holy Land.[82]

The verse predicts that from being told "you are not My people," the nation will become "children of the living God." In the context of the current return, the title *Not My People* can be applied to some of the founders and subsequent leaders of the State. It is certainly hard to confer the title *My People* upon atheists.

Yet from this sorry state, the people are destined to rise once more to the elevation of their original status. In the wilderness, after their miraculous departure from Egypt, the nation was told, "Children are you to the Lord your God" (Deuteronomy 14:1). Eventually, the declaration will once again come forth: "Children of the living God."

THE UNCONDITIONAL COVENANT

We have explained how the secular foundation of the State was a stroke of Divine providence; we have also shown how the process was foretold in Biblical prophecy. Yet a nagging question remains: *Why?*

Surely, God could have conducted the gathering of the Jews to their homeland in any manner He wished. The method, whatever it would have been, would have been written into the prophetic word, just as the current process has been. Why, then, did God choose to found the process of ingathering on such seemingly shaky legs – on Herzl, who had reached the farthest distance from the traditional faith of the Jews[83]

---

82. This assumes that the current ingathering includes, or will ultimately include, the Lost Tribes of Israel. See Appendix C, which details what is known today concerning the Lost Tribes.

83. As mentioned, Herzl did not even have his son circumcised. Today, although the percentage of secular Jews in Israel hovers around forty percent, only some five percent of Jews do not circumcise their sons. Taking into account those "Jews" who are not considered Jews according to Torah law, the actual number is probably closer to two percent or less.

(falling short only narrowly of conversion to another faith), and on his secular followers?

Moreover, the Talmud teaches that God "brings good things through the worthy, and evil through the unworthy" (Shabbat 32b, Bava Batra 119b). "Worthy" in this context refers to a righteous and pious individual, whose dedication to the service of God renders him a suitable vehicle for the advent of great things. The example offered by the Midrash is of Daniel, whose advice was pivotal in bringing Esther to the royal palace.[84] Daniel's righteousness earned him the merit of being the stepping stone to national salvation in the Purim episode.

Notwithstanding significant flaws, the Jewish State has in many ways been a good thing for the Jewish People. It has revitalized the nation, prevented wholesale assimilation, fostered the rebirth of Jewish religious and cultural activity on all levels, and played an integral role in the fulfillment of several prophecies of ingathering and redemption. Forty years before the event, Herzl himself made a prediction that was to come tragically true: "The Hungarian Jews, too, will meet their fate, and the later it comes, the more bitter and cruel it will be. Meantime, we, the Zionists, will be building a spacious home for those who do not wish to know us."[85] In 1943, the Rebbe of Belz used a Zionist passport to escape to from Hungary to Palestine. The tragedy, of course, was that only few were able to accompany him.

Yet, Zionist leadership, beginning with Herzl and continuing with equally secular personalities, hardly fits the religious bill of "good things through the worthy." Of course, human eyes are weak judges of inner virtue, but by religious standards, somebody as distant from Jewish practice and belief as Herzl and his followers cannot be described as "worthy." Why, then, was an exception to the talmudic dictum made in this most significant case?

Nobody can be certain of the answer to this question. God alone knows the hidden depth of His own guidance over the world: "The hidden," writes the verse, "are for the Lord, our God" (Deuteronomy

---

84. *Pirkei Derabbi Eliezer*, Chap. 48.

85. Cited by Meir Shalev, "*Mitz Petel*," Supplement to *Yediot Aharonot*, Aug. 6, 1993.

28:29). Our suggestion is, therefore, not so much an answer, but a possible line of thought.

God, perhaps, wished us to know that the Eternal Covenant with Israel is *unconditional*. When God promised the Land to Abraham, there were no provisions attached: "To your seed, I shall give this land" (Genesis 12:7). Future generations were warned that if they would disobey Divine instruction, the Land would not tolerate them: "Let not the Land disgorge you for having contaminated it, as it disgorged the nation that was before you" (Leviticus 18:28). Eventually, however, the Covenant will prevail. By ways that we cannot know, devices that are revealed to Him alone, God will bring His creation to its destiny. It will be done through the People of Israel: in belief or in unbelief.

In fact, Herzl's own life, distant as it was from Judaism, may serve as a microcosm of sorts of the eternal and unconditional Jewish Covenant. Even prior to his December entry describing how a visiting rabbi was distressed at the sight of Herzl lighting a Christmas tree (rather than a Chanukah candelabrum), an entry in Herzl's diary reveals an awakening of his Jewish roots: "I am taking up once again the torn thread of the tradition of our people."[86] Two years later, in 1897, Herzl published an essay, titled "The Menora," in which he described an unnamed German-Jewish intellectual – an obvious reference to himself – who had "long since ceased to care about his Jewish origin or about the faith of his fathers." In spite of this apathy, the subject of the essay had always been "a man who, deep in his soul, felt the need to be a Jew" – a need that slowly developed into a full awakening of his Jewish roots:

Gradually, his soul became one bleeding wound. Now this secret psychic torment had the effect of steering him to its source, namely his Jewishness, with the result that he experienced a change that might never have taken place in better days. . . . He began to love Judaism with a great fervor. At first he did not fully acknowledge this . . . but finally it grew so powerful . . . that there was only one way out . . . namely, to return to Judaism.[87]

---

86. *Herzl Diary*, June 10, 1895, p. 64.

87. Herzl, "The Menora," *Die Welt*, December 31, 1897; quoted by Yoram Hazony, "Did Herzl Want a Jewish State?," in David Hazony, Yoram Hazony, and

Throughout his life, Herzl remained deeply distant from any form of religious practice. Despite the "return to Judaism" he prescribed (which can be understood in a cultural rather than religious sense), Herzl's son testified that he never failed to light the Christmas tree, irrespective of the Chanukah candles that "became a parable for the kindling of a whole nation." Yet, although his conscious abandonment of religious practice scarcely betrayed it, Herzl did remain a Jew. Later, reiterating his opening words at the First Zionist Congress of 1897,[88] he would write that "the greatest triumph of Zionism is having led a youth lost to his people back to Judaism"[89] – a Judaism, as Herzl's diaries demonstrate, pigmented with classical tradition, and aware of its unique relationship with "the historical God."[90] Herzl had strayed far afield – yet the flame of his Jewish spirit was not extinguished.

The same can be said of the Jewish nation on a macroscopic level. Although the returnees to Israel were predominantly secular, content to leave their traditional faith for the new god of Zionism, their Jewish souls lived on. On a layer hidden from the naked eye, the current return did not emerge from the European Enlightenment, from the militant secularism of its followers, or from the political winds of the twentieth century. We might even say that it was achieved in spite of these factors. The soul of the return is the soul of the eternal Jewish spirit – the spirit of a Divine Covenant.

Michael B. Oren eds., *New Essays on Zionism* (Shalem Press, Jerusalem, 2006), p. 368.

88. Herzl stated that "It may be said that we have returned home. Zionism is a return to Judaism even before it is a return to the Land of the Jews. . . . In the ancient home we receive a warm welcome, because it is abundantly clear that we do not raise the brazen thought of undermining holy foundations. This matter will be revealed when the Zionist plan will be unveiled before us." [Basel, August 29, 1897; cited in Anita Shapira (ed.), *We Hereby Declare: Sixty Chosen Speeches in the History of Israel* (Hebrew) (Kinneret, Zmora-Bitan, Dvir – Publishing House, 2008), p. 15.]

89. Letter to Chaim S. Schor, January 30, 1900. *Herzl, Briefe und Tagebuecher*, vol. 5, pp. 302–303; quoted by Yoram Hazony, "Did Herzl Want a Jewish State?," p. 369.

90. *Herzl, Briefe und Tagebuecher*, vol. 2, p. 241; quoted by Yoram Hazony, "Did Herzl Want a Jewish State?," p. 369.

THE SHIELD OF ABRAHAM

The very first section of the weekday *Amidah* prayer concludes with the theme of redemption: ". . . and recalls the kindnesses of the Patriarchs, and brings a Redeemer to their children's children, for His Name's sake, with love."

This opening sets the tone for the entire prayer: From the first benediction through to the nineteenth, its complete structure describes a process of redemption. The last words of the section refer to God by a unique title: the *Shield of Abraham*.[91] Throughout the ages, God *shields* Abraham, protecting the flame of the Jewish spirit lest it be extinguished, and ensuring that the unconditional Covenant will ultimately be fulfilled.

Having reached this point, the question *why* will perhaps lose its sting. Facing the will of God and the Covenant integral to it, it can no longer be reasonably posited. Doing so is perhaps akin to somebody living in a two-dimensional world of shadows, for whom a body of three dimensions defies all comprehension. There are some things that as limited human beings, we cannot comprehend.

The Germans and their accomplices in the Holocaust did not discriminate between Jews. For them, all the Jews were equal – believers, non-believers, and even "half-Jews" and "quarter-Jews";[92] all of them were judged to be evil personified and treated accordingly.[93] With their vile malice, the Nazis ordained that a Jew is a Jew, whatever his professed beliefs, and whatever his deeds. The same lesson, taught by the excruciating pain of the Holocaust, is destined to be taught in elation and glee when the people are finally gathered to their Land. However

---

91. This is based on the promise of God to Abraham: "I am a shield for you" (Genesis 15:1).

92. *Mischlingen* were products of mixed marriages, and the rules governing them were very complicated, depending on their marital status, their children, and what degree of Mischling they were. Some were deported to their deaths, while others survived.

93. Even Karaites, who severed their connection with mainstream Judaism long ago, were almost totally exterminated in countries occupied by the Germans, despite claims that they were not Jews.

distant he may stray, a Jew remains a Jew, destined to fulfill his special part in the Divine plan for the world.[94]

Even Herzl could initiate the return of the Jewish people to their homeland.

Bring My sons from afar, and My daughters from the ends of the earth, everyone who is called by My name, and for My glory have I have created him; I have formed him; even I have made him. (Isaiah 43:7)

Everyone means *everyone*: every single one. Why? Because it is His will; because it is His Covenant.

---

94. The idea of comparing God's selection of Jews for His purpose, with the Nazis' selection of Jews for death and slavery, was proposed at a Purim feast by the late Rebbe (Grand Rabbi) of Zanz (a Hassidic group), who survived the Nazi camps and emigrated to America.

Chapter 4

THE TIME OF EVENING-MORNING

Within the historical framework of the current ingathering of Jews to their Biblical homeland, the most momentous event is undoubtedly the establishment of the State of Israel. The acceptance or negation of Zionist ideology has no bearing on the truth of this statement. Whatever our leanings concerning political Zionism, the historical implications of the State, by virtue of which millions of Jews have immigrated to the Holy Land, are indubitably profound. Even if we maintain theological neutrality, it is important to place this focal point of history into a Biblical context.

PROPHECY OF THE JEWISH STATE

The presence of the Jewish State in Biblical prophecy, which we will discuss in greater detail in chapter 6, is a matter worthy of investigation. Had the establishment of the State immediately brought about the final ingathering of Israel from their lengthy exile, there would, of course, be little need for inquiry. The ultimate redemption is well chronicled in countless prophecies scattered throughout Biblical revelation. The Jewish State, in the final scheme of things, would be the Kingdom of God itself.

The final deliverance, however, has not yet come about. Only after the advent of the long-awaited Messiah, in whose time the Jews of the

Diaspora will be entirely gathered in,[1] will the Temple stand in all its future glory. On this day knowledge of God will prevail throughout the world (Isaiah 11:9) – and only then can the redemption be considered complete. Of that time, the prophet foretells the following:

And He shall judge between the nations, and shall decide for many peoples; and they shall beat their swords into plowshares, and their spears into pruning-hooks; nation shall not lift up sword against nation, neither shall they learn war any more. (Isaiah 2:4)[2]

This prophecy has obviously not been fulfilled. The world is filled with wars and international tensions – not least in the Middle East, where the fledgling State of Israel has from its inception been perceived as a thorn in the sides of its Arab neighbors. The wolf does not live with a lamb; nor does the leopard lie down with a kid.[3] The Temple Mount, on which the Third Temple is destined to stand, remains firmly under Muslim jurisdiction. Barring an all-out war, this state of affairs does not seem likely to change in the foreseeable future.

Knowledge of God, moreover, which is destined to be widespread in the age of Messiah,[4] is all too scanty. Although in global terms, the total number of believers still outnumbers non-believers, there are at least one billion complete non-believers in the world today. In some countries and provinces – notably those with little modern religious tradition – the non-believers even greatly outnumber believers.[5]

What is more, although the number of monotheistic believers across

---

1. Isaiah 27:13: "And it shall come to pass in that day, that a great horn shall be blown; and they shall come that were lost in the land of Assyria, and they that were dispersed in the land of Egypt; and they shall worship the Lord in the holy mountain at Jerusalem." Opinions differ concerning the translation of Ashur, Assyria.

2. The reference to the judge, in the opinion of all the commentaries, is to the Messiah, himself; this is clearly indicated by in another prophecy of Isaiah (11:4).

3. As prophesied in Isaiah 11:6.

4. See Isaiah 11:9.

5. In Sweden, for instance, non-believers outnumber their believing fellows by 6 to 1. The global ratio of believers to non-believers, however, is something like 4 to 1 on the side of the believers.

the globe reaches an enormous four billion, the *quality* of belief must also be taken into consideration. Defining a person's belief by issues such as the presence and manifestation of God in the world, His role as Creator, His constant control and guidance over creation, His partnership or lack thereof with other spiritual, celestial, or physical beings, and further similar criteria, we will find extremely little common ground between the myriad faiths extant around the world.[6] Great masses in Eastern countries continue to worship various deities, exhibiting a belief system entirely foreign to Judeo-Christian tradition. Furthermore, the Western tendency toward secularism relegates belief in God, even among professed believers, to the backseat of everyday life.[7] To say the least, it is hard to believe that today's "knowledge of God" approaches the picture outlined by the prophet.

It thus emerges that without any doubt, the establishment of the State of Israel is not in itself the manifestation of the longed-for Messianic Age. As the central focus of the current return to the Land, however, it does remain a highly significant event, and certainly worthy of theological investigation.

Numerically, the return of the twentieth century would seem more impressive even than the Second Commonwealth, which was established by Ezra and his contemporaries at the end of the Biblical era. The autonomous rule that Jews of today enjoy over (a large part of) the Holy Land, while remaining to some degree dependent on the grace

---

6. Even within a single religion, such as Christianity, there are tens of different sects, such as Roman Catholic, Protestant, Evangelical, Presbyterian, Methodist, Unitarian, Amish, Mormon, Quaker, Adventist, and so on, each possessing its own individual belief system. The differences between the groups range from subtleties to distinctions in central religious tenets.

7. A fair yardstick, which I was handed by my Mentors, of how much we involve God in our everyday lives, is the dedication of our own achievements to Divine assistance. It is one thing to turn to God in prayer in times of need; it is quite another, in times of success and affluence, to acknowledge that our achievements are solely by the grace of God (who may, in turn, have certain demands related to those achievements). A sign of a believer is that after completing a lucrative business deal, he credits God, rather than stating "my strength, and the might of my hands, have brought me this glory" (Deuteronomy 8:14).

of foreign powers, is a political status the returning Babylonian exiles could only have dreamed of.[8] But whereas the second coming of Jews to the Holy Land, an event far removed from the final redemption,[9] was well chronicled by the prophets,[10] the establishment of the State is far harder to locate.[11]

The Biblical prediction of a future Jewish autonomy in the Land of Israel will be discussed in chapter 6. In the present chapter, we will

---

8. Though permitted to conduct their own affairs, the Jews were continually subject to Persian taxation, and were not permitted military independence. Only during the short period of the Hasmonean revolt did they achieve a semblance of independent self-government.

9. Although they were granted permission to return to the Land of Israel and to rebuild the Temple, the Jews never received the freedom to re-establish the monarchy, and continually lived under the shadow and interference of the controlling imperial power. Furthermore, the Second Temple lacked much of the glory possessed by its predecessor, built by King Solomon. See Talmud, *Yoma* 12b, which lists the differences between the two Temples.

10. See Jeremiah 25:11–12; Daniel 9:24.

11. The question of finding, or rather *not finding* the State of Israel (of the establishment of a Jewish autonomy before the coming of the Messiah) in Biblical prophecy, was raised by Rabbi Mordechai Pogramansky, whose words are transmitted by Rabbi Moshe Sternbuch, *Teshuvot VeHanhagos*, vol. 5, *Yoreh De'ah*, no. 297.

The response given by Rabbi Pogramansky was that the Bible, the sages, and the later commentaries were all silent concerning the establishment of the Jewish autonomy prior to the Messianic Age because the period of Jewish autonomy is only a trial, whose purpose is to sort the faithful from the non-faithful, in preparation for future redemption. It stands to reason that prophets should not mention anything of future trials, for their mention in prophecy threatens the free will of those who must stand the trial.

This approach appears to be somewhat strained, the more so from the vantage point we have today, which surely presents the establishment of the Jewish state as part of a historical process rather than merely a trial. It therefore stands to reason that the Jewish autonomy should be mentioned in prophecy. The reason why the Jewish State does not figure *prominently* in prophecy is perhaps because, as explained below, the Jewish State in itself is only an intermediary stage in the process of redemption, and it is therefore to be expected that it merits only limited attention in prophetic writings.

focus on one specific prophecy, which is possibly a direct, if indistinct, reference to the tumultuous events of the year 1948.

EVENING-MORNING 2,300

Of all the books of the Bible, the setting that would most suit a prophetic revelation concerning the State of Israel is without question the Book of Daniel. No Biblical text dwells on the Latter Days as does the Book of Daniel; virtually all eschatological calculations throughout the generations have based themselves on visions recorded therein.

A foretelling of the State in the Book of Daniel would also account for the difficulty of locating such a prophecy. The eschatological revelations of Daniel are cryptic; the visions were "sealed," obscured, making them particularly difficult for the reader to decipher. As the Talmud states, the concealment of End-time affairs, in which the State of Israel might have a major part to play, was entirely intentional (*Yoma* 9b).

Upon close inspection, I believe we can find a passage in Daniel that predicts the advent of the Jewish State with remarkable precision. The relevant prophecy begins as follows:

Then I heard a holy one speaking; and another holy one said to that certain one who spoke – "How long shall be the vision concerning the continual burnt-offering, and the transgression that causes devastation, to give both the Sanctuary and the host to be trampled underfoot?" (8:13)

To understand the magnitude of this question, it is important to place it in its context within the vision of Daniel.

In chapter 8 of his book, Daniel describes a vision of a powerful double-horned ram, which conquers universally. Commentators explain that this animal represents the empire of the Medes and the Persians (hence the two horns), which took over the reins of power from the fallen Babylonian Empire. Finally, the ram is overcome by the power of a single-horned goat: the irresistible force of Alexander the Great, before whom no nation could stand.

The great horn, however, broke without outside intervention – Alexander died off the battlefield – to be replaced by four smaller horns. Three represent the officers who inherited the Greek Empire.

The fourth, a "Little Horn," sprouted forth from one of the three, and proceeded to "grow exceedingly," and to touch even the heavenly host. The consensus of commentaries is that this horn was Antiochus Epiphanes (Antiochus IV), who ruled over Syria and Judea from 175–164 BCE. Daniel predicted that Antiochus, unlike his Greek predecessors, would interfere with the service of God, persecuting His servants and desecrating His Temple.

The scriptural description of this event contains a marked repetition, which is suggestive of hidden meaning:

And it waxed great, even to the host of heaven; and some of the host and of the stars it cast down to the ground, and trampled upon them. Even to the prince of the host; and from him the continual burnt-offering was taken away, and the place of his Sanctuary was cast down. And the host was given over to it together with the continual burnt-offering through transgression; and it cast down truth to the ground, and it wrought, and prospered. (Daniel 8:10–12)

Abarbanel explains that the *second* reference to the cessation of the continual burnt-offering refers to the evils of Rome (the Fourth Kingdom), and not to those of Greece (the Third). Ultimately, it was Rome, not Greece, which caused the termination of the continual burnt-offering, cast Truth to the ground, and grew to enormous proportions.[12]

TWO THOUSAND THREE HUNDRED DAYS?

Against a backdrop of unparalleled evil, a force that would conquer even the "host of heaven," Daniel saw two celestial beings, who addressed each other with the question of all questions: Until when? For how long will this sorry state continue on? The answer was given:

And he said to me: "Until evening and morning two thousand and three hundred; then shall the Sanctuary be victorious." . . . And I heard the voice of a

---

12. The magnitude to which the kingdom of Rome grew is depicted in chapter seven of Daniel. It is striking to note that from both the third kingdom of Greece, and the fourth of Rome, there sprouted a "Little Horn" (one of them mentioned in Daniel chapter seven, and one in chapter eight), which grew to terrible proportions, and encapsulated the essential evil of the kingdom. As noted by Abarbanel, these two Little Horns are described in almost identical scriptural terms.

man between the banks of Ulai, who called, and said, "Gabriel, make this man understand the vision." So he came near where I stood; and when he came, I was terrified, and fell upon my face. But he said unto me: "Understand, son of man, for the vision belongs to the time of the end. . . . And the vision of the evening and morning which has been told is true; but you, seal the vision, for it belongs to many days to come." (Daniel 8:14–26)

Abraham Ibn Ezra (1089–1164), a leading Jewish scholar of the twelfth century – and with him the vast majority of Christian scholarship and Bible translations – has explained the "two thousand and three hundred" as two thousand and three hundred *days* – literal evenings and mornings.[13] The prophecy, according to this view, has already come to pass. Antiochus invaded Jerusalem in 170 BCE, and desecrated the Temple by offering a foreign sacrifice on the holy altar. The temple was closed from the autumn of 170 BCE until December 25, 164 BCE – 2,300 days – in exact fulfillment of Daniel's prophecy. The principal source for this historical overview is the Book of Maccabees.[14]

Though superficially pleasing, this interpretation is not without difficulty, and a number of questions quickly arise.

One immediate problem is that the angel-interpreter sent to Daniel clearly states that the vision "belongs to the time of the end," which seems quite incompatible with the time of Antiochus and the Maccabee revolt. Suppressing one's basic intuition, one might suggest that the "time of the end" refers to the end of a particular era, during which the vision came to pass – yet this idea is not especially convincing.

More disturbingly, perhaps, the expression "evening-morning" is surely an odd way of referring to simple twenty-four-hour days. If the

---

13. Commentary to Daniel 8:25.

14. The First Book of Maccabees was probably written about 100 BCE, after the restoration of an independent Jewish kingdom. It tells the story of the conquest of the Land by the Greeks under Alexander the Great, the attempt by the Greeks to impose Greek culture on the Jews, and the final miraculous victory of the Maccabees over the massive Greek forces. Though not included in the Hebrew canon of Holy Writ, the book is considered an accurate historical representation of the events it chronicles.

verse had wished to convey a number of days, why should he not have used the normal word for days?

Furthermore, the angel concludes, "And the vision of the evening and morning which has been told is true." The singular form of *evening and morning*, used in both instances of its mention, is striking.[15] Why is the singular form used, rather than the more appropriate plural, *evenings and mornings*?

Also, the very reference to such a large number of days is unheard of in Scripture. When the verse describes more than seven days, units of weeks are used; when the period in question is longer than four weeks, the verse refers to months; and when more than twelve months are involved, the verse resorts to years. If the intended meaning of the prophecy was so great a number of days, why does the verse insist on using units of days rather than the more appropriate unit of years?

A further point of difficulty is the sudden change in the prophetic medium that Daniel experienced. The vision of the Ram and the Goat, their horns indicating the immense power they wielded, ended with the terrible havoc wreaked by the Little Horn, which reached "even unto the prince of the host, casting down the continual burnt-offering, and wrought, and prospered." Why, unlike the horns before it, did Daniel not see the ultimate fate of the Goat, its defeat at the hands of the Maccabees, or the breaking of its Horn at the hand of God Himself?[16]

Additionally, the instruction given to Daniel to "seal the vision, for it belongs to many days to come" (8:26) is unique in the Book of Daniel, apart from one similar instance in the final chapter. Why was this vision decreed for sealing, any more than other visions depicted in the Book of Daniel? The reason given by the verse for sealing the vision is that "it

---

15. Naturally, most translations render 'evenings and mornings.' Our translation of the verses highlights this anomaly.

16. The armies of Antiochus were defeated by the far smaller group of Hasmoneans, under the leadership of Judah Maccabee. This event continues to be celebrated annually by Jews in the Feast of the Dedication (Chanukah). Antiochus himself became ill with a foul illness, as described in I Maccabees, which led him to admit his wrong in making war against the people of God and their religion. He eventually died of his illness.

belongs to many days to come." Was Daniel to reveal only prophecies that pertain to the short-term, sealing up all the others?

Lastly, it is noteworthy that Daniel concludes the chapter by stating that he did not understand the vision: "And I was appalled at the vision, but understood it not." What particular point of the vision was beyond Daniel's understanding? The matter of the Four Kingdoms was by this time familiar material for the experienced prophet; he had previously interpreted an epic dream of Nebuchadnezzar as an allusion to the same Kingdoms. A prophecy that merely extended Daniel's previously acquired knowledge should not, it seems, have been so difficult to comprehend.

THE TIME OF EVENING-MORNING

Applying the Abarbanel's interpretation, we can find a theme, hidden between the lines, which will serve to explain all of these observations.

As previously mentioned, Abarbanel maintains that the vision we have dwelt upon, though pertaining chiefly to the two empires of Medea-Persia and Greece, also hints at the later Roman Empire. Following in the footsteps of the wicked Antiochus, the Empire assailed the Jewish People and their service of God, ultimately destroying the Temple, and sending Israel into a long and harsh exile. Of this, Abarbanel explains, was asked the question of the "holy one": "How long shall be the vision concerning the continual burnt-offering?"

The reply, in this context, cannot be a matter of days; rather, the two thousand and three hundred units must be understood as *years*. As the angel concluded, the prophecy was *for many days to come*, indicating a period of a great order of magnitude – far longer than the relatively short time until the days of Antiochus. This, indeed, is how Abarbanel, and a number of prominent ancient Jewish commentators, understand the prophecy.[17] After two thousand and three hundred years, the evil of Rome will finally be thwarted.

17. Notably, Rabbi Saadiah Gaon, Rashi (Rabbi Shlomo Yitzchaki), Nachmanides, Ralbag, Metzudat David, and Malbim. Some of these commentators are content to understand the entire vision of the Little Horn prior to the

In this light, we can readily understand why this particular vision was designated for *sealing*. In contrast to other visions of Daniel, here was a prophecy that pertained directly to the End of Days, to the destiny of creation that remains concealed by its very nature. Fittingly, the vision of the last chapter of Daniel (Chap. 12), which the prophet is also instructed to seal, similarly relates to the time of the End. Daniel himself confessed – a confession unique to this particular vision – that he did not understand the vision. The explanation he received may have unraveled the mystery of the beasts and the horns, but the matter of the End remained hidden.

This neatly explains the sudden change in prophetic medium that Daniel experienced in the middle of Chapter 8. The prophetic revelations pertaining to the coming kingdom of the Medes and Persians, followed by that of Greece, were represented graphically by beasts (for kingdoms) and horns (for kings). Deeds that will come to pass only at the End-time, however, cannot receive so graphic an embodiment. The time of the End is by nature hidden: it could not be seen as a prophetic vision, but was hinted at through the angelic conversation that Daniel was made to overhear.

The term "evening-morning," according to this interpretation, will likewise take on new meaning. Rather than a reference to a number of days, the expression defines the mode of redemption that the prophet forecast. It will not be a complete redemption, as the light of the dawn that dispels the gloom of night; instead, the prophetic revelation refers to *the eve of the morning* – the evening before the light of day re-appears. It is not the day of redemption itself, but the period preceding the coming of the Redeemer.[18]

Before we come to actually dating the onset of the Evening-Morning period, we may add that the interpretation of the prophecy in terms of years does not necessarily preclude a corresponding interpretation as a number of days. On the contrary, the possibility of *correctly* interpreting

---

question, as referring to Antiochus; nevertheless, the question, and the response of two thousand and three hundred, refers to the End of Days.

18. This interpretation is stated by Nachmanides; Abarbanel, Ralbag, and other commentators offer alternative explanations to the unique term.

the prophecy in terms of days can itself be construed as an added obscurity to the hidden reference to the End of Days. The problems we have raised, which make the interpretation of days almost untenable, may thus be understood as indicators of an inner, hidden meaning, without necessarily negating the interpretation of two thousand three hundred units of days (which was fulfilled at the time of Antiochus).

One way or another, it is clear that the prophecy may be referring to 2,300 years, pertaining to the actual End of Days.

TWO THOUSAND THREE HUNDRED YEARS — CHRISTIAN CHRONOLOGY

The great question now concerns the commencement of the period of 2,300 years. There is a significant discrepancy between Jewish and Christian scholars in ascribing a date to Daniel's prophetic visions. Naturally, this is of great importance for approximating the conclusion of this period.[19]

---

19. In the opinion of Christian and secular scholars, the Persian Empire was established far earlier than the date given by accepted Jewish tradition. Because the Persian Empire displaced the Babylonian kingdom of Nebuchadnezzar, Christian scholarship was thus forced to set the date of the destruction of the First Temple far earlier than the 420 BCE of Jewish tradition. (In *Seder Olam*, a Tannaic source dating back to the Second Temple era, the date for the destruction is given as 3,338 years from the creation of the world, which is equivalent to 422 BCE.)

It is unnecessary for us to examine the evidence that led historians to their assumptions regarding the Persian Empire. Suffice it to note that the history of the Persian nation is shrouded at least to some degree in a veil of mystery, and that sources that might shed light on its roots and early development are fairly sparse, leaving room for conjecture and hypothesis. The traditional Jewish position does have certain backing from the general lack of recorded history in the 'additional years' of the Persian Empire, which historians designate The Silent Years. According to traditional Jewish sources, these years (of return to Zion under the Persian Empire) simply did not exist, which explains the dearth of information. On the other hand, the Christian-secular version has the backing of several external historical sources. As a fairly unlearned layman, I cannot express serious opinion on the subject.

In the Talmud, the entire length of Persian rule during the Second Temple era is reckoned as thirty-four years (*Avodah Zarah* 9a), which yields a total of fifty-two

In the opinion of Christian scholars and most historians, Daniel lived in the sixth century BCE. Calculating the 2,300 years from the time of the vision itself, therefore, would yield a date somewhere in the eighteenth century CE. The widely accepted position among Christian scholars, however, was to calculate the 2,300 years from the time at which Israel received the final consent for rebuilding the destroyed Temple.[20] According to the Christian system, this would place the beginning of the count at around 450 BCE, and its end somewhere in the middle of the nineteenth century.

Approximately thirty-five writers between 1810 and 1844 calculated that the period of 2,300 years would end in 1843 or 1844, which is based on a starting date of 457 BCE derived from Archbishop Usher's chronology. A further twenty-five or so looked to 1847.[21]

---

years when the eighteen years of the Temple's construction are added. If this seems historically short, it is noteworthy that even after the advent of the Greek Empire it is likely that Persian rule lingered on in Judea in the form of minor government clerks and governors. Combined, the Persian-Greek era in Israel lasted for 214 years, and was replete with important occurrences and personalities.

For general reading on the subject, see Brad Aaronson, "Fixing the History Books, Dr. Chaim S. Heifetz's Revision of Persian History," at http://www.star ways.net/lisa/essays/heifetzfix.html (accessed 05/09/12); for the secular rebuffal of this argument, see Alexander Eterman, "Fixing the Mind," at http://www.talk reason.org/articles/fixing1.cfm. See also Sheldon Epstein et al, "A Y2K Solution to the Chronology Problem," In *Hakira*, vol. 3, p. 67, available at http://www .hakirah.org/Vol%203%20Epstein.pdf; additional sources are cited in note 15.

20. This is based on the same starting point as the seventy-week prophecy of chapter nine of Daniel, which referred, from the Christological viewpoint, to the crucifixion (or another key event in the life of Jesus). Final consent for the rebuilding of the Temple was given by King Artaxerxes, of the Persian dynasty.

21. L. E. Froom, *Prophetic Faith of Our Fathers*, vol. 4. Although there was only a small difference of opinion concerning the exact chronology, the actual event that was to come after 2,300 years was interpreted in several ways. Miller's predecessors had suggested various possibilities, such as the purification of the Church, the liberation of Palestine from the Muslims, the end of the Papacy or of Islam, the restoration of true worship, or, in some cases, the return of Jesus to set up a kingdom on earth. Miller's view on the matter underwent something of an evolutionary process. Untimately, he included the cleansing of Palestine (the place of God's Sanctuary) and of the whole earth in the final fires. This fiery cleansing,

The rest is history. In 1843, the due date was corrected to 1844, taking into account the extra year at the beginning of the Gregorian count. During 1844, several more corrections were made, in accordance with various methods of dating the Jewish year. Finally, all the dates expired uneventfully, and for those who had awaited the Second Coming, the period became known as "the Great Disappointment." Most Adventists (after October 22, 1844) concluded that their chronology was in error. A sizeable minority, however, held that the error was not in the reckoning of the period, but in the interpretation of the event to be expected at its culmination. Among these was a minor group who came to form the nucleus of the Seventh-day Adventist organization.[22]

Before coming to the traditional Jewish chronology of events, it is worth noting the calculations of Sir Isaac Newton – a man revered more for revolutionary scientific discoveries than for theological musings, but who valued the latter no less than the former. Newton understood that the 2,300 days of the profanation of the Temple were not fulfilled in literal days in the time of Antiochus Epiphanes. Instead, he placed the period within the context of the final Jewish captivity, arguing that the Little Horn (which for him was the Papacy) was to act until "the last end of the indignation" that was not yet complete. During this period, "the sanctuary continued cast down 2,300 days before it was cleansed, and days in sacred prophesy are put for years."[23]

---

he believed, would destroy the last trace of sin and purify the earth in preparation for the Divine Kingdom, which would then be established for eternity.

22. For more details, see *Daniel and Revelation*, by Uriah Smith (one of the leading Millerite proponents of the nineteenth century, and the leading Adventist writer of his time), which is available electronically on the Internet. See also Daniel 8:14, by Desmond Ford, *The 2,300-day Prophecy of Daniel 8*, Bible Advocate Press; and *Exposition of the Bible*, by John Gill. Although belonging to a slightly different genre, Sydney Cleveland's *White-Washed: Uncovering the Myths of Ellen G. White, "The Great Disappointment,"* provides an interesting perspective. Many of the anti-Adventist reproaches made in the latter books will not apply to our own approach, as based on Abarbanel and other Jewish sources.

23. Mint Papers 19/5, f. 12v (written on the back of a letter from George Needham dated 16 May 1725); quoted by S. Snobelen, *The Mystery of This Restitution of All Things: Isaac Newton on the Return of the Jews* (Kluwer Academic Publishers, 2001).

Concerning the starting-point of the 2,300 days, Newton was not struck by apocalyptic fever as were other Restorationists. Instead of searching for a suitable date in the near future, Newton makes three suggestions for the start of the count, which place the conclusion of the period somewhere between 2370 and 2446 CE. Finally, and with eminent wisdom, he puts forward another suggestion: "Some other period that time will discover."[24]

Although the proposition below is made with the benefit of hindsight, I nonetheless add the same addendum.

TWO THOUSAND THREE HUNDRED YEARS – JEWISH CHRONOLOGY

According to Jewish tradition, the commencement of the 2,300 years is seen from an altogether different historical perspective from that of Christian scholarship, which places the destruction of the First Temple at 586 (or 587) BCE. Jewish authorities from the time of the Second Temple until the present day place the date of the destruction in the year 3338 (422 BCE).[25]

Based on Hebrew chronology, Ibn Yechia, a renowned Jewish scholar who wrote his commentary to Daniel roughly five hundred and fifty years ago, comments as follows:

Then the angel answered him that [the desecration] will last . . . two thousand three hundred years, after which the Sanctuary shall be cleansed for eternity. Now see, that three thousand, three hundred and ninety-one years passed from the creation of the world until Cyrus of Persia became king. It [the vision of Daniel] was then, and a little before then, during the reigns of Belshazzar and Darius [the Mede].[26] It thus emerges that at the end of five thousand and seven hundred years from creation [around 1940 CE], our destiny shall come.

24. Newton, *Observations*, p. 122.

25. The most ancient source for this date is the *Beraita* (Tannaic text) of *Seder Olam* (Order of the World).

26. Historians have encountered difficulty in placing the Darius of Daniel in a historical context. He is mentioned in the book of Daniel, in the writing of Flavius Josephus, and in Jewish midrashic sources, but not in other historical sources. This issue is not relevant to our specific discussion.

Based on the vision of Daniel, Ibn Yechia thus predicted what he believed to be the complete redemption, which he dated at somewhere around 1940.

By shifting the starting point by a few years, we may be able to further pinpoint the intended year. It was foreknown – at least to Daniel – that the redemption granted by Cyrus and the kings who followed him, and the rebuilding of the Second Temple that was accomplished with their permission, was not to be the ultimate redemption.

It follows that the end of the seventy-year exile is a suitable starting point for the count of 2,300 years, effectively extending the initial seventy-year exile by an additional 2,300 years. The exile in Babylon ended seventy years after the Destruction, in the year 3408 (352 BCE). If the span of 2,300 years is calculated accordingly, the period expired in 5708 (1948 CE). This was the year in which the State of Israel was established, and in which the Holy Land returned to autonomous Jewish rule after an intermission of almost two millennia.

Alternatively, we may reach the same conclusion based on the chronology of Abarbanel. Basing his calculation on the years of kings as chronicled in Scripture, Abarbanel dates the Destruction twenty years later than the traditional Jewish opinion, at the year 3358 (402 BCE). Many later authorities agree with Abarbanel's careful computation.[27] Based on this method, the date of Daniel's vision can thus be calculated as the year 3408. Using the vision as the starting point for the count of 2,300 years, we once again reach the termination year of 5708, or 1948 CE.[28]

---

27. See introduction of Abarbanel to the Book of Kings; Ezekiel 24:2. Isaac Halevi, in his historical magnum opus (*Seder Hadorot*), writes that many scholars adopted Abarbanel's dating scheme as being wholly accurate.

28. The calculation of years is based on the Talmud (*Megillah* 11a). Combined, the reigns of Nebuchadnezzar and his son Evil Merodach spanned forty-eight years after the Destruction. According to Abarbanel, Belshazzar, the king (or ruling authority) who reigned during the time of the vision we are discussing, thus took the throne in the year 2406. Adding two years of Belshazzar's reign (Daniel's vision was on the third year of Belshazzar's reign), we reach the year 3408 (352 BCE).

BIRTH PANGS OF THE MESSIAH

Based on traditional Jewish chronology (as opposed to the widely accepted academic view), it thus emerges that the year 1948 (5708) is at least a reasonable candidate for the expiry date of the crucial 2,300-year period mentioned in Daniel.

Yet, we have already mentioned that the current state of world affairs, both within and without the State of Israel, is entirely incongruous with the final redemption. The post-State world remains full of violence and wars, corruption, immorality and vice, and it generally exhibits no obvious signs of the idyllic age of the Messiah. Undoubtedly, the State of Israel is therefore not synonymous with the long-awaited redemption that Jews anticipate. The event that occurred at the end of the 2,300 years, if attributed to 1948, will therefore need careful examination.

Reaching the year 1948 from an entirely different angle, Rabbi Moshe David Walli (1697–1777), the foremost disciple of the great luminary Rabbi Moshe Chaim Luzzato (Ramchal), offers a stimulating clue toward understanding the nature of the current era.

The Talmud teaches that "this world spans six thousand years" (*Rosh Hashanah* 31a), each thousand-year period corresponding to one of the six weekdays in which the world was created. The sanctity of the Sabbath, on which God rested from the labor of creation, is manifest in the utopian existence of the "seventh thousand," during which the spiritual condition of the world will entirely transcend its current state. Leaning on principles of Lurianic kabbalah, Rabbi Walli explains that the first stirring of the mundane weekdays toward the holiness of Sabbath occurs on midday of Friday – or more precisely, seven hours before the commencement of Sabbath (at the beginning of the sixth hour of Friday). The first stirring of this world's six thousand years toward the utopia of the "seventh thousand" similarly takes place at the point in the "sixth thousand" that corresponds to this time of the day.

Dividing a full Jewish day (which commences at the fall of dusk) into twenty-four sections, we may derive that each hour of Friday is equivalent to forty-one years and eight months of the "sixth thousand." Multiplied by seven to yield the number of years during the "sixth thousand" in which the "seventh thousand" has begun to stir, the result is 291 years and eight months. Subtracted from the year 6,000, the result is the year 5708 of the Jewish calendar, or 1948. Based on Rabbi Walli's analysis, the first stirring toward the "seventh thousand" – the first historical awakening toward a time of purity and transcendence – took place in 1948.

Rabbi Walli does not predict 1948 as the year of Messiah's coming. Instead, he calls it the time of *Chevlei Mashiach – Pangs of Messiah.* The State of Israel has not brought peace and harmony to the Jewish People. It has not emerged as the spiritual utopia that its religious proponents described; neither has it proven itself as the tangible panacea its secular leaders hoped for. What it has brought, however, is hope. It has stoked the fire of an ancient, desperate hope for better times.

THE EVE OF MORNING

Nachmanides, who also understood Daniel's 2,300 to mean a count of years, explains that the vision does not refer to the actual coming of the Messiah. Commenting on the words "evening-morning," he writes that had the verse not mentioned the expression we would infer that the count of 2,300 years reaches the arrival of the Messiah. The word *evening,* however, implies that the count does not reach the actual End, but a time close to the End. It is a stage before redemption, and not re-demption itself.[29] The current ingathering, we have already mentioned, may be likened to the *remembrance* (as opposed to *redemption*) of the First Return to Jerusalem during the reigns of the Persian kings Cyrus and Darius.[30]

The final redemption is anticipated as a great light: "Then your light will burst forth like the dawn, and your healing will speedily sprout; your righteous deeds will precede you, and the glory of the Lord will gather you in" (Isaiah 58:8). Zechariah, describing the day on which

---

29. *Sefer Hageulah,* printed in *Kitvei Ramban* (Mossad Harav Kook, 1994), p. 293. In his volume of 'debates' (between himself and Christian scholars), Nachmanides writes that there is no reference in the Book of Daniel to the com-plete redemption, other than at the end of the book. This likewise implies that the vision we discuss does not pertain to the final redemption.

30. See p. 63.

God will reveal Himself to save His people from the enemy, similarly pictures a day of wondrous light: "There shall be one day, which shall be known as the Day of the Lord, neither day nor night; but it shall come to pass – toward evening time there shall be light" (14:7).

This light is the *morning* of Daniel's vision, which represents the actual redemption – the time of the End when the light of Israel, itself the light of the Lord, will fill the world. Before that time, there will come an *evening*. Daniel envisaged this time as Evening-Morning: the eve before the final break of dawn. As befits an evening, which defines a time of darkness, the period will not be without hardships; among the trials and tribulations will be the great war of Gog and Magog, as the verses of Zechariah imply. Nevertheless, it is a period that clearly leads toward the morning. The radical events of recent years, and particularly the historic return of Jews to their homeland, surely match the description.

Religious Zionists have applied the expression *atchalta degeulah* – "the commencement of the redemption" – to the establishment of the State of Israel.[31] In fact, the expression was already used by the disciples of the Vilna Gaon, who considered their achievements of rebuilding the Jewish (Ashkenazi) community of Jerusalem in a similar light:

For had it not been that God desired us, He would not have shown us all of these, to bring us to our resting-place and our heritage. It is a sign of *atchalta degeulah*.[32]

Although the incentive to invoke the "commencement of the redemption" is clear and appealing, perhaps the definition derived from Daniel is more appropriate. The time we are in is a period of darkness that heads inexorably toward light; it is the "Eve of Morning."

---

31. The source of the expression is the Talmud, *Megillah* 17b.

32. P. Greivsky, *Miginzei Yerushalayim*, book 2, p. 3; cited in Morgenstern, *Natural Redemption: The Disciples of the Vilna Gaon in Eretz Israel*, p. 89. The text is a part of a fundraising letter that was sent by the *Perushim* to European communities.

CLEANSING OF THE SANCTUARY

Yet, the meaning of the "cleansing of the Sanctuary" – the event forecast by Scripture for the termination of the 2,300 year period – remains obscure. The secular Jewish State that was established in 1948 had no intention of rebuilding the Temple and re-establishing the Sanctuary, and to this day no such plans officially exist. Due to the mosque that stands on the site, the very existence of any such program would cause a political confrontation of gargantuan proportions. If the Sanctuary does not refer to the Temple (which has not been "cleansed"), to what does it refer?

In order to understand this, we open a new chapter, and arrive at a fundamental theme in Jewish history and theology: the Eternal Covenant.

℘ Chapter 5

THE ETERNAL COVENANT

RELEVANCY

After establishing a possible correlation between the expiry date of the 2,300 years in Daniel's vision and the establishment of the State of Israel, we ended the previous chapter of this book with a question. The event at the expiry of the 2,300-year period is described in Daniel's vision as the "cleansing of the Sanctuary."[1] How does this description match the events of 1948?

To answer the question, we must reconsider our translation of the Biblical words describing the event. Following most traditional versions, we have translated the words as "then shall the Sanctuary be cleansed." The literal meaning of the Hebrew words *venitzdak kodesh*, however, implies an entirely different concept. The word *nitzdak*, which is derived from the root *tzedek*, implies vindication in judgment. The Darby Bible Translation thus reads, "then shall the Sanctuary be vindicated." The word *kodesh*, in turn, literally means *holy*. Together, the expression *venitzdak kodesh* thus means, "then the Holy shall be vindicated."

Translated in this manner, we may find a very real fulfillment of the prophesied event in the foundation of the Jewish State. Whatever positive or negative emotions the State of Israel evokes, one particular property has become increasingly prominent over the decades: *relevance*. Whether one loves and supports it, or hates and condemns it,

---

1. See page 123.

the State of Israel is relevant – not to Jews or Israeli citizens alone, but on a universal scale.

In contrast to what most would say about the two millennia prior to the foundation of the State, it is no longer possible to relegate the Jewish nation to the periphery of world history. Their fate, and in particular that of their tiny State in the Middle East, is often a central and pivotal focus of global affairs. Though he committed his life to the establishment of the Jewish State he envisioned, Ze'ev Jabotinsky never hid his love of his hometown of Odessa, a harbor city of international importance, where (as he put it) "every corner of local life used somehow to get entangled with affairs and questions of worldwide range."[2] How ironic that the same description applies today to the State of Israel, of which Jabotinsky was arguably the first "virtual citizen."

The content of international news bulletins serves to accentuate the point. In terms of the earth's population, how much does the Jewish nation constitute? Next to nothing.[3] The size of the Jewish State, in global terms, is likewise negligible.[4] When listening to or watching international news broadcasts, however, you will probably hear the name of the tiny Jewish State more frequently than that of any other country. At the very least, we can say that the prominence of Israel on the international scene is entirely disproportionate to its size and population.

Although the political relevance of Jews is a novelty of the twentieth century, the similarly disproportionate contribution of Jews to humanity is not. As Winston Churchill wrote, "Some people like Jews and some do not, but no thoughtful man can doubt the fact that they are beyond all question the most formidable and most remarkable race which has ever appeared in the world."[5] In religion and broader fields

---

2. Quoted in Joseph B. Shechtman, *Fighter and Prophet: The Life and Times of Vladimir Jabotinsky* (Eshel Books, Silver Spring), p. 553.

3. The number of Jews in the world today is approximately 14 million, some 0.25 percent of the world's population. The number of Jews living in Israel is close to 6 million, a little more than two-thirds of the population of London.

4. Approximately the size of New Jersey, or Wales.

5. *Illustrated Sunday Herald*, February 8, 1920; quoted by Martin Gilbert, *Churchill and the Jews* (Henry Hold & Co., 2006), p. 38.

alike, the historical influence of Jews has been immeasurably greater than their proportion of the world's population. The point is easily illustrated by a small sampling of individuals listed in Michael Shapiro's *Ranking of the Most Influential Jews of All Time*: Abraham, Moses, King Solomon, the Prophets, Jesus (and Mary), and St. Paul in ancient times, and, in the twentieth century, Albert Einstein, Paul Ehrlich, Niels Bohr, Sigmund Freud, Henry Bergson, Martin Buber, Franz Kafka, and Karl Marx.

Many thinkers, such as Sigmund Freud and Thorstein Veblen,[6] have contemplated the secret of Jewish success in the scientific and intellectual advances of the modern era, generally citing local psychological factors as the solution to the conundrum.[7] It is possible, however, that the secret lies in some higher purpose defining the centrality of the Jewish People in the historical progression of humanity – this central role being at times more revealed, and at times hidden.

THE MISSION OF JUDAISM

Recognition of the State as a significant factor in the collective fate of the planet and its inhabitants affirms a central tenet in Jewish faith: the Eternal Covenant between God and the Jewish People. From its inception, this Covenant, made with Abraham and repeated with his descendants, was intended as a permanent definition of the relationship between God and Israel:

---

6. Set out in his paper, "The Intellectual Pre-Eminence of Jews in Modern Europe," 1919, *Political Science Quarterly*.

7. A wealth of material has been written, and continues to be written, about the question of where the disproportionate Jewish representation in so many fields stems from. For a fairly recent article on the subject, see Jennifer Senior, "Are Jews Smarter?" (*New York Magazine*, October 16, 2005), which dwells on the possible genetic advantages of Ashkenazi Jews (available online at nymag.com/nymetro/news/culture/features/1478/ – accessed 01.06.12). For a wholesale rejection of the attribution of Jewish successes in all fields to some inherent and inborn quality, see Yeshayahu Leibovitz, *Al Olam U'Mlo'o* (Jerusalem: 1987), pp. 43–45.

And I will establish My covenant between Me and you and your seed after you throughout their generations, for an everlasting covenant, to be a God unto you and to your seed after you. (Genesis 17:7)

Later in the same chapter, the *seed* with which the Covenant would continue was specified as Isaac: "But My Covenant will I establish with Isaac, whom Sarah shall bear unto you at this set time in the next year" (17:21).[8] Following Isaac, his father, Jacob – whom God later called "Israel" – continued the lineage of the Covenant.[9] Subsequently, the Jewish People, or the "the Children of Israel," were created as a national entity in the miraculous redemption from Egyptian exile.[10] Upon Mount Sinai the Jews received the Torah, which defined the actions befitting the People of the Covenant; the actual Covenant, however, remained the same as that which was initiated with the Forefathers.[11] Thus a thousand years after the age of the Hebrew Forefathers, King David affirmed the continuing validity of the original Covenant:

He [God] has remembered His covenant forever, the word which He commanded to a thousand generations; the covenant which He made with Abraham, and His oath to Isaac; then He confirmed it to Jacob for a statute, to Israel as an everlasting covenant. (Psalms 105:10)

Although its expression may change and evolve over time, the perennial duty of the Jews is to live by the Covenant of the Patriarchs, thereby bringing the Divine blessing of monotheistic morality to the world: "Nations will walk by your light, and kings by the brilliance of your shine" (Isaiah 60:3). In the declaration of the Covenant, God stated that He would be Abraham's God – of Abraham and his descendants. God

---

8. The covenant was likewise reaffirmed with Isaac in Genesis 26:1–5.

9. Genesis 28:3–4, 13–14 and 35:10–12; see also Exodus 2:24.

10. See Exodus, Chap. 12; see also Ezekiel 16:4, in which the event of the Exodus is described as a literal birth. In a national sense, Israel was born out of Egypt.

11. The original oath and covenant made with the Patriarchs is referred to by the Bible several times in the continuing sojourns of the Jewish People through the wilderness, and is likewise occasionally mentioned in the later writings of Scripture – for instance, see II Kings 13:23.

is of course Master over all peoples and all creatures; yet his *revelation* as God, as an omnipotent Essence that continually guides the creation He fashioned, depends on His nation Israel (which is why He is known as "God of Israel"). The late Lord Immanuel Jacobovitz, former Chief Rabbi of the United Kingdom and the Commonwealth, summed up the matter as follows:

Yes, I do believe in the Chosen People concept as affirmed by Judaism in its holy writ, its prayers, and its millennial tradition. In fact, I believe that every people – and indeed, in a more limited way, every individual – is "chosen" or destined for some distinct purpose in advancing the designs of Providence. Only, some fulfill their mission and others do not. Perhaps the Greeks were chosen for their unique contributions to art and philosophy, the Romans for their pioneering services in law and government, the British for bringing parliamentary rule into the world, and the Americans for piloting democracy in a pluralistic society. The Jews were chosen by God to be *peculiar unto Me* as the pioneers of religion and morality; that was, and is, their national purpose.

Those peoples aware of a particular calling or purpose that describes their place in world history – nations such as England and France, Italy, Greece, Germany, and the United States – have been dubbed by Yoram Hazony "historic nations."[12] These nations realize that aspects of their national inheritance are of true global significance, a realization that infuses nationalistic sentiment with a deep undercurrent of purpose. Too many Jews today, as Hazony laments, fail to appreciate that the Jews, more than any other people, have always understood themselves to be a "historic nation." Indeed, their contribution to humanity is unquestionable. We return to Churchill, writing the following in 1920:

We owe to the Jews . . . a system of ethics which, even if it were entirely separated from the supernatural, would be incomparably the most precious possession of mankind, worth in fact the fruits of all other wisdom and learning put together.[13]

12. Yoram Hazony, "The Guardian of the Jews," writing in David Hazony, Yoram Hazony, and Michael B. Oren (eds.), *New Essays on Zionism* (Shalem Press, Jerusalem: 2006), p. 49.

13. *Illustrated Sunday Herald,* February 8, 1920; quoted by Martin Gilbert,

The fact that much of the "other wisdom and learning" is also the product of Jewish thinking is beside the point. The disproportionate success of Jews even in fields far removed from their inborn calling – the reader is referred to Dan Senor and Saul Singer's *Startup Nation* for an updated version of Jewish influence – appears to be a consequence of an inherent calling.

But whereas the "historic" nature of other nations is a matter for self-definition, the significance of the Jews as a historic nation is defined by Scripture. The words of the prophet leave no doubt as to this definition: "This nation I have fashioned for Myself, that they should declare My glory" (Isaiah 43:21); "You are My servant, Israel, in whom I will be glorified." (49:3). By Biblical designation, the Jews exist to tell the praise of God, to glorify His name. If the system of ethics that the Jews introduced to the world could be separated from the supernatural – as Churchill suggested – the purpose would be inherently incomplete. The raison d'être of the Jew is to reveal God within the world of mankind.

In midrashic writings the three Hebrew Patriarchs are collectively called "the Chariot" (*Genesis Rabba* 47:6); the Creator is known as *their God*, because He revealed Himself through their persons – through the Chariot they formed. Ever since the Jews became a nation, He is thus referred to in hundreds of verses in the Tanach and in other holy writings and prayers as *God of Israel*. The concept of "Chosenness," writes Joseph Telushkin, means to make God known to the world:[14] to form a Chariot by which He enters His own creation, revealing His infinite presence before the eye of man. The Jews are thus "a kingdom of Priests and a Holy Nation" (Exodus 19:6), destined to lead the earthly revelation of God, to preach His ways and to make known His service.

Churchill and the Jews (Henry Hold & Co., 2006), p. 38.

14. *Jewish Literacy: The Most Important Things to Know About the Jewish Religion, Its People and Its History* (Bell Tower/Crown Books, New Edition 2001); he adds that Chosenness is unconnected with race, as evidenced by the Jewish belief that the Messiah will descend from the Biblical Ruth, a non-Jewish woman who converted to Judaism.

THE TRADITIONAL GENTILE (CHRISTIAN) VIEW

Jews have always cherished this fundamental tenet of their faith. Whatever their social position, their financial means, and their political status, they have traditionally maintained the same Divine service, as ordained by the Torah of Sinai and the interpretations of the Oral Law, knowing that their words and deeds are not for naught, and forever anticipating Divine revelation and salvation.

Moreover, the age-long suffering experienced by the Jews over the bi-millennial exile was seen as a part of the same Covenant – certainly not a pleasant facet of Chosenness, but an integral aspect nonetheless. In the words of the prophet, "You alone have I singled out of all the families of earth: therefore will I visit upon you all your iniquities" (Amos 3:2). As nations around them vanished into the mists of history, the commitment of Jews to the concept of their fundamental purpose has kept them afloat in the raging sea of exile.

But, while remembered by the Jews, the Eternal Covenant was long forgotten by the rest of humanity. In the long-standing opinion of traditional Christianity, the eternal suffering of the Jews was just punishment for their rejection of the one whom Christianity crowned Messiah. For instance, Hippolytus of Rome (born 170 CE), one of the founding Church Fathers, ominously declared, "And surely, you [the Jews] have been darkened in the eyes of your soul with a darkness, utter and everlasting."[15]

Hippolytus insisted that unlike the exile of the Jews in Egypt, and later in Babylon, the post-Biblical exile would continue throughout the course of human history.[16] The writings of Origen (185–254 CE) describe a similar basic theology: "And we say with confidence that they

---

15. Hippolytus, *Treatise Against the Jews* 6, ANF 5.220.

16. Hippolytus further avouched, "Now then, incline thine ear to me and hear my words, and give heed, thou Jew. Many a time dost thou boast thyself, in that thou didst condemn Jesus of Nazareth to death, and didst give him vinegar and gall to drink; and thou dost vaunt thyself because of this. Come, therefore, and let us consider together whether perchance thou dost boast unrighteously, O Israel, and whether thy small portion of vinegar and gall has not brought down

[the Jews] will never be restored to their former condition. For they committed a crime of the most unhallowed kind. . . ."[17] According to this doctrine, the suffering of Jews is not part of an Eternal Covenant; on the contrary, it shows that the initial Covenant was rescinded, transferred to a people more faithful than the former. Thus, Lactantius (304 CE) asserted that the Jews were abandoned by God because of their disobedience:

For unless they [the Jews] did this [repent], and laying aside their vanities, return to their God, it would come to pass that He would change His covenant, that is, bestow the inheritance of eternal life upon foreign nations, and collect to Himself a more faithful people out of those who were aliens by birth. . . . On account of these impieties of theirs, He cast them off forever.[18]

More than a millennium later, Martin Luther saw the same fundamental ideology reinforced by historical evidence:

Listen, Jew, are you aware that Jerusalem and your sovereignty, together with your temple and priesthood, have been destroyed for over 1,460 years? . . . For such ruthless wrath of God is sufficient evidence that they assuredly have erred and gone astray. . . . Therefore this work of wrath is proof that the Jews, surely rejected by God, are no longer His people, and neither is he any longer their God.[19]

On account of their sinfulness, Luther recommended such sanctions as setting fire to Jewish synagogues, destroying their homes (relocating the occupants to communal barns), confiscating their prayer books, and forbidding their rabbis to teach religious practice (under penalty of death) – among others. Although he may have taken them to an extreme, Luther's ideas were by no means original; the measures he prescribed, and a great many besides, had already been aired, written, and sporadically implemented over centuries of Christian intolerance.

---

this fearful threatening upon thee and whether this is not the cause of thy present condition involved in these myriad of troubles."

17. Origen, *Against Celsus* 4.22, ANF 4.506.
18. Lactantius, *Divine Institutes* 4.11, ANF 7.109.
19. Martin Luther, "On the Jews and Their Lies," in *LW* 47:138–39.

Ultimately, however, it took the secular or pagan malice of Nazi Germany, which gave vent to the traditional hatred of Jews in a new racial context, to fully realize the Lutheran suggestions.

Even Karl Barth of the twentieth century, a man recognized as the greatest Protestant theologian since Calvin and whose writings about the Jews are ambivalent, could not hide his deep-seated and ideologically rooted sentiments. Though staunchly anti-Nazi, and though strongly opposing anti-Semitism, he did not flinch at joining with many colleagues in charging the Jews with the death of Jesus. In 1942, from his base in Switzerland, Barth castigated Judaism as a "synagogue of death," a "tragic, pitiable figure with covered eyes," a religion characterized by "conceited lying," and the "enemy of God." Like the original Fathers of the Church, he saw the Jews as a mirror of man's rebellion against God, against which Christians must continually struggle.[20]

The Islamic Koran, in its own unique style, exhibits a similar theme to Christian substitution theory: "But on account of their breaking their covenant, we cursed them and made their hearts hard" (Koran 5:33); "[B]ut Allah has cursed them [the Jews] on account of their unbelief, so they do not believe but a little" (4:46). Moreover, the Koran uproots the essential Jewish claim of Divine Election: "Ibrahim [Abraham] was not a Jew, nor a Christian, but he was [an] upright [man], a Muslim, and he was not one of the polytheists" (3:67); "Nay! Do you say that Ibrahim and Ismail and Yaqoub and the tribes were Jews or Christians? Say: Are you better knowing or Allah?" (2:140).

In view of these clear religious attitudes, in particular those of the Christian teachings so influential on the inhabitants of European countries that were home to the majority of the Jewish population, it is

---

20. The citations are from Barth's "Church Dogmatics." See H. Jansen, "Antisemitism in the Amicable Guise of Philo-Semitism in Karl Barth's Theology Before and After Auschwitz," in *Remembering for the Future: Papers Presented at the International Scholars' Conference* (Pergamon Press, 1988), p. 74. When Yeshayahu Leibowitz, who was certainly no lover of Christianity, wished to convey the problems that Christianity has with the Jewish religion, he pointed out Karl Barth; see Yeshayahu Leibowitz, *Al Olam U'Mlo'o*, pp. 58–9. For a deeper look at Barth's theology concerning Jews and Judaism, and how this theology changed in the aftermath of the war, see Mark R. Lindsay, *Barth, Israel, and Jesus* (Ashgate, 2007).

hardly surprising that the Jews were relegated to a peripheral role in the course of human affairs. They were damned, a wretched people, maintained only as a relic of an ancient past – a "fossil record" that serves to remind the "New Israel"[21] of the terrible fate of the unfaithful.

THEOLOGICAL TURNABOUT

The establishment of the State of Israel in 1948, and the astonishing military success of its early history, caused a revolution in the Gentile view of Jews. No longer could the Jews be reduced to the annals of historical irrelevance. For the first time in two thousand years, the Jews suddenly had autonomous control over their own affairs. Moreover, the location of their independent State was the very location of their Biblical heritage, in the same area that God promised Abraham in the Eternal Covenant.

To many Christians, the new political reality urgently demanded a revision of their traditional attitude toward the Jews. It appeared that the perpetuity of the Abrahamic Covenant, which gave the Jews a Divine right to their Promised Land, had been affirmed by the hand of Providence. The image of the "wandering Jew," the homeless traveler doomed to endless wandering in exile and subjected to eternal suffering, had been dispelled. Over time, the theological implications of the State infiltrated even the bastions of Catholic Christendom.

The turnabout in Christian doctrine was made official in chapter 4 of *Nostra Aetate* (1965), a text agreed on by the vast majority of Bishops of the Second Vatican Council, which set in motion a veritable revolution in the attitude of the Roman Catholic Church toward the Jews. In the 1970 Missal of Paul VI, the traditional Good Friday prayer for the conversion of Jews was replaced by a positive prayer recognizing the Jews' Eternal Covenant with God, a principle to which Pope John Paul II was deeply committed.

In the 1985 *Vatican Notes*, the permanence of the Jewish People was portrayed as a "historic fact," and a "sign to be interpreted within God's

---

21. Justin Martyr (100–165 CE): "For the true spiritual Israel . . . are we who have been led to God through this crucified Christ."

design." John Paul II was not the first non-Jew to make this observation. It is told that King Louis XIV of France asked Blaise Pascal, the renowned seventeenth-century philosopher, to give him proof of the supernatural. Pascal answered: "Why, the Jews, your Majesty – the Jews." The well-known anecdote is affirmed in Pascal's writings:

This people are not eminent solely by their antiquity, but are also singular by their duration, which has always continued from their origin till now. For, whereas the nations of Greece and of Italy, of Lacedaemon, of Athens and of Rome, and others who came long after, have long since perished, these ever remain, and in spite of the endeavours of many powerful kings who have a hundred times tried to destroy them, as their historians testify, and as it is easy to conjecture from the natural order of things during so long a space of years, they have nevertheless been preserved (and this preservation has been foretold); and extending from the earliest times to the latest, their history comprehends in its duration all our histories which it preceded by a long time.[22]

Other prominent thinkers and writers such as Mark Twain, Leo Nikolaivitch Tolstoy, and Nikolai Berdyaev, have articulated their wonder at the supernatural survival of the Jews into the twentieth century.[23] None, of course, were expressing a novel insight; the point has already been stated with eloquence in the Talmud (*Yoma* 69b),[24] and it is

---

22. *Pensées*, Christian Classics Ethereal Library (Grand Rapids, MI: 2002), par. 620, p. 116.

23. Berdyaev, in *The Meaning of History* (1935), wrote the following: "The Jews have played an all-important role in history. Their destiny is too imbued with the 'metaphysical' to be explained either in material or positive historical terms. . . . Its survival is a mysterious and wonderful phenomenon demonstrating that the life of this people is governed by special predetermination, transcending the process of adaptation. . . . The survival of the Jews, their resistance to destruction, their endurance under absolute peculiar conditions, and the fateful role played by them in history; all point to the particular and mysterious foundations of their destiny." Another prominent thinker to see the survival of the Jews as a clear sign of Divine Providence was Sir Isaac Newton, some of whose thoughts are discussed in chapter four of this book.

24. The Talmud states that the Men of the Great Assembly are so called because they "restored the crown to its former glory." While previous prophets had

firmly sourced in Scripture.[25] Yet, the official affirmation of the Eternal Covenant of the Jews by the Vatican, as proven by their unnatural permanence (1985 Vatican Notes), is not without significance.

Are these Christian doctrinal reforms sincere? It is hard to say, and there seems to be a range of opinions within the Church as to how to proceed in matters concerning the Jews.[26] The main point to which we wish to draw attention, however, is that *Christianity was forced into changing its mind.* The Christian endeavor to usurp the name of Israel from its true bearers, an enterprise that for centuries seemed as though

---

omitted the awe and might of God from their prayers, for these attributes lacked expression in the state of Jewish exile, the Men of the Great Assembly found these qualities of God expressed in the exilic condition itself. If not for the awe of God upon His people, how could the nation continue to survive in the midst of hostile neighbors?

25. The "permanence theory" is plainly expressed by Jeremiah: "'I am with you to save you,' says the Lord; 'I will make a full end of all the nations among whom I scattered you, but of you I will not make a full end'" (30:11). Thus, the Assyrians, the Babylonians, and the Romans, who scattered Israel – even the great Greeks and the ancient Egyptians – all have disappeared, but the Jews have survived. "'I have loved you with an everlasting love,'" the prophet continues, "'therefore I have continued My faithfulness to you'" (31:3).

26. In particular, the current Pope (Benedict Benedict XVI) has made a number of moves and statements that have brought something of a regression in Jewish-Christian relation. In July 2007 the Pope released motu proprio, which effectively reinstated the 1962 version of the Good Friday prayer for the Jews. This step, which permits a prayer that calls for the conversion of the Jews, and beseeches God to "lift the veil" from Jewish hearts, was construed by some (notably the Anti-Defamation League) as a setback in interfaith relations between Jews and Christians. (The decision to reinstate the 1962 prayer was amended in February 2008, but still contains a plea for the Jews to be converted.) Pope Benedict XVI has also moved to bring Pope Pius XII toward sainthood, a move that has upset Jewish rabbis and groups who feel Pius did too little (at best) to prevent the Nazi Holocaust. Furthermore, he has lifted the excommunication of Bishop Richard Williamson, who has been accused of Holocaust denial, and endorsed the U.N. World Conference Against racism, which was boycotted by both Israel and the United States on account of its virulent anti-Zionist (and by implication anti-Semitic) slant.

it might succeed, has been shattered by the very existence of the State of Israel.

Well before the landmark declaration of *Nostra Aetate*, Rabbi Joseph B. Soloveichik noted the theological barrier that Christianity faced in the form of the Jewish State:

[T]he theological arguments of Christian theologians to the effect that the Holy One has taken away from the Community of Israel its rights to the Land of Israel, and that all of the Biblical promises relating to Zion and Jerusalem now refer in an allegorical sense to Christianity and the Christian Church, were all publicly shown to be false, baseless contentions by the establishment of the State of Israel. (*Kol Dodi Dofek*, p. 34)

The same idea was later expressed by Rabbi Shlomo Wolbe, a leading spiritual mentor among Orthodox Jewry in Israel, who emphasized the significance of the State of Israel in contradicting conventional Christian doctrine. In his view, no "theological acrobatics" on the part of Christians will suffice to explain the resurgence of the Jewish People and their return to their Biblical homeland: "The theologians are paralyzed in seeking to rebuild, in an intellectually meaningful way, their crumbled tower of lies."[27]

Although it is not generally found in documentation of official Christendom, personal conversations with a number of Christianity scholars have confirmed that the establishment of the Jewish State has indeed had a major impact on Christian doctrine. The age-old doctrine of Christian supersession – a doctrine so basic to Christian theology – appears to no longer be viable.

Apart from the strictly theological repercussions of the State, the effect of the State of Israel on the broader attitude of Christians toward Jews also deserves a mention. The popular rise of Christian Zionism, whereby Christians manifest their support of the Jewish State in recognition of its Messianic connotation, is only one of several related phenomena.[28] The impact on popular opinion is reflected in the results

27. Rabbi Shlomo Wolbe, *Bein Sheshet LeAsor* (later renamed *Olam Hayedidut*), pp. 183–184.

28. Several recent works have researched the interesting alliance of Jews and

of a 2006 survey by the Pew Forum on Religion and Public Life, in which American Protestants strongly supported Israel in the Israeli-Palestinian conflict. Fifty-three percent of participants believed that Jews were justified in saying that the Land is theirs and that God gave it to them.

On a different note, who can fail to be touched by the tireless work of Father Patrick Desbois on behalf of nameless Jewish millions who perished in the Holocaust. Desbois's work has been described by Paul A. Shapiro, director of the Center for Advanced Holocaust Studies of the U.S. Holocaust Memorial Museum, as having "memorial and testimonial significance beyond anything we have encountered for a long time."[29] If, in the past, a Catholic priest would have devoted himself to locating mass graves of Jewish dead, telling their stories, and arranging for *kaddish* to be said for them, he would surely not have done so publicly. Most probably, so radical or even heretical a thought would never have crossed a Christian mind. Today, Desbois is a hero of both Judaism and Christianity.

The point we wish to highlight is the impact seemingly made by the State of Israel on Christians and Christianity. On both doctrinal and popular levels, the State of Israel, by means of its very existence, has played a significant role in catalyzing a revolution.

VINDICATION OF THE HOLY

If not for the Covenant – if not for the Jews' Divinely ordained purpose that unfolds continuously over history – there is no reasonable explanation for the pivotal phenomenon of the Jews and their Land. The

---

Christian Zionists in recent times. See Zev Chafets, *A Match Made in Heaven: American Jews, Christian Zionists, and One Man's Exploration of the Weird and Wonderful Judeo-Evangelical Alliance* (HarperCollins, 2007); Victoria Clark, *Allies for Armageddon: The Rise of Christian Zionism* (2007); Irvine Anderson, *Biblical Interpretation and Middle East Policy: The Promised Land, America, and Israel, 1917–2002* (University Press of Florida, 2005).

29. Foreword of Paul A. Shapiro to Patrick Desbois, *The Holocaust by Bullets: A Priest's Journey to Discover the Truth Behind the Murder of 1.5 Million Jews* (Palgrave, Macmillan, 2008), p. xii.

chances, if you will, in a natural or Darwinian sense, of such a tiny segment of humanity possessing such a central place in world destiny, are
negligible. The only logical conclusion in the view of many believers,
Jew and Gentile alike, is that the Covenant – the unique relationship
between God and Israel – is, indeed, eternal.[30]

Ibn Yechia, in his commentary to Daniel, explains that the expression
venitzdak kodesh, to which this chapter is dedicated to interpreting,
refers to the vindication of the Jews: "It will be shown that justice lies
with them, and not with their enemies." The greatest *vindication* is
surely given the Jews by their traditional enemy: the Roman Catholic
Church. After almost two millennia of oppression, persecution, ex-
pulsion, massacres, burnings, and forced conversions, the Church
now officially recognizes the fact that one need not be Christian to be
"saved;" one may be Jewish, too, belonging to the ancient group, the
"elder brother" of the Church,[31] whose Eternal Covenant with God was
never revoked, and will never be revoked.[32] Moreover, the Church has
no choice but to recognize it.

Marking the 37th anniversary of the Second Vatican Council declaration, Walter Cardinal Kasper, president of the Pontifical Commission
for Religious Relations with the Jews, made the following statement:

[W]e Catholics became aware with greater clarity that the faith of Israel is that
of our elder brothers, and, most importantly, that Judaism is as a sacrament
of every otherness that as such the Church must learn to discern, recognize,
and celebrate. It is therefore proper [on] this date for the Pontifical Council to
welcome and to encourage any initiative favoring the growth of a bond with

---

30. Thus, J. Dwight Pentecost, writing in *Things to Come* (Zondervan, 1978)
on the subject of the Abrahamic Covenant, states, "This covenant . . . promises of
the preservation of a nation, and the possession of a land by that nation. . . . [It]
was given to a specific covenant people. Since it was unconditional and eternal,
and has never been fulfilled, it must await a future fulfillment. Israel must be
preserved as a nation, must inherit her land, and be blessed with spiritual blessings
to make this inheritance possible."

31. An expression that was often used by Pope John Paul II.

32. John Paul II, "Address to the Jewish Community in Mainz, West Germany,"
November 17, 1980.

Judaism, with its theological and spiritual wealth, and with the culture that is expressed by it.[33]

The choice of the word "sacrament," a Catholic theological term that denotes mediation of the Divine to the Church community, is striking. In the context of two millennia of Jewish-Christian history, it is impossible. It is a vindication of the Holy: *venitzdak kodesh*.[34]

WHEN ONE RISES, THE OTHER FALLS

In the context of the prophecies contained in the Book of Daniel, the significance of the Christian doctrinal reforms is greatly amplified. According to the 2,300-year theory to which, as we have shown, many Jewish Bible commentators (both ancient and modern) subscribe, the year 1948 can be perceived as a major milestone in the process of Hebrew redemption from the exile of the Fourth Kingdom.

Chapter 7 of Daniel describes the power of this Fourth Kingdom as a Little Horn, which "had eyes, and a mouth that spoke great things," and was "diverse from the former [powers]," and which "shall speak words against the Most High, and shall wear out the saints of the Most High"

---

33. Walter Cardinal Kasper, "Address on the thirty-seventh Anniversary of *Nostra Aetate*," Oct. 28, 2002.

34. This is not to say that there are no 'traditionalists' who cling to replacement theology, and apply it even to the situation in the State of Israel. One prominent figure who appears to fit this category is Archbishop Emeritus of South Africa, Desmond Tutu. After explaining that Palestinians are more oppressed by the State of Israel (where Arabs enjoy the right to vote, to parliamentary representation, to a Supreme Court justice, and equal rights at least on a formal level) "than the apartheid ideologues could ever dream about in South Africa," he explains that "prophetic voices have been calling this empowered people who were once oppressed and killed, to their deepest values of justice and compassion, but they have refused to listen even to the most reasonable voices." Though it would not be politically correct to make them explicit, overtones of replacement theology are quite clear. [Extracts above taken from Desmond Tutu's letter in support of "Church divestment from Israeli occupation," published by "rabbisletter.org": (http://www.rabbisletter.org/endorsement-by-south-african-archbishop-demond-tutu/, accessed 21.06.12).]

(Daniel 7:8). Nachmanides,[35] and after him Abarbanel, explain that the vision of the Little Horn refers to the Roman Catholic Church, destined to inherit the immense wealth and political power of the Roman Empire.[36] The words of a nineteenth-century Pope ironically confirm this assessment:

It is, therefore, by a particular decree of Divine Providence that, at the fall of the Roman Empire and its partition into separate kingdoms, the Roman Pontiff, whom Christ made the head and center of his entire Church, acquired civil power.[37]

It is perhaps not by chance that while the power of Rome, manifest in the Church that bears its name, remained extant, the Jews remained altogether powerless. Even as twin fetuses, sharing the same womb of their mother, Jacob and Esau were proclaimed to be eternal foes. The balance of power between them was moreover defined as a dynamic constant: "One nation will be stronger than the other nation" (Genesis 25:23). "When one rises," explains Rabbi Shlomo Yitzchaki (Rashi) of the two brothers – and by implication of the Fourth Kingdom and Israel – "the other falls."[38] While the power of Rome lasted, the power of the Jews could not exist.

---

35. *Sefer HaGeulah*, pp. 239–240.

36. The suggestion of Nachmanides, that the Little Horn was represented by the papacy, was adopted by many Christians in the Reformation Era, and even before it. John Wycliffe, the leading fourteenth-century theologian, was perhaps the earliest of these, and he was followed by many leading figures in the Protestant Movement, among them Martin Luther, Andreas Osiander, Johann Funck, David Chytraeus, Johann Oecolampadius, William Tyndale, and many others. Post-Reformation figures who upheld the same interpretation included James I of England, Henry More, Sir Isaac Newton, and many others. For a more comprehensive list, see http://christiantrumpetsounding.com/Antichrist/Reformation%20Views.htm (accessed January 3, 2010).

37. Pope Pius IX, Apostolic Letter Cum Catholica Ecclesia, March 26, 1860, quoted in *Papal Teachings: The Church*, selected and arranged by the Benedictine Monks of Solesmes, translated by Mother E. O'Gorman, R.S.C.J., Manhattanville College of the Sacred Heart, St. Paul Editions, Boston: p. 160.

38. Commentary to the words "and the one nation shall be stronger than the other nation" (see previous footnote).

The ultimate downfall of the Fourth Kingdom is shrouded in ambiguity: In contrast to the fall of Babylon, Persia, and Greece, that of Rome is not described in the verses of Daniel. In a similar vein, a midrashic source describes how Jacob was shown the rise and fall of three of the Four Kingdoms that would exile his descendants.[39] Of the Fourth Kingdom, he was shown only its rise; its downfall at the hands of God Himself was promised, but not shown. Indeed, its immense power would last for many centuries, far longer than the reign of its predecessors. Yet, after the long years during which the Roman Empire and its Christian heirs held the reigns of power, recent decades have seen it decline, quickly losing its grip over world domination to nations that pay it little or no homage. Simultaneously, the State of Israel was established.

The doctrinal reverses that the Christian faith has recently experienced can be seen as an integral part of the Jacob-Esau relationship. As the power of the Church has declined, that of Israel has ascended, and as the Jews have returned to autonomous rule over their homeland, Christianity has been forced to reverse its age-old stance on the question of the Jews.

The establishment of the State, though remaining far from the end of the road, represents a major landmark in the conflict of the Jews and the *Little Horn* of Daniel's vision. Two thousand three hundred years after the vision declared it, *the Holy* – in a Jewish, Christian, and even universal sense – had been vindicated.

---

39. *Pirkei Derabbi Eliezer*, Chap. 35.

✍ Chapter 6

THE STATE OF ISRAEL

With regard to the State of Israel, the mention of the word "prophecy" – which was brought up in chapter 4, and to which we will return later in the present chapter – is often cause enough to elicit a heated response.[1] Well before its establishment, and the more so once it became a tangible reality, the theological definition of the State of Israel had been a subject of fiery debate and deep division within Jewish Orthodoxy.

Three distinct ideologies can be identified, each of them involving significant practical ramifications in relation to conduct vis-à-vis the State. History has not yet decided the issue, and barring an extreme turn of events, it is hard to foresee any of the sides backing down from their respective positions. At the same time, historical fact has certainly been a factor in molding the positions, forcing those at the extremities of the debate to adjust their stances in reaction to a dynamic of unfolding events.

This, of course, is a question of Zionism – and Zionism is not the subject of this book. Moreover, we have already mentioned[2] that the place of the Jewish State in prophecy, which is the subject of this chapter, does not necessarily confer upon the State any degree of holiness.

---

1. Concerning the presence or otherwise of the State of Israel in prophecy, see also above, beginning of chapter 4.

2. See Preface.

Nevertheless, there remains scope to discuss the theological status of the Jewish State in light of prophetic revelation. In this context alone, and without seeking to encompass (and barely to touch upon) the broad issue involved, I wish to dedicate a brief section to the theological definition of the State of Israel.

THE JEWISH STATE: HALLOWED OR DEMONIC?

Although the ideas had been articulated before his time, Rabbi Avraham Yitzchak Kook is widely credited with providing Zionism with a coherent, sweeping, and specifically messianic framework within religious theology. Rabbi Kook certainly expressed his dismay at the secular influences that were molding the future state, and articulated his desire that Zionism should be cleansed of "all the filth and mire smeared upon it by reckless writers"; yet, secularism in itself did not dissuade him from giving the State-to-be an exalted and even hallowed definition:

An ideal state, one that has the highest of all ideals engraved in its being . . . the most sublime happiness of the individual . . . this shall be our state, the State of Israel, *the pedestal of God's throne in this world,* for its only aim shall be that the Lord be acknowledged as one and His name one, which is truly the highest happiness.[3]

After the State came into existence, the followers of Rabbi Kook, and most prominently his son, Rabbi Zvi Yehudah Kook, were not hesitant to confer a Divine status on the secular state. In the words of Rabbi Zvi Yehudah, "The State of Israel is a Divine entity, our holy and exalted state!"[4] Rabbi Zvi Yehudah believed wholeheartedly that "the Statehood of Israel is totally *Kadosh,* without any blemish at all,"[5] irrespective of the religious level of the State:

The intrinsic value of the State is not dependent on the number of observant Jews who live here. Of course, our aspiration is that all of our people will

---

3. *Orot Hakodesh* (Jerusalem: 1963), p. 160.

4. Zvi Yehudah Kook, *Lehilchot Tzibbur* (Jerusalem: 1987), pp. 244, 246.

5. Zvi Yehudah Kook, *Torat Eretz Yisrael* (Jerusalem: 1991), p. 346.

embrace the Torah and the mitzvot. However, the Statehood of Israel is *Kadosh* whatever religious level it has.[6]

From the darkness of the Holocaust, the light of the Messiah had finally shone forth, manifested in the State of Israel. Rabbi Shlomo Aviner, a leading figure in the Religious Zionist camp, expressed the messianic belief in the State so central to Religious Zionism:

If someone whispers in your ear that he has "not seen the Messiah lately, either in the field of the Golan or in the expanses of the Sinai," he may be an honest man. . . . But if he goes a step further and says, "Since I have not seen it, it does not exist," his words are words of falsehood and seduction. Say to him, "You may not have seen it, but others have." . . . We declare the absolute certainty of our imminent redemption. . . . All the troubles, delays, and complications we have endured are merely momentary and cannot obscure this mighty overall trend, this Messiah, whose power has been concealed since ancient times in the treasure house of history, and who is now being revealed in actuality.[7]

The exile, according to this position, is a thing of the past. Although the Messiah is not yet revealed in person, he is revealed in essence, in the spirit of the State of Israel. This conception of the Jewish State led inevitably to the hallowing of national institutions, bestowing Divine elevation upon the concrete actions of the State. Thus, Rabbi Zvi Yehudah Kook stated that

The holiness of the Divine service, the service of the Temple, is extended to the work of the State as a whole, both practical and spiritual, both public and private. (*Lenetivot Yisrael*, 1:183)

When an Israeli cabinet minister entered Yeshivat Merkaz Harav (the elitist Torah academy of the Religious Zionist school) during Independence Day celebrations, students felt no ideological discomfort in dancing and chanting around him, as is the norm for leading Torah luminaries.

A second, no less extreme approach presents the State of Israel in

6. Ibid., p. 344.
7. Shlomo Aviner, *Am Kelavi* (Jerusalem: 1983), 2:192–94.

the very opposite light. Instead of emanating from a source of Divine holiness, the Jewish State is seen as a manifestation of satanic forces (as mentioned at the beginning of Chap. 3) – the very embodiment of evil. Rabbi Yoel Teitelbaum, the renowned Rebbe of Satmar Hassidim and spiritual leader of the Eidah Haredit (the chief organization of the "old settlement" of Jerusalem), was the foremost proponent of this vehemently anti-Zionist ideology. Commenting on the verse, "May the Lord rebuke you, O Satan who chooses Jerusalem" (Zechariah 3:2), Rabbi Teitelbaum wrote:

May the Lord rebuke Satan, for [he] has chosen Jerusalem in order better to overcome those who dwell there . . . to seduce and corrupt the entire world wrapped in the mantle of Jerusalem's glory. . . . And 'outrages have been committed by the enemy in the sanctuary' (Tehillim 79:1) in the hallowed land . . . for vicious people have come there and defiled it with their heretical government, may God protect us.[8]

In the view of Rabbi Teitelbaum and his followers, the very notion of a Jewish State in advance of the Messiah is heretical. As Yerachmiel Domb, a vocal ideologue of the Neturei Karta faction, put it, "This Zionism, the idea that we ought to be a nation and have a state, is a pollution that encompasses all other pollutions, a complete heresy that includes all other heresies" (*Kuntress Et Nisayon*, p. 4). Taking the passivity of traditional Judaism to its greatest extreme, Rabbi Teitelbaum saw the Jewish state as heretical and evil, irrespective of the virtue or otherwise of its leaders:

Even if the cabinet ministers were all beloved of God, all pure; even if they were all talmudic sages, nevertheless, because they have seized freedom and sovereignty before the appointed time, they have committed heresy against our holy Torah and faith. The kingdom of [Bar Kochva] was, after all, ruled by the Torah . . . and his contemporaries were all saints. . . . Yet see how grievously they were punished, heaven spare us the like, for [their actions, in rebelling against Rome] amounted to a forcing of the End before the appointed time.[9]

---

8. *Vayoel Moshe* (Jerusalem: 1978), sec. 149.
9. Rabbi Yoel Teitelbaum, *Essay on the Three Oaths*, sec. 77.

It should be noted that the actual following of this most extreme ideology is marginal, amounting to several thousands in Israel, and somewhat greater numbers in the United States. Nevertheless, the influence of this school of thought spans far beyond its numeric following, and mainstream elements of Haredi Jewry are certainly influenced, to a greater or lesser degree, by the ideology of the more radical factions.

Dwelling on the two radically conflicting approaches of religious Zionism and religious anti-Zionism, it might be tempting to see the possible presence of the State in prophecy as contradicting the latter, and affirming the former. Even leaving aside the actual presence (or otherwise) of the State in prophecy, the fulfillment of Biblical prophecies in the wake of the State, as outlined in earlier chapters, can be seen as backing up the theological legitimacy of the State. Indeed, Rabbi Teitelbaum is careful to refute the modern association of some of the prophecies outlined in chapter two of this book (that appear to have been fulfilled in the present era), rightly fearing that an appreciation of their fulfillment in a modern context might confer an air of legitimacy on the Jewish State.

Yet, although it does not seem plausible to think that the "vindication of the holy" mentioned in the previous chapter should have come through a satanic manifestation, it is likewise false to infer from the fulfillment of prophecy that the State of Israel is "holy." Cyrus, whose permission to rebuild the Temple embodied the prophecy of redemption, was neither holy nor evil. His neutrality in respect of holiness did not prevent him from being a tool for the fulfillment of prophecy; nor did it deny him the title of "My Messiah" (Isaiah 44:28). As we will see, the state might be inherently *unholy*, and even destined for ultimate decline, yet still play a central role in the fulfillment of Biblical prophecy.

This brings us to a third theological perspective on the State of Israel. Whereas the two opposing outlooks outlined above present a concrete religious definition of the Jewish State, many reject both definitions in favor of a wholly neutral position. The State of Israel is neither good nor evil (in a theological sense), neither hallowed nor satanic. It is, rather, a state among states of the world. The fact, according to this outlook, that the State is ruled and run by Jews, does not imply an emergence from exile. This position is shared by the majority of secular and ultra-Orthodox Jews (an unusual alliance). In the words of the Haredi leader Rabbi Elazar Menachem Schach, "The Jewish People is still in exile, until the arrival of the Redeemer, even when it is in Eretz Israel; this is neither redemption nor the beginning of the redemption."[10]

In the (mainstream) Haredi Weltanschauung, the State of Israel is not to be judged by theological standards. Zionism, of course, was and is still seen in a harshly negative light – but this is chiefly because of its secularist manifesto, and not because of the objection in principle to Jewish power. Rabbi Chaim Soloveichik, among the leading figures of ultra-Orthodoxy at the turn of the century, castigated the Zionists whose "purpose [is] to uproot the fundaments of [our] religion . . . to destroy religion, and is a stumbling block to the House of Israel."[11]

This position criticizes Zionism for its secular nature, but makes no sweeping statement that sheds theological light on the future Jewish State.

The "undefined" approach to the State of Israel is theologically explained in the following words of Rabbi Joseph Epstein:

Both camps, those who affirm the vision of the revealed End as well as those who deny it, force themselves, as it were, into the secrets of the Almighty, as if the upper world were unfolded before them like a garment. But the heavenly voice has not yet emerged![12]

Rather than yardsticks of theology, according to this outlook the criterion for judging the State (as with all other worldly things) is only its worthiness in promoting the performance of and study of the Torah. If the State can serve in bringing Jews closer to their Father in Heaven, and in supporting the study of Torah, then it is to be judged favorably; if not, or if it hinders these goals, then it is judged negatively.

This "neutral" outlook on the Jewish State avoids the patent theological difficulties encountered by the extreme positions at each end

---

10. Rabbi Elazar Menachem Schach, *Michtavim U'maamarim* (Bnei Brak: 1980), p. 9.

11. S. Z. Landau and Joseph Rabinowitz, eds., *Or Layesharim* (Warsaw: 1900), p. 55.

12. Joseph David Epstein, *Mitzvat HaShalom* (New York: 1970), p. 605; quoted in Ravitzky, *Messianism, Zionism, and Jewish Religious Radicalism*, p. 155.

of the spectrum. It has no problem, for instance, with the ostensibly miraculous salvation of the Six Day War – in which the Temple Mount was taken and Jerusalem united under Jewish rule – an event that the Satmar Rebbe was forced to attribute to forces of evil. At the same time, it has little ideological difficulty with the disengagement from areas of the Biblical Land of Israel (such as Judea and Gaza), which for the Religious Zionist camp implies a deep betrayal by the State, and a theological paradox for which there is no resolution.[13]

Yet, the adoption of a noncommittal stance concerning the definition of the State does not preclude the recognition of its place in prophecy; similarly, it does not deny the import of events connected with the Jewish State. In spite of their general anti-Zionist stance, many Haredi leaders, including such luminaries as the *Chafetz Chaim* (Rabbi Israel Meir Kagan) and Rabbi Yosef Chaim Sonnenfeld, saw the Balfour Declaration in the context of Divine Providence.[14] The fact that the declaration was a Zionist achievement did not prevent them from seeing it as such. When he heard about the establishment of new cities in the Land of Israel such as Rechovot, Rishon LeZion, and

---

13. Betrayal by the State of the theological definition bestowed upon it by Religious Zionism, through acts such as disengagement and forced evacuation of Jewish settlers, have compelled even staunch Religious Zionists to reconsider their position vis-à-vis the inherent "holiness" of the State. In the wake of these considerations, some Religious Zionists have suggested disconnecting the two terms: One may be Zionist, acknowledging the virtue of self-rule, and one may be Religious, but the two should not be combined in giving statehood religious significance. The idea of "doing away with the hyphen" that links the two terms has been mentioned by Rabbi Dr. Michael Abraham, in "The Third Way, or: On Religious Zionism Without the Hyphen" [Hebrew], in *Tzohar*, issue 22.

14. According to the testimony of Isaac Breuer in *Moriah* (Jerusalem: 1980), p. 104, Rabbi Sonnenfeld reacted with the following words: "Let us assume that rain had not fallen for two thousand years, and a small cloud was suddenly seen in the sky. Would not everyone become excited and say, 'Perhaps, nevertheless.' And is not the British Mandate at least such a cloud?" For the reaction of the Rabbi Yisrael Meir Kagan (the Chafetz Chaim), see the testimony of his son in Shmuel Grainemann, ed., *Chafetz Chaim al HaTorah*, p. 101, which quotes the Chafetz Chaim as exclaiming that the Balfour Declaration was a form of Divine intervention in favor of the redemption.

Gedera, the *Chafetz Chaim* could even comment: "Behold, the thing [the coming of the Messiah] has already begun!"[15] Indeed, when the State of Israel was formed, even the Brisker Rav (Rabbi Yitzchak Zev HaLevi Soloveichik), a vehement anti-Zionist, saw the event as a "smile from Divine Providence."

In the present chapter, we will present first the rise, and then the possible decline of the State of Israel, from a perspective of prophecy. Those who adopt radical positions of Zionism or anti-Zionism concerning the State of Israel will have trouble with the first and second assertions, respectively. The more neutral approach, which sees the State of Israel as neither holy nor satanic, will encounter no theological problems with either.

FROM DOMINION TO KINGDOM

We have already had occasion to mention the two distinct stages of the redemption: At first, Israel will take the initial tentative steps toward national and religious freedom; later, she will be redeemed in glory as God reveals Himself to the world.[16] These two stages can be discerned in the following verse from the Book of Micah:

And you, Migdal-Éder [Tower of the Flock], the hill of the daughter of Zion, it shall return unto you; the former dominion shall come, the kingdom of the daughter of Jerusalem. (4:8)

A clear distinction separates the concepts of a *dominion* and a *kingdom*. The structure of a *mamlachah* (kingdom) implies a hierarchical order in which the subjects of the king, all of them eager to do his bidding, form the essential cogs of the machinery of the kingdom. The king is enthroned by his people, either actively in an elected monarchy, or passively in an inherited kingdom.

By contrast, the term *memshalah* (dominion) denotes a constitution of government or power that lacks the structure of a kingdom.

---

15. This comment was reported by the Chafetz Chaim's son, Rabbi Aryeh Leib, to Rabbi Zvi Yehudah Kook; *Torat Eretz Yisrael*, p. 345.

16. See above, Chap. 2, text adjacent to notes 3-11.

One who rules by force, for instance, without the consent or support of the people, is termed *moshel* (ruler) rather than *melech* (king).[17] A kingdom implies majesty and splendor; a dominion implies power, but little glory.[18]

Based on this distinction, Malbim explains that the two terms mentioned by Micah refer to two stages of Jewish return. The "former dominion" refers to the initial stage of return, in which the Jews will rule by a "small government," allowing them a degree of power and self-rule, yet lacking the distinctive splendor of monarchy. Malbim writes that this is likened to the *former dominion* of Israel, referring to the days of the Judges, before a king arose to rule over the nation. The second stage will be the establishment of a full kingdom, as the heyday of Solomon's rule over Israel.

The difference between the epoch of the Judges and the era of the Kings is defined by Ibn Yechia:

One system of government [for Israel] consists in self-rule by the people, managed by their priests and elders, and above them, the Judge; this [system of government] is termed *senate*, as found in Venice and Florence. [The system corresponds to] the rule of Israel by its elders, before the king ruled over them, and at their head was a single Judge, such as Samson and the like.[19]

Applying this to the present day, we find that a "small Jewish government" has indeed arisen, embodied in the current State of Israel, which follows the self-rule style that prevailed during the times of *former dominion*. It may not be glorious or majestic, yet this only strengthens its claim to be the return of *the former dominion* that Micah foresaw.

---

17. See Genesis 37:8, which uses a double expression of dominion and rule, and the commentary of Rabbi Eliyahu of Vilna (the Vilna Gaon) in Kol Eliyahu; see also *Sefer Hashorashim* (Moshel), among several sources.

18. For instance, the sun and the moon were "given dominion" over the day and the night (Genesis 1:18). By Divine ordination, the celestial bodies were given power and control over their respective times; their dominion, however, lacks majesty and glory. It is a *memshalah* (government or regime), and not a *mamlachah* (kingdom).

19. *Commentary of Ibn Yechia to Psalms* 2:10, commenting on the mention in the verse of kings and judges.

Based on the prophecy and Malbim's interpretation, at a later stage this government will be transform into a permanent kingdom.

The Biblical context of the verse in the Book of Micah is also revealing. The preceding verses predict the ingathering of the people:

On that day – the word of the Lord – I will assemble the lame, and gather in the one driven away, and whomever I afflicted. I will make the lame into a remnant, and the one cast far off into a mighty nation; and the Lord shall reign over them at Mount Zion, from now and forever. (4:6–7)

The gathering described, the beginning of which we have witnessed in recent times, sets the scene for the return of the *former dominion*, and ultimately for the Messianic Kingdom. Today, the afflicted Jew is no longer afflicted – certainly not by the standards of times of old; his scattering is much diminished, and his State is powerful.

Additionally, we have already noted the significance of recent upheavals in official Christian policy concerning the Jews,[20] which came hand in hand with the establishment of the State. The above verses of Micah present the greatest possible contradiction to the traditional New Israel doctrine of Christianity, which claims prophesies of future glory for itself and leaves those of doom and calamity for sinful Israel. Indeed, Malbim writes that the following verse from Micah makes an explicit reference to this doctrine: "And now, many nations shall gather upon you, saying, 'Let her be guilty, and our eyes shall take hold of Zion'" (Micah 4:11). As Malbim explains, the nations take hold of Zion for themselves, claiming to be the true subject of eschatological Biblical prophecy.[21]

In amending the distortion, the prophecy speaks of "assembling the lame," a promise that leaves no doubt as to identification. If ever there was "the lame," "the one driven away," and "the afflicted," it was the Jew. Downtrodden and oppressed for so long, the same people are presently returning once more to build and to plant. "Just as I watched over them to uproot, to smash, to destroy, to annihilate, and to bring

---

20. See mainly chapter five of this book.

21. Significantly, Malbim mentions that the Arabs (today implying the Muslims) have annexed the replacement doctrine for their own religious theology, and are therefore destined to wage war on Jerusalem.

evil," declares God, "so will I watch over them to build and to plant" (Jeremiah 31:27). The *scattered sheep* (50:17) of Israel will once more be a powerful nation.

With which stones, however, is the path from dominion to kingdom paved? The ensuing verses, which follow the prediction of a Jewish dominion and kingdom, indicate that the route toward destiny – the day on which "the Lord shall reign over them" – is one of hardship:

Now, why do you seek alliance? Is there not a king in your midst? Has your counselor become lost, that pains have gripped you like a woman in child-birth? . . . And now, many nations have assembled against you. . . . But they do not know the thoughts of the Lord, and do not understand His counsel, for He has gathered them like sheaves to the threshing floor. (Micah 4:9–12)

In the opinion of many commentators, the passage, which refers to exile in and ultimate salvation from Babylon, refers to Micah's own era. Nonetheless, the description of a gathering against Jerusalem, in which the nations are destined to be as sheaves on a threshing floor, surely relates to a later time – the *latter days* with which the fourth chapter of Micah begins. Before the End is reached, times of hardship must be endured; the road from *dominion* to *kingdom* will not be smooth.

THE FINAL EXILE: WINTER'S RAIN?

The verses of Micah give no indication as to how the prophesied transition from dominion to kingdom is destined to take place. According to Rabbi Shlomo Kushelevsky (*Asher Tavona Yagidu*, pp. 90ff), a possible scenario is the actual collapse of the Jewish State, which would then be followed by the revelation of the Messianic Kingdom. He bases this on a prediction made by the *Zohar*, interpreting the following verse in Song of Songs:

For behold, the winter is past, the rain is over and gone; the blossoms have appeared on our land, the time of pruning has come, and the voice of the turtledove is heard in our land. (2:11–12)

The *Zohar* teaches that these verses describe an integral part of the final redemption. "The winter" refers to the dominion of the foreign nations over Israel; the first stage in the redemption will be the termination of foreign rule over Israel. Following this, however, another power will arise to rule over Israel: "'The rain is over and gone' – this is the rule of the *erev rav*" (*Tikkunei Zohar* 144a). This constitutes the final phase of Jewish exile.

It is not possible to identify the *erev rav* in a present-day context. The term actually refers to the Mixed Multitude of Egyptians who emerged from Egypt together with the fledgling nation of Israel (Exodus 12:38). The Bible writes very little about this *erev rav* contingency, and later sources are also extremely sparse on the subject. Early Jewish Sages clearly didn't dedicate a great degree of significance to the subject.

However, a talmudic tradition confirms a continual presence of the *erev rav* group among the Jewish People. The Talmud records how one of the sages chanced upon a group of individuals whose behavior, despite their Jewish lineage, conflicted sharply with established Jewish dispositions. "These," he declared, "are from the *erev rav*" (*Beitzah* 32b). Although their ancestry cannot be traced, some (interpreting the comment literally) therefore see the Mixed Multitude as remaining an integral part of the Jewish people. Notwithstanding its genealogical Jewishness, this element continues to embody a foreign element that amalgamated with the Jewish nation at its inception.[22]

According to the prophetic statement of the *Zohar*, the dominion of foreign nations is destined to pass, to be replaced by a new power that will arise over Israel: the rule of the *erev rav*. The foreign element that was grafted into the nation is destined to seize the reins of power.

Following a tradition that has been articulated by a number of Haredi leaders past and present,[23] Kushelevsky (pp. 92-96) suggests in this light

---

22. See *Zohar* 1:25a, and commentary of *Or Hachamah*, who emphasizes that even an individual of purely Jewish lineage could possess a soul from Amalek – a particular branch of the Mixed Multitude; see also Rabbi Shlomo Elyashuv, *Hakdamot U'She'arim* (Pyetrykaw, 1909), *Shaar* 6, Chap. 5.

23. An example of a past leader is Rabbi Elchanan Wasserman, in his Ikveta De-Meshicha, section 4; for a present (and relatively moderate) Haredi leader who has voiced such expressions is Rabbi Aharon Leib Steinmen; see http://ebookbrowse.com/rabbi-steinman-secular-jews-erev-rav-1-4-2012-pdf-d325803714 (17.1.13).

that among those who established the State of Israel were members of the *erev rav* sector. The accusation is that from an all-embracing religion, leading Zionists would have transformed Judaism into a manifestation of modern nationalism, the membership of which demanded no commitment beyond subscription to the manifesto of the Zionist cause. The slogan coined by Max Nordau, "Zionism has nothing to do with religion," may not have been an official declaration of the 1897 Zionist Congress (as Rabbi Kook, later Chief Rabbi of Palestine, thought it to be[24]). Herzl, perhaps out of sensitivity to popular opinion, and perhaps because of his (albeit fragile) continued attachment to the religion of his fathers,[25] distanced himself from the proclamation. Yet, it closely reflected the prevailing spirit of the Zionist movement, and of the State in which the movement culminated.

It is interesting to note that according to the *Zohar's* interpretation, the Gentile nations are termed *winter*, while the foreign element within Israel is termed *rain*. In many climates, and prominently in the Holy Land in which the Song of Songs was composed, rain is specifically associated with the winter; during the summer months there are barely any clouds to be seen, let alone actual rain. As was the case in the first manifestation of the Mixed Multitude, the comparison thus suggests that the power of Israel's foreign element will emerge from the Gentile powers, as rain emanates from the winter season.

This was the case in the background of the leadership that founded the State of Israel. Herzl and his followers were not products of the *yeshiva* (talmudic college) or the traditional *cheder* (school for boys in which religious subjects are taught almost exclusively), but of the culture, ideology and politics of contemporary European society. Herzl's drive to found a Jewish state was based primarily on the acute need for national self-defense. His inspiration, however, and that of the other early Zionists who eagerly joined him, did not stem from religious fervor, nor even from love of the Land or the nation, but from the

---

24. Rabbi Kook harshly censored the statement, which he believed was given official status at the Zionist convention.

25. See end of chapter three of this book.

nationalistic zeal typical of early-twentieth-century Europe, tinged with the socialist ideals budding in Eastern Europe.[26]

Ze'ev (Vladimir) Jabotinsky, whose moral clarity as founder and leader of the Revisionist Zionists was perhaps sharper than other Zionist leaders, and who prophetically preached the urgent need for the "evacuation" of European Jewry to Palestine, understood well the ideological dependency of Zionism on Gentile foundations. At the Second Revisionist World Conference held in Paris in 1926, he coined the epigram *morenu verabbenu hagoy* – "our master and teacher, the Gentile."[27] In this worldview the winter had perhaps passed, but not before it produced rain.[28]

But notwithstanding the temptation to make use of the *erev rav* idea in a modern context, I believe it mistaken to do so. Beyond the esoteric writings of the *Zohar*, the eschatological concept of an "exile among Jews" and the expanded identity of the *erev rav* as a "threat from within" is not present in ancient Jewish texts. Certainly, the use thereof sets a mystical tone inappropriate for this volume, whose focus is on prophecies and their interpretation and not on Kabalistic material. However, it is significant that a mainstream Haredi writer such as Kushelevsky, among many others, feels comfortable in adducing the idea as part of his ideological and interpretational source material.

The anomalous entry of the esoteric *erev rav* idea into mainstream dialogue and terminology reflects a need of the ultra-Orthodox

---

26. In particular, the Russian Communist model served as a beacon for the early Zionist pioneers, and Russian literature, folksongs, and theology were common among the youthful settlers. See Shlomo Avineri, *The Making of Modern Zionism: The Intellectual Origins of the Jewish State* (Basic Books, NY: 1981), who has expounded on the contemporary European model on which Zionism was founded.

27. Joseph B. Shechtman, *Fighter and Prophet: The Life and Times of Vladimir Jabotinsky* (Eshel Books, Silver Spring), p. 349.

28. It should be stressed that those who uphold the doctrine cannot say which individuals are from the Mixed Multitude, and which are "authentic" Jews. See Rabbi Joel Teitelbaum's *Al Hageulah ve'al Hatemurah*, sections 61–62, who highlights the significant difference between ordinary sinners and actual heretics. Rabbi Teitelbaum cites Rabbi Yisrael Meir Kagan (the *Chafetz Chayim*) in labeling the Zionists an Amalekite element within Israel.

community to present a theological framework for an exilic condition that includes Jewish sovereignty over (much of) the biblical Land of Israel.[29] At the beginning of this chapter, we mentioned dissenting opinions among religious figures concerning the status of the Jewish state. At times, this difference of opinion caused tangible friction even within the Haredi camp, as radical groups condemned mainstream co-operation with the Zionist movement. Yet, the common denominator that united all Haredi groups was a professed belief that the exile had not terminated with the establishment of the Jewish State. The exile had only changed its face. Identifying the State of Israel (the "Jewish State") with the continued exile naturally leads to a pessimistic view concerning its future.

It was this sentiment that Rabbi Shlomo Wolbe wished to convey in relating a conversation he had with the one of the luminaries of the pre-war generation, Rabbi Mordechai Pogramansky.

I shared with him one of the last discourses I heard from Rav Yerucham [Leibovitz], the spiritual mentor of Mir Yeshiva, who had a deep love for the Land of Israel and would follow developments therein with great interest. In 1936, Rav Yerucham said that sinners would never succeed in building the Land of Israel, and that the Land of Israel can only be built in a spirit of holiness and with commitment to Torah law.

Rabbi Mottel responded: "They cannot establish it; however, they are able to build it. Its prolonged existence must be granted by Divine Providence."[30]

Rabbi Wolbe, perhaps disturbed by the fact that history was seemingly disproving Rabbi Leibovitz's axiomatic belief that "sinners" could not succeed in building the Land of Israel (though it was still two years before the State was formally established), consulted with Rabbi Pogramansky. The latter replied that "sinners" can, indeed, build the Land (contrary to Rabbi Leibovitz's assertion), but clarified that they cannot grant it prolonged existence. The secular pioneers of Zionism

---

29. See Rabbi Eliyahu Weintraub, *Ha-Tekufa Bise'arat Eliyahu* (Bnei Braq, 2007).

30. Rabbi Shlomo Wolbe, *Bein Sheshet LeAsor* (later renamed *Olam Ha-Yedidut*).

could provide the Land with a temporal body, as it were; the provision of an eternal soul is a quite different matter.

At the same time, based on all we have seen thus far it seems difficult to accept that the building of the Land, albeit by secular Jews, was not "granted by Divine Providence."

SMASHING THE HAND OF THE HOLY PEOPLE

An interesting scriptural prophecy (also mentioned by Kushelevsky) that might be of relevance to the future of the State is found in the book of Daniel. Standing by the Tigris River, in the wake of a great vision of angels who appeared to him, Daniel beheld "two others" standing on either side of the bank:

> One said to the man clothed in linen, who was above the waters of the river, "How long until the concealed end?" I heard the man clothed in linen, who was above the waters of the river, as he lifted his right hand and his left hand to the heavens and swore by the Life of the Worlds that after a period, periods, and a half, upon the completion of the smashing of the hand of the holy people, all these would be finished. (12:6–7)

The verse, which refers to "the smashing of the hand of the holy people," is cited by the Talmud (Sanhedrin 98a) as proof that the final redemption will come in spite of the people's remaining unrepentant.[31] Commenting on the verse itself, Rabbi Shlomo Yitzchaki (Rashi) explains:

> When their upstanding and the strength of their hands, which hitherto gave them the power to spread forth hither and thither, will end; then, when their might will be no more, and they will be humbled to a great extreme, will the troubles end, and the Messiah come.[32]

---

31. We have already mentioned this prophecy, and explained how its talmudic context pertains to the present-day state of affairs, in chapter two of this book. See above, text adjacent to note 26.

32. Rashi, Commentary on Talmud, *Sanhedrin* 98a.

The implication is that before the arrival of the Messianic Age, the Jewish nation will wield a degree of power, and will even procure the military prowess required for national expansion – "hither and thither." Finally, however, this power will dissipate. Kushelevsky thus suggests that only following a certain decline in strength, "the smashing of the hand of the holy people," will the troubles end and the Messiah come.

PRUNING THE VINE

The Talmud itself articulates this prophetic idea in quite explicit terms.

In an eschatological prophecy, which concludes with the promise of how the nations will bring the People of Israel as gifts to God on Mount Zion, Isaiah opens with the words, "Woe to the land of clamorous wings" (18:1). Much speculation has been made, in particular in recent times, as to the identity of this land. Although traditional commentaries have pointed at Ethiopia, India, or another unknown country, the implication of "clamorous wings" has always been a point of contention.[33] The jet-age of the twentieth century has opened up the possibility that the prophecy may refer to the United States, where aviation came into being, and which remains the long-established world leader in aviation power and technology.[34] The location of the land is described as "on the other side of the rivers of Cush." This, it might be surmised, is the prophet's method of describing a land that is far away, beyond even the great rivers of Northern Africa, past all civilization known to contemporary humankind.[35] Furthermore, the land is described as a nation that *sends envoys upon the sea*, which also fits the description of a distant, rather than a relatively nearby country. The reference to *papyrus vessels*,

---

33. Classical commentaries (Radak, Malbim, and *Metzudot Zion*) explain that this refers to the sound of ships, whose sails resemble wings, or to the sound of birds.

34. Wilbur and Orville Wright made the first engine-powered flight in Kitty Hawk, North Carolina, on December 17, 1903. Ever since, the U.S. has always been at the forefront of airplane manufacture and technology, and its air force is the most powerful in the world.

35. *Targum Yonatan*, which is the most ancient of Jewish Bible translations, refers to the Land as a "distant land," but makes specific reference to India.

however, accords less with the America theory; an aircraft is constructed out of thin, papyrus-like material, but surely not of papyrus itself. In the context of an ancient prophecy this can perhaps be forgiven.[36]

Yet, and despite claims of some modern extrapolators who search for apocalyptic predictions relating to the great superpower, the ensuing verses certainly do not refer to the United States, but rather to the Nation of Israel:

Go, swift messengers, to the nation that is dragged and plucked, to the people that inspired awe from the day it came into being and onward, the nation that is detested and trampled, whose land was ravished[37] by rivers. (Isaiah 18:2)[38]

We would like to focus on verse 6 of the same chapter:

For before the harvest, when the flower is finished and the bud turns to grapes approaching ripeness, He will cut down the young branches with pruning hooks, and He will remove and chop off all the twigs.

This is not the only place in which Israel is portrayed as a vine; the same simile appears in Psalms: "You plucked a vine out of Egypt . . . and planted it" (80:9). The verse in Isaiah describes how before harvest-time, as the grapes approach ripeness, there will be buds and blossoms: As Israel nears the ultimate achievement of their national purpose, it will go through a stage of blooming and thriving. In tandem, the foreign branches, which must be amputated for the sake of the vine itself,[39] will be cut away. Following this, the next verse predicts a glorious future: The same People of Israel, a people oppressed and trampled, will be brought to Zion as an offering to God.

The Talmud reveals the identity of the harmful branches that must be pruned from the vine: "Rabbi Chama son of Chanina taught, the Son

---

36. See Introduction, above.

37. Classical commentaries explain that this is a reference to Gentile kings, who ravished the Land like rivers.

38. Note that Christian translations, such as the King James I edition, render several words of this verse entirely differently from the classical understanding of the Hebrew words. Nevertheless, the implication is certainly Israel, and not the U.S. or any other Gentile nation.

39. *Commentary of Malbim*, Isaiah 18:5.

of David will not come until the shameful dominion is terminated from Israel, as it says, 'He will cut down the young branches with pruning hooks'" (*Sanhedrin* 98a). According to this talmudic interpretation, the coming of the Messianic Age will be preceded by a "shameful dominion," whose power will ultimately be terminated.

In the contemporary setting, the State of Israel has become the political representative of the People of Israel. For better or for worse, philo-Zionism is virtually synonymous with philo-Semitism, and anti-Zionism with anti-Semitism. As the Jewish ambassador to the world, the State has not always embodied the "kingdom of ministers and holy nation" (Exodus 19:6) that the verse impels. Rather than a "holy nation," the State has sometimes strived, with a measure of success, to be "as all the nations" (Ezekiel 20:32). Instead of a sanctification of God, the secularism espoused by the State has at times constituted a desecration.

RESTORATION OF THE JUDGES

We return once more to the *Amidah* – the nineteen-blessing prayer instituted by the Men of the Great Assembly (which included both elders and prophets)[40] which has been recited thrice daily by Jews over the course of two millennia. We have already noted how the twelve central blessings form a continuum toward the final blessings of redemption (the rebuilding of Jerusalem, the sprouting of the seed of David, God's acceptance of our prayers, and the return of the Holy Presence to Zion). Furthermore, we have shown the connection between the sixth and seventh blessings – the rebirth of the Land, and the ingathering of its people.[41] We now turn to the relationship between the eighth and ninth blessings.

Following the blessing of the ingathering, where it seems we stand today on the time-continuum of the prayer (although the ingathering is still incomplete, the first stage certainly appears to be underway),

---

40. See Talmud, *Megillah* 17b; the *Jerusalem Talmud* (*Berachot* 4d) mentions 120 elders and approximately 80 prophets. These included such great prophets as Ezra and Nehemiah.

41. See above, p. 41.

the theme of the prayer moves on to the Restoration of the Judges. We have noted that a parallel can be drawn between the *former dominion* of Israel, which will return prior to the coming of the Messianic King, and the Biblical period of the Judges, prior to the establishment of the Davidic dynasty. Within this stage, which follows the first ingathering of the people, we pray that our national leaders should be as in former times – righteous leaders whose primary objective is true justice.

The ninth blessing, which is a later addition of talmudic times, relates to the other side of the same coin: "And for slanderers, let there be no hope; and may all wickedness perish in an instant; and may all Your enemies be cut down speedily." The prayer that enemies of God should be *cut down* strikes a chord of familiarity; the Hebrew form for *cut down* is identical to the form used by the verse of Isaiah: "He will *cut down* the young branches with pruning hooks" (18:5). An integral element of the new period of Judges, prior to the re-establishment of the Davidic dynasty, is the cutting down of the wicked who stand in the path of the new order.

Based on Talmud precedent (*Berachot* 10a), our hope in this context is that the wicked repent their ways rather than their actual destruction. God does not desire the destruction of the wicked, but only of the evil they bring to the world.

HE WILL NOT FORSAKE HIS HERITAGE

To Zionist and non-Zionist alike, the State of Israel presents itself as one of the modern Wonders of the World.[42] Its foundation, achieved against all the odds, was surely something of a miracle. The military sensation of the Six Day War, in which Jerusalem was united as part

---

42. One camp – followers of the late Rabbi Joel Teitelbaum of Satmar – takes exception to this definition. In his writings on the subject, Rabbi Teitelbaum painstakingly pointed out that the events involved in the foundation of the State, and in particular, the Six Day War, were not miracles in the full sense of the word. He added that whatever successes the Zionists had were inspired not by powers of holiness, but by satanic forces (see *Al Hageulah ve'al Hatemurah*, sections 5–7). Though sometimes vociferous, radical groups that fully embrace his views constitute a very small minority of Orthodox Jewry.

of the massive defeat of Israel's foes, consolidated the perception of Israel as something beyond the natural.[43] The same can almost be said of Israel's economic success, going against all the odds and under the constant threat of war and terror. But what does the future hold? We cannot know.

In this context it is worth noting how the ways of God are beyond human comprehension: "As high as the heavens over the earth, so are My ways higher than your ways, and My thoughts than your thoughts" (Isaiah 55:9). Prophecy allows us no more than a glimpse behind the scenes, brief chapter headings of a script whose inner meaning we cannot know.

By way of illustration we can perhaps picture a world of shadow-creatures – beings whose entire existence is limited to two dimensions alone. Can such creatures understand the ways of a three-dimensional world? They cannot do so for the very concept of a third dimension is beyond their existential consciousness. In a similar sense, humankind, whose existence is confined to three dimensions, cannot fathom the ways of an infinite God: "For My thoughts are not your thoughts, and your ways are not My ways – the word of the Lord" (Isaiah 55:8). God conducted and oversaw the establishment, expansion, and prosperity of the State. And he will oversee its future, whatever it may be.

Though the State may undergo a process of metamorphosis, we are assured that God will keep His Biblical promise: "For the Lord will not cast off His people, nor will He forsake His heritage" (Psalms 94:14). The process will be none other than that which brought the State into existence. Ultimately, it will be revealed as another step in the same direction – a further progression along the path of Jewish destiny (as outlined by the *Amidah* prayer), whose climax is the rebuilding of Jerusalem and the coming of new age.

---

43. A part of this miraculous feat was the entry of Trans-Jordan into the war, despite pleas on the part of Israel that it not join the fray. Had Jordan not entered the cataclysmal war, Jerusalem would have remained divided.

$\mathscr{B}$ *Chapter 7*

WHO OWNS THE LAND?

Wwe have already noted numerous Biblical predictions of the Jews' return to their homeland. As we have seen, some of these prophecies can be understood to include the current return to the Land, which began in the first half of the nineteenth century, and, with the advent of modern Zionism, gained momentum toward the beginning of the twentieth. We must now deal in greater depth with the significance of the Land itself, and with the Jews' Biblical (and historical) right to it. These matters form a central tenet of Judaism, and have taken on special significance in the light of current affairs.

MY LAND

Before addressing the matter of actual rights to the Land, we first turn our attention to the fundamental nature of the Land itself. As we have already mentioned, the attention of the media on the Middle-Eastern region that includes the State of Israel and its immediate surroundings is completely disproportionate to its size. This attention is partly related to the unique people who occupy the tiny country. Only since the return of Jews en masse to their homeland has the global fascination with the region come into being, indicating that the primary factor of this focus is the people of the Land, rather than the Land per se. Nevertheless, there is no doubt that the Land itself shares some common denominator with its people. What is its secret?

The answer to this is found in the following verses:

For the Land, which you come to possess, is not like the land of Egypt that you left, where you would plant your seed and water it on foot like a garden of herbs. But the Land, to which you cross over to possess it, is a Land of mountains and valleys; from the rain of heaven it drinks water;[1] a Land that the Lord, your God, seeks out; the eyes of the Lord, your God, are always upon it, from the beginning of the year to year's end. (Deuteronomy 11:10–12)

Although he never set foot there,[2] Moses proclaimed the uniqueness of the Land in the direct nature of its relationship with Divine guidance. The figurative reference to the "eyes of the Lord" implies the concept of Divine supervision – of God's constant watching over the Land, never leaving its fate to chance or to determinative factors of nature. The time span "from the beginning of the year to year's end" denotes the agricultural cycle, which is based on the seasons of the year. The verse promises that every season, every aspect of the yearly cycle, is firmly under God's direct supervision.

In numerous places we find that God calls the Land of Israel by the title *My Land*.[3] On the part of God, Who created the entire world, the use of *My Land* for a particular location is somewhat surprising. God Himself declares that "the heaven is My throne, and the earth, My footstool" (Isaiah 66:1). If the entire world is His, what is the particular significance of calling the Land of Israel *My Land*?

The explanation of this title, however, is that the Land of Israel is special in its being preconditioned, to a greater degree than the rest of the world, for the revelation of God. Nachmanides explains that in contrast to other lands, no "celestial minister" wields authority over the Land of Israel: God Himself, and no other, watches over the Land. Confirming this principle, the Talmud makes a remarkable statement:

---

1. We will return to explain the significance of rainwater, as opposed to the river-water irrigation of Egypt, toward the end of this chapter.

2. Moses died in the wilderness, on the verge of the nation's entry into the Promised Land.

3. See, for instance, Jeremiah 2:7 and Ezekiel 38:16, among several other references.

Anyone who lives in the Land of Israel is considered as if he has a God; and anyone who lives outside the Land of Israel is considered as if he has no God, as the verse (Leviticus 25:38)[4] says, "To give you the Land of Canaan, to be God unto you." (*Ketubot* 110b)[5]

The complete dependence of the Land of Israel on Divine guidance, to the extent that someone living in the Land earns a special relationship with God, renders it a spatial medium for the earthly manifestation of this same guidance. As the place of Divine revelation, the Land of Israel is fittingly labeled *My Land*.

MY PEOPLE AND MY LAND

There is a nation whose inherent purpose matches the fundamental nature of the Land of Israel: the People of Israel. "This nation I have fashioned for Myself, that they should declare My glory" (Isaiah 43:21). The essential role of Israel as a people is defined by Scripture as the glorification of God. For this purpose, He brought them forth from Egypt; for this purpose, He gave them the Torah; and for this purpose, He is destined to redeem them and to found His Kingdom upon them: "Let this [King David's prayer] be recorded for the final generation, so that the newborn people will praise God" (Psalms 102:19).

We find that together with the labeling of the Land of Israel as *My Land*, the People of Israel are labeled *My People*:

I will gather all of the nations and bring them down to the Valley of Jehoshaphat and I will contend with them there concerning *My people*, My inheritance Israel, that they dispersed among the nations, and they divided up *My land*. And they cast lots upon *My people* . . .[6]

---

4. See also Genesis 17:8.

5. More precisely, the Talmud concludes that someone living outside the Land of Israel is considered as if he worships other gods. The underlying theme, however, is identical: He who lives in the Land enjoys the direct guidance of God, and has the ability to relate to God in a manner that cannot be achieved outside the Land.

6. Joel 4:2–3 (emphasis added).

A similar combination of *My Land* and *My People*, which occurs in Ezekiel, suggests the central theme that binds together the Land and the People:

You will advance against *My people* Israel like a cloud covering the earth. It will be at the End of Days that I will bring you upon *My land*, in order that the nations may know Me, when I become sanctified through you before their eyes, O Gog! (Ezekiel 38:16)[7]

The subject of the great war at the End of Days, by means of which God will "become sanctified" before the entire world, will be the People of Israel; the location will be the Land of Israel. The human aspect of the vehicle upon which the glory of God is contingent is Israel; the spatial aspect is the Land. Both are appropriately defined by God as being *His*.[8] The special connection between the Land of Israel and the People of Israel is articulated with characteristic directness by the Vilna Gaon:

"Who is like Your nation Israel, one nation upon the earth" (II Samuel 7:23). For both of them are singular: Israel and the Land of Israel – Israel among the seventy nations, and the Land of Israel among all the lands. Just as [God] is called the "God of Israel,"[9] so He is called "God of the Land"[10] . . . therefore

---

7. Emphasis added.

8. We have already offered the same explanation for the common scriptural reference to God as the God of Israel (Exodus 5:1 and Joshua 5:13, among hundreds of references), or the God of Abraham, Isaac, and Jacob (Genesis 23:24 and Exodus 3:6, among many references). At first glance, this mode of reference appears difficult. Surely, the Creator of heaven and earth is God over the entire world, and not only of Israel, or their Forefathers? A possible solution to this is that the expression "God of Israel" does not imply that God is master over Israel alone; as demonstrated to Pharaoh in Egypt, God is master over the entire universe: "There is none like Me in the entire world . . . so that My Name may be declared throughout the world" (Exodus 9:14, 16). Rather, the implication is that the revelation of the Creator as God over the world depends on Israel, and on the patriarchs who founded the nation. The Creator is termed God of Israel because his "Godliness" – His revelation to the world as God – is dependent on Israel's fulfilling its fundamental role. This role, as this chapter clarifies, is inextricably linked with the Land of Israel.

9. Exodus 5:1, among several sources.

10. II Kings 17:26.

even the revelation of Torah is in the Land of Israel, as the sages have said, "The air of the Land of Israel imbues wisdom" (Bava Batra 157b); and even prophecy is confined to the Land of Israel . . .[11]

Scripture makes repeated mention of the Land of Israel as the place in which the Jews must perform the Law of Sinai: "Behold, I have taught you decrees and ordinances, as the Lord, my God, has commanded me, to do so in the midst of the Land to which you come, to possess it" (Deuteronomy 4:5); "These are the decrees and the ordinances that you shall observe to perform in the Land that the Lord, the God of your forefathers, has given you, to possess it" (ibid., 12:1). Settlement of the Land is, in this sense, a prerequisite for the fulfillment of the Law. The mitzvah (commandment) of dwelling in the Land of Israel is one specific mitzvah out of six hundred and thirteen; yet the Midrash equates it to the performance of the entire Torah.[12] As Nachmanides adds (based on a midrashic source), observing the dictates of the Law outside the boundaries of the Land, while remaining obligatory, is required only as a "rehearsal" for observing them in the Land.[13] The role and duty of Israel (*My People*), which is accomplished by means of the Torah they were given, is specifically fulfilled on the soil of the Land of Israel (*My Land*).

THE LAND COVENANT

The special relationship of the People of Israel to the Land would itself be sufficient for a potential "claim to ownership" – for the concept of ownership is closely related to the use of an item. Ownership implies the reservation of an item for the personal use of its owner, excluding the use thereof by others (unless the owner permits it, in which case the other's use is itself an extension of the owner's use). If the use of

---

11. Rabbi Eliyahu Kremer of Vilna (the "Genius of Vilna"), *Aderet Eliyahu*, Deuteronomy 1:6.

12. *Yalkut Shimoni*, Deuteronomy, Chap. 12, no. 885.

13. *Commentary to Torah*, Leviticus 18:25, quoting from *Sifri, Eikev* 33.

a particular item is inherently reserved for a particular individual, it might follow that ownership of the item is automatically vested in him.

Based on a midrashic text, Rabbi Shlomo Yitzchaki (Rashi) writes that "Adam did not bring an offering from stolen property, because all things were his."[14] By virtue of his being the only man in the world (together with his wife), all things were fundamentally reserved for his use; every item to which the concept of ownership could be theoretically applied belonged to Adam. Conversely, Jewish law dictates that an item from which it is prohibited to derive any benefit[15] is fundamentally ownerless.[16] Because the item cannot be used in any way, or even sold to another party, it ceases to be the property of its owner. In a similar vein, because Israel alone is able to realize the elevated potential of the Land, it can be suggested that the ownership of its soil automatically transfers to them.

God, however, through the words of the prophets, left no room for such theoretical musing. In several covenants with, and promises made to the Patriarchs,[17] the Land was given to the future nation as an everlasting inheritance. The first instance of an instruction given by God to Abraham was to ascend to the Land; upon arrival, God promised Abraham that the Land would be given to his descendants (Genesis 12:7). Later, the Covenant[18] is referred to as being *everlasting*:

I will establish My covenant between Me and you and between your offspring after you, throughout their generations, as an everlasting covenant, to be a God to you and to your offspring after you; and I will give you and your descendants after you the land of your sojourns – the whole land of Canaan – as an everlasting possession; and I shall be a God unto them. (Genesis 17:7–8)

---

14. *Commentary to Torah*, Leviticus 1:2.

15. One such example is bread or other leavened products during the Passover festival.

16. See *Ketzot Hachoshen* 200; there is a wide-ranging debate concerning this issue among medieval talmudic authorities.

17. Abraham, Isaac, and Jacob.

18. This refers to the Covenant Between the Parts (Genesis Chap. 15), on which we will later dwell in greater detail.

Lest there be any doubt as to which of Abraham's descendants the Land Covenant referred, a later verse explicitly singles out Isaac as the sole inheritor of the Covenant, to the exclusion of any other child: "But regarding Ishmael, I have heard you:I have blessed him. . . . But I will establish My Covenant through Isaac, whom Sarah will bear to you by this time next year" (ibid., 17:20–21). Later, the Covenant is confirmed to Isaac, himself: "For to you and your offspring I will give all these lands, and establish the oath that I swore to Abraham your father" (26:3). Completing the picture of the Land Covenant made with the three Patriarchs, we find that the promise is repeated to Jacob: "The Land that I gave to Abraham and to Isaac, I will give to you; and to your offspring after you I will give the Land" (35:12).

The great significance of the Land Covenant is highlighted by the following passage from Psalms, with which the *Shacharit* prayer opens daily:

He remembered His covenant forever – the word He commanded for a thousand generations – that He made with Abraham, and His vow to Isaac, and He established it with Jacob as a statute, for Israel as an everlasting covenant, saying: "To you I shall give the land of Canaan, the lot of your inheritance" (Psalms 105:8–10)

The array of terms used by the verse to describe the Land Covenant cannot be taken lightly; it is called a covenant, a word, an oath, a statute (or decree), and, finally, an everlasting covenant. Also noteworthy is the fact that the *Shacharit* prayer begins with this chapter of Psalms every day of the year.[19] National Jewish identity is not founded on the three Patriarchs as simple individuals; it is founded on the Patriarchs as individuals with whom God struck a unique covenant. The *Shacharit* prayer fittingly begins with an expression of gratitude for the original Covenant.

There are many other verses, scattered throughout Scripture, which attest to Israel's ownership of the Land. In some instances, this

---

19. The chapter opens with an expression of gratitude to God, before describing the covenant He made with the Patriarchs.

ownership is mentioned in passing;[20] in others, it is mentioned as part of the promise to ultimately return the people to their homeland. One prominent instance is the following verse:

When I gather in the House of Israel from the peoples among whom they were scattered . . . *and they will dwell on their land that I gave to My servant, to Jacob.* (Ezekiel 28:24)[21]

Equally telling is the following passage:

For behold, days are coming – the word of the Lord – when I will return the captivity of My people Israel and Judah, said the Lord, *and I will return them to the land that I gave their forefathers, and they will inherit it.* (Jeremiah 30:3)[22]

Prior to the nation's departure from Egypt, God declares that "I shall bring you to the Land about which I raised My hand to give it to Abraham, Isaac, and Jacob, and I shall give it to you as a heritage – I am the Lord" (Exodus 6:8). The Jerusalem Talmud notes the double expression: the Land is both *given*, and given as a *heritage*. "After He gave it as a gift," explains the Talmud, "He gave it once again as a heritage" (*Bava Batra* 23a). The difference between the two forms of giving is elucidated in the same chapter of the Talmud. A gift can be given on condition, or given for limited duration. A heritage, however, is eternal: "Heritage cannot be interrupted" (ibid., 129b, 133a).

The picture painted by the verses is abundantly clear: Whenever the Jews return to the Land of Israel, they return to their own land. Ownership, in the light of Scripture, is not in issue.

OWNERSHIP AND THE RIGHT TO DWELL

The Land, as we have shown, fosters a dynamic relationship with God. This is highlighted by the verses that we quoted at the beginning of this chapter, which stress the fundamental difference between the Land of Israel and Egypt:

---

20. See, for instance, Jeremiah 35:15.
21. Emphasis added.
22. Emphasis added.

For the Land, to which you come to possess it, is not like the land of Egypt that you left, where you would plant your seed and water it on foot like a garden of herbs. But the Land, to which you cross over to possess it, is a Land of mountains and valleys; from the rain of heaven it drinks water; a Land that the Lord, your God, seeks out; the eyes of the Lord, your God, are always upon it, from the beginning of the year to year's end. (Deuteronomy 11:10–12)

By contrast with Egypt, which receives its irrigation from the Nile (". . . water it on foot"), the total dependence of the Land of Israel on rainfall ("from the rain of heaven it drinks water") indicates direct dependence on Divine goodwill for basic human existence. Whereas the Egyptian irrigation channels promote an ecosystem that is essentially self-sufficient, displaying no dependence on the rain of the skies,[23] the Land of Israel requires its inhabitants to turn their eyes constantly heavenward, in the hope of coming rainfall.

Of all aspects of the physical world, none embodies the constant influence of Divine guidance as vividly as rain; through rain, the keys of life and death are retained firmly in the hands of God.[24] In lands that require it, the absence of rainfall – which implies famine, hunger, and even death – is every citizen's greatest fear. Other than praying, which is the archetypical act of *relating* to God, there is nothing that human inhabitants can do to influence it. In Egypt, one could theoretically live alone, a life detached from any Divine association; indeed, Pharaoh went so far as to declare himself God of the Nile (Ezekiel 29:3).[25] In the Land of Israel, existence itself is revealed as a function of a relationship with God.

The Land of Israel, in this sense, is a demanding place in which to live. For those who do not follow the path of God, the Land presents a particular danger: "You shall observe all My decrees and all My ordinances and perform them; then the Land to which I bring you to

---

23. Although the Nile, at its source, is of course entirely dependent on rainfall, this dependence is in no way manifest for those residing in Egypt. For the Egyptian farmer, there is no *awareness* of the dependence on distant rainfall.

24. Based on Talmud, *Taanit* 2a.

25. Pharaoh declared: "Mine is my river, and I have made it for myself."

dwell will not disgorge you" (Leviticus 20:22). Elsewhere, this threat is defined in terms of the dependence on rain: "Beware for yourselves, lest your heart be seduced and you turn astray. . . . He will restrain the heaven so there will be no rain, and the ground will not yield its produce; and you will be swiftly banished from the goodly Land that the Lord gives you" (Deuteronomy 11:17). Conversely, following the path of God earns direct results: "It will be that if you hearken to My commandments that I command you today . . . then I shall provide rain for your Land in its proper time" (11:13–14). Even in simple, day-to-day life, the guidance of God over the world is thus accentuated by living on the soil of the Land.

Yet, although the right to live in the Land is a matter of continual Divine guidance, and evil deeds can cause the Land to "disgorge" its inhabitants, the actual fact of ownership is never placed in doubt. The Covenant and promises made to the Patriarchs, and the continued reference to them throughout Scripture, implies that ownership itself is unconditional.

In the Land Covenant with Abraham, God instructed the first Jewish patriarch to divide three animals into two: a heifer, a she-goat, and a ram. Abraham proceeded to lay the halves one against the other, such that a trail was formed between the pieces (Genesis 15:10). Although the Covenant involved two parties, the verse describes that only a "flaming torch" passed between the pieces (15:17). This indicates that the Covenant was made unilaterally. The promise uttered by God, following the act of Covenant, leaves no room for doubt: "On that day the Lord made a Covenant with Abram, saying: 'To your descendants I have given this Land, from the river of Egypt to the great river, the River Euphrates'" (15:18).

As history has borne out, Israel's fundamental ownership of the Land does not necessarily bequeath her the Divine consent to dwell there. Apart from the issue of ownership, the right to dwell in the Land is contingent on the dynamic relationship between the Jews and God. This relationship depends in turn on both human deed and the hidden ways of Divine guidance. Divine consent, however, is a matter for God alone to decide on. As far as humankind is concerned, Israel's Divinely granted ownership of the Land gives it the national right to live, or at least to endeavor to live, within the Biblical boundaries of the Land.

THE THRUST OF DIVINE REVELATION

The repeated statements of Scripture affirming Israel's ownership of her Biblical homeland are made for a purpose. For two thousand years, this ownership had little practical significance: scattered across the globe, the Jewish People were in no position to realize it. Accustomed to their national homelessness for so long, they all but forgot their national claim.

The Land was always considered God's Land: In all three daily prayers, Jews have forever stood facing toward the Land of Israel, as the holy location through which their prayers ascend heavenward.[26] Furthermore, in the liturgies that promise a glorious return, the Land is repeatedly mentioned as "our Land."[27] Yet in a pragmatic sense, the Jews, with few exceptions, had no nationalist or political ambition to consummate their rights as owners.[28]

In recent times, after the return of Jews to their Land on a national scale, the Land has entered an era of comparative prosperity. From a sorry state of ruin and desolation, the Land has flourished in every possible respect: agricultural, demographic, and social.[29] *My Land* rejoices in its reunification with *My People*; the spirit of the Land resonates with the return of its long-lost owners. After so long an absence, the Mother – as the Jerusalem Talmud refers to the Land (*Berachot* 18b) – is once more surrounded by her sons.

Yet, the actualization of Israel's ownership of the Land remains incomplete. Judea and Samaria, which are integral parts of the Biblical Land, remain virtually unoccupied by Jews. The enemies of Israel,

---

26. See Talmud, *Berachot* 28b.

27. For instance, in the blessing before the reading of the *Shema*: "Bring us in peacefulness from the four corners of the earth, and lead us with upright pride to our Land."

28. See above, p. 83.

29. See chapter two, in which we have expounded on the prophetical aspect of the flourishing Land.

moreover, bitterly contest even such parts as the Jews have built and settled, all of which are entitled "occupied territory." The Jews may live – or so at least goes the claim – but not in the State of Israel.

After languishing for two millennia in the realm of theory, the scriptural statements concerning ownership of the Land have today come alive in the most practical sense.

A midrashic source[30] highlights the importance of the scriptural message. Why, asks the Midrash, was the initial creation of the world and its aftermath included in the Bible? Would it not have been sufficient to begin the Bible with the Divine instruction to the Jewish People, informing them of their duties toward God, giving them the Torah, and leading them into the Promised Land? The Midrash answers its own question: The purpose of chronicling the Creation is to address the issue of the Land. In future generations, a nation may claim that the Land does not rightfully belong to the Jews; they stole it from the Seven Nations who dwelled upon it before their coming. The answer to them is that the entire world belongs to God – for He created it! Formerly, He gave the Land to the Seven Nations, and it was theirs; later, He gave it to Israel, and it became rightfully theirs (*Genesis Rabba* 1:2).

This midrashic teaching offers us a profound insight into the importance of the Land Covenant and its modern implications: *The entire Creation was only included in Scripture for the sake of ratifying the Land Covenant.* It is little wonder, bearing this teaching in mind, that the issue of the Land and the right to dwell upon it has reached the center of the global political stage. The repeated mention by Scripture of the Covenant, the promise, and the actual ownership of the Land, is focused on the current period, in which the matter of the Land has come to the fore.

THE CHAPTER OF ISRAEL

It is ironic that at the time when *My People* returned on a national scale to *My Land*, after so many years of absence, they did so largely in a

---

30. The Midrash is especially well known among Bible students, since it is the subject of the very first comment of Rashi on the Torah.

state of unbelief. Obsessed by the goals of Zionism, or simply fleeing from malice and persecution, they barely acknowledged the identity of the Land as *My Land*, and their own as *My People*.[31] The returnees knew and cared little for the religious significance of the Land, the deep relationship with God that it implies, and the weighty responsibility of Jews living in the Land of the Jews. Nevertheless, such was the manner in which the Jewish People returned to their historical homeland – to the Land that God bequeathed to their Fathers as an everlasting inheritance.

The felicitous decision to name the new State the "State of Israel," rather than one of several other options such as Zion, Eiver,[32] and Yehudah (Judah), embodied a further stroke of Providence. The name *Eretz Yisrael* (The Land of Israel), with which Scripture renamed the original Land of Canaan,[33] confirms the ownership of the Land by Israel – the descendants of Jacob and the Patriarchs. The current name of the Jewish State similarly recalls the divinely sanctioned ownership of the Land. By virtue of the name Israel, Jews are associated with their spiritual heritage, and their Land is associated with its ancient Jewish ownership.

Concerning nomenclature, it should be noted that the name Palestine was only bestowed on the Land by the Romans, after the revolt of Bar Kochva was finally quashed and the Second Temple reduced to rubble. Emperor Hadrian, who wanted to blot out the Jewish connotation of the Roman name "*Provincia Judaea*," renamed the Land "*Provincia Syria Palaestina*," which was later shortened to Palaestina, the forerunner of the modern "Palestine."[34] The name is derived from the chief Biblical enemy of the Jews, the Philistines,[35] whose misdeeds are recorded by

---

31. We have discussed the "return in unbelief" in detail in chapter three of this book.

32. After one of the sons of Shem; the word also implies *Ivri*, an Israelite.

33. See, for instance, I Samuel 13:19, Ezekiel 40:2.

34. Fortunately, the proposed name for Jerusalem, "*Aeolia Capitolina*," never became accepted in the common language.

35. The Philistines were not Arabs, nor even Semites, but were most closely related to the Greeks originating from Asia Minor and Greek localities. The current

Scripture even during the patriarchal era.[36] Although the Philistines had long been extinct, the name became a part of the common language; it was later employed by the Crusaders during the twelfth century, and once more by the British during the Mandate period in the twentieth century. Nevertheless, the name of the Land remains *Eretz Yisrael*: The Land of Israel.

The translation of these principles into political theory is not simple. Some, who might be termed "fundamentalists" for their religious adherence to fundamentals, believe that Israel must seek to expand the Jewish State until it spans its full Biblical dimensions. Others, who deem themselves pragmatists, are prepared to give their support to some version of the "two-state solution," while continuing to hope and pray that the Biblical homeland should return in its entirety to its people. It has already been mentioned that the nature of this book is apolitical, and this debate is therefore outside its bounds.

For our purposes, suffice it to note that with the return of the Jews to their Land a new chapter in Jewish history opened – a new phase in the continued guidance of God over His people. It is an exciting time to be alive: a time when Land and People are united, and when the issue of the Land occupies the central stage in global politics it deserves. Whether we are Jewish or not, whether we live in the Land of Israel or outside it, and whatever our political vision for two nations in conflict – each of us can take a part in the process. Those who have the means can lend their support – be it political, financial, or moral – to the Jewish settlement of the Land; those who do not, can believe and pray, adding their supplications to the daily prayers of more than two thousand years.[37] We continue to pray, and await the conclusion of this intriguing chapter of world history.

---

use of the title by local Arabs is an attempt to breathe life into an entity that did not exist in the past, and by no means implies any historical claim to the Land.

36. See Genesis 26:1–18.

37. See Appendix A, where we have elaborated on the importance of prayer in a national sense.

✒ *Chapter 8*

ISHMAEL AND THE END-TIME

The eschatological significance of Ishmael, the ancestor of the Arab peoples according to Jewish, Christian, and Muslim tradition, is considerable. Even the name Ishmael, which literally means *the Lord will listen*, is interpreted by some Jewish sages as a reference to events of the latter days:

Why is his name Ishmael? Because God is destined to hear the cries of the nation [of Israel] out of the persecution that the descendants of Ishmael will perpetrate in the latter days – therefore his name is Ishmael.[1]

THE FUTURE WARS OF ISHMAEL

The following passage, which occurs in a number of ancient midrashic sources,[2] gives us a general idea of how the role of the Arab peoples in the End-time is perceived by classical sources:

In the latter days, the descendants of Ishmael are destined to wage three tumultuous wars in the Land, as the verse states, "For they will wander because of swords" [Isaiah 21:15], and there are no swords other than [in times of] wars. One will be in the forest in the eve, as it says, "because of the outstretched sword" [ibid.]. One will be in the sea, as it says, "because of the drawn bow." And one will be in a great city, which will be heavier than both, as it says,

1. *Pirkei Derabbi Eliezer*, Chap. 31; *Yalkut Shimoni*, Genesis no. 45.
2. See *Pirkei Derabbi Eliezer*, Chap. 29; *Yalkut Shimoni*, Isaiah no. 421.

"and because of the severity of the war." From there will the son of David spring forth, and he will see the destruction of all of these; and from there, he will come to the Land of Israel, as it says, "Who is this coming from Edom?" (Isaiah 63:1)

The reference to Edom in these writings does not refer to the ancient nation of Edomites, which neighbored the Biblical kingdom of Judah. The ancient Edomites ceased to exist during the Jewish-Roman wars at the end of the Second Temple Era, and End-time predictions can hardly involve the long-extinct people. Rather, the name *Edom* in the writings of Jewish sages is a specific reference to the Roman Empire and its subsidiary powers, including the European nations that emerged as a result of its breakup.[3] Thus, it is certainly possible that a talmudic passage which discusses whether Persia is destined to fall into the hands of Rome, or Rome into the hands of Persia (*Yoma* 10a),[4] is related to the midrashic teaching.

Only time will reveal exactly how these three wars are destined to come about, the manner in which they will be fought, and their global repercussions. What the Midrash makes clear is that the parties involved will be Edom and Ishmael.

THE EDOM-ISHMAEL UNION

Although the previously quoted Midrash implies that Ishmael and Edom are destined to wage war *against* one other, Maimonides, in his famous letter to the Jews of Yemen, views the End-time clash of nations from a different perspective:

Yet, it has already been clarified from the words of Daniel and Isaiah, and from the writings of our Rabbis of blessed memory, that the time [of the Messianic Age] will come when the hands of Edom and of Arabia will be mighty, and

---

3. See, for instance, Talmud, *Avodah Zarah*, p.10b. In midrashic and later sources, the Fourth Exile, foreseen by Daniel, from which the Jewish nation has not yet emerged, is labeled the Exile of Edom.

4. Elsewhere (*Avodah Zarah* 2b), the Talmud writes that the two kingdoms of Persia and Rome are destined to retain their power until the time of the End.

when their kingdoms will spread throughout the world, as they have today. Of this there is no doubt, and this cannot fail to be. The last words of Daniel relate the Kingdom of Ishmael, and the arising of Muhammad, and afterwards the coming of the Redeemer, in close proximity. Similarly, Isaiah explained that the proof of the coming of the Messiah is the coming of Muhammad, for so he wrote, "He will see a chariot, a pair of horsemen, a donkey chariot, a camel chariot; and he will listen intently, with much to hear" (Isaiah 21:7). [The meaning of this is that] the *donkey chariot* is the Messiah, of whom it is written "poor and riding upon the donkey, upon a foal, a calf of she-donkeys" (Zecharia 9:9), who will come immediately after the rising of the *camel rider*, the King of Arabia. That which it writes, *a pair of horsemen*, refers to the union of two nations, which are Edom and Ishmael.

The implication of some form of union between Edom and Ishmael, as Maimonides predicts, is not a novel concept. Over three thousand years ago, their respective ancestors (Esau and Ishmael) formed a bond through the marriage of Esau to Machalat, the daughter of Ishmael (Genesis 28:9). The sages explain the underlying thought that prompted Esau to form the union: his burning desire to kill Jacob (after the latter denied him the parental blessing of Isaac).[5]

In a modern historical context, it is fascinating to observe how the intense hatred of Jews that has become so widespread in the Arab and Islamic world is largely the product of a relatively recent bond between Esau and Ishmael. In this instance, the parties are represented by Germany on one side, to which the Talmud refers explicitly as *Germania of Edom* (*Megillah* 6b),[6] and the Muslims on the other – the inheritors of the Ishmaelite legacy.

Though not without sporadic instances of violence and persecution, Jews had enjoyed centuries of relatively cordial relations with their Muslim hosts. The Muslim world sympathized with the Jewish

---

5. See *Midrash Tanchuma*, Exodus 1; see also *Commentary of Rabbeinu Asher [Rosh] to Torah*, Genesis 28:9, which outlines the elaborate plan by which Esau meant to take Jacob's life.

6. The Talmud writes that if they were to "go out," they would destroy the entire world.

experience of Christian hatred, and generally respected the People of the Book. This history of respectful coexistence was brought to an abrupt end during the short time in which the Nazi regime had a direct influence over the Arab world. Apart from funding and encouraging the expanding work of the anti-Jewish Muslim Brotherhood, the German government ran an Arabic radio service between 1939 and 1945, which combined classical anti-Semitic propaganda with Arabic music and quotations from the Koran.[7] The broadcasts, which were supervised by Amin al-Husseini (the pro-Nazi Mufti of Jerusalem), were eagerly received by millions of Arabs;[8] the vociferous Nazi propaganda made an impression that was to prove lasting.

Thus, the Jewish killing of Muslim children and the ritual use of their blood, the Jewish plot for world domination,[9] and the fact that Jews are descended from apes and pigs (or *are* apes and pigs),[10] have become common knowledge for Muslims worldwide.[11] Only the universalism of this national consciousness could allow Hamas, the Palestine branch of the Muslim Brotherhood, to adopt in 1988 a charter that sounds, in the words of former PLO representative Sari Nusseibeh, "as if it were

---

7. Kuntzel, *Islamic Antisemitism and its Nazi roots* (2003).

8. The Nazis possessed the most powerful short-wave transmitter in the world, which was used with great effect in the Arab transmissions.

9. *The Protocols of the Elders of Zion* is part of the school curriculum in some Arab countries, and is a widely used source in Arab anti-Semitic propaganda. A statement of the Palestinian Authority's Minister of Agriculture, Abdel Jawed Saleh, which was quoted in *Al-Hayat Al-Jahidah* (November 6, 1997), is typical: "The Jews seek to conquer the world. . . . We must expose the Zionist-Colonialist plot and its goals, which destroy not only our people, but the entire world."

10. The connection between the Jews and apes and pigs is already made by the Koran (2:62–65, 5:59–60, and 7:166), albeit in quite a different context. Today, it is used as a method of dehumanizing the Jews, much as the Nazis did in their propaganda campaign against the Jews.

11. All these aspects were central to the Nazi propaganda machine; the idea of a "solution" to the "Jewish problem," and the ultimate thrust toward the extermination of the Jews, has also been taken up by Arab propagandists and cartoonists. See Kuntzel, *Islamic Anti-Semitism and its Nazi roots*. For an insider's account of the Jew-hatred that Arabs are indoctrinated with (in "friendly" Egypt), see Nonie Darwish, *Now They Call Me Infidel* (Sentinel, 2006), pp. 10, 14, 48, 202.

copied from the pages of *Der Stürmer*." Hamas defines itself as "the spearhead and the avant-garde" of the struggle against "world Zionism."

The Jews, the charter explains, "were behind the French Revolution [and] the Communist Revolution. . . . They were behind World War I . . . they were behind World War II, through which they made huge financial gains by trading in armaments, and paved the way for the establishment of their state. . . . There is no war going on anywhere, without having their finger in it. . . ." Article 32 states that "their plan is embodied in *The Protocols of the Elders of Zion*, and their present conduct is the best proof of what we are saying."

This rhetoric is no less absurd now than it was in 1939, but to a sizable proportion of modern Arabs, just as to the Germans before them, it is perfectly acceptable. In the words of historian Yehuda Bauer, the Islamists who have seized the helm of the Muslim world are very much "Hitler's Islamic heirs."[12]

Another aspect that may relate to the union of Edom with Ishmael is the so-called phenomenon of *Eurabia*: the political reality by which the European bloc allies itself with, and even merges with the Arab world.[13] Many critics have played down the imminence or even the long-term threat of an Islamic takeover of Europe. Nevertheless, the markedly pro-Arab stance adopted by many of Europe's leading nations is undeniable.[14] One result of Europe's pro-Arab policy has been a distinctly

---

12. Professor Bauer has outlined his views on the connection between the anti-Semitism of radical Islam and its European precedent in a December 2006 lecture at a Yad Vashem symposium. The lecture, in audio or transcript form, is available online at http://www1.yadvashem.org/about_yad/departments/audio/symposium.html, accessed February 24, 2009.

13. The term "Eurabia" was suggested in this context by Bat Ye'or, in her 2005 book, *Eurabia*.

14. A case in point is the treatment of the aforementioned Al-Husseini. Al-Husseini had directed the Muslim SS divisions in the Balkans between 1941 and 1945, and had been personally responsible for blocking negotiations that might have saved thousands of Jewish children from the gas chambers. Freeing the Mufti provides an early example of what can only be described as political irresponsibility for the sake of placating the Muslims. In spite of his Nazi past, Britain and the United States chose not to prosecute him, in order to avoid spoiling their relations with the Arab world. France, which was holding al-Husseini, *deliberately* let him

anti-Israel stance on many issues, and the at times outrageous bias of its media – the notorious al-Dura case[15] being only one of a great many – when reporting aspects of the Arab-Israeli conflict.

In terms of population, conservative demographic projections indicate that by 2050, Muslims will comprise at least twenty percent of Europe's population, compared to five percent today.[16] For the first time in history, Muslims are building large communities across Western Europe – choosing for economic, social, or political reasons, to make their homes in non-Muslim countries. In the last thirty years, Muslim populations have more than tripled, and the three largest cities in the Netherlands are soon expected to have a Muslim majority.[17]

In their strict Biblical sense, the terms *Edom* and *Ishmael* refer to nations, rather than religions. Nevertheless, the course of history has served to associate the names with particular religious significance. *Ishmael*, in this sense, refers to the religion of Islam, which soon after

---

get away. This effective amnesty was naturally interpreted in the Arab world as a vindication of his actions; al-Husseini's Nazi past was viewed with pride and not shame, and Nazi criminals on the wanted list in Europe began to flood into the Arab world.

15. A twelve-year-old boy named Mohammed al-Dura became a rallying-call for the cause of the Palestinian Intifada (uprising) after video footage of his merciless murder by IDF forces was screened by France 2 TV. Years after the "tragic event" had made its impression, and notwithstanding continual use of the footage in worldwide anti-Israel propaganda, it was proven beyond reasonable doubt that the whole affair had been staged by the Palestinians themselves: Either they had killed al-Dura for PR purposes, or else he wasn't dead at all. When journalist Philippe Karsenty continued agitating against the obstinate stance of France 2 TV, the TV station decided to take proceedings against him for defamation and duly lost the case. For the first time, the TV station released footage showing Palestinian operatives staging a false fight with far-away Israeli security forces, and also revealed fake rescues of unharmed people, fake casualties, and staged injuries. Predictably, the revelations of the malicious fraud received little coverage in world media outlets, and the image of the martyred al-Dura will undoubtedly continue to play an important role in worldwide anti-Israel and anti-Semitic propaganda.

16. Timothy Savage, "Europe and Islam: Crescent Waxing, Cultures Clashing," *The Washington Quarterly*, vol. 27, no. 3, summer 2004, pp. 2–5.

17. See David Masci, "An Uncertain Road: Muslims and the Future of Europe," *The Pew Forum on Religion and Public Life*, December 2004, pp. 2–3.

its inception became the national religion of the entire Arab world, and was later adopted by various non-Semitic peoples in Asia and Africa. *Edom* refers to the Roman Empire: to Christianity, the religion it adopted, and to the Christian European powers that inherited its legacy. Malbim sums up the traditional approach to Edom:

[The] Romans are called by the name Edom, because the city of Rome was settled by Edomeans, who later founded their faith [Christianity] . . . which later became widespread, whereupon all the followers of the faith carry the title Edom.[18]

Although trends can change, and nobody can tell how events will unfold, recent religious and political trends indicate that whether by war, by political union, or by some combination of the two, the two ideologies – Islam on the one hand, and the West on the other – will play a major role in the events of the End-time.

---

18. Commentary of Malbim to Obadiah 1:1. That Edom was a synonym for imperial Rome was the opinion of early Jewish sages (see, for instance, Talmud, *Megillah* 6b and *Makkot* p. 12a), although they do not reveal whether the connection is ideological or genealogical. The actual descent of the Romans from the Edomites is the subject of a lengthy dissertation of Abarbanel, who based his theory mainly on Josephus (see Commentary of Abarbanel to Isaiah 34, and *Announcer of Salvation*, p. 19). Certainly, the equation of Edom with Rome does not imply that the entire nation of Edom became Roman, but more probably that the Romans were among the descendants of Edom.

Although some Christian scholars, such as the Biblical commentator Nicholas de Lyra (see *Announcer*, p. 17), have accepted this position, others have considered the identity of Edom-Rome as being a Jewish fabrication, invented out of hatred of the Christians. We have already mentioned the later identification of Edom with Christendom at large in quoting the interpretations of Nachmanides and Abarbanel, who explained that the "Little Horn" of Daniel 7, which is part and parcel of the Fourth Kingdom of Rome, refers to the Roman Catholic Church (see p. 138). See also, for instance, Ibn Ezra's Commentary on Genesis 27, concerning the blessings of Esau.

ABARBANEL'S PREDICTION

Before we proceed further, a word of caution is in order, which will also serve as a fitting introduction to the forthcoming section concerning the war of Gog and Magog. Writing in 1496, no one was more acutely aware of the harsh trials faced by contemporary Jewry than Don Isaac Abarbanel – one of the greatest luminaries of Jewish history, who was at once statesman, financier of royal courts, respected scholar, renowned philosopher, and religious leader.

Choosing the path of exile as a Jew over the comforts of wealth and power as a convert to Christianity, Abarbanel found the exiled people broken to a point of despondency. Three hundred years of spiritual and physical assault on the bastion of Spanish Jewry had brought the nation to near capitulation. In particular, the last century of their Spanish sojourn saw the golden era turn markedly sour for the shrinking number of faithful. The final decree of exile, issued by the Christian monarchy in 1492, was the last act of a lengthy process.

Abarbanel's response lay in the perennial messianic hope, a hope that had been all but forgotten in the ongoing troubles of exile and the incessant challenge of Christian rhetoric – yet a hope that prevailed as a dim flicker in the heart of each Jew. Abarbanel focused his formidable understanding of philosophy and power of interpretation to refute the Christological arguments that dominated contemporary messianic thought and literature. In three works – *Wells of Salvation, Announcer of Salvation*, and *Salvation of His Anointed* – Abarbanel established a lucid and remarkably coherent picture of the process by which the Messiah was destined to arrive.

An astounding feature of Abarbanel's Messianic treatise was the timescale he proposed: Just seven years in advance of the projected year, Abarbanel confidently stated that the Messiah would arrive in 1503. As Professor Benzion Netanyahu has pointed out, this act of daring cannot be judged by modern standards. Whereas somebody making such a prediction today would be branded a lunatic or a charlatan, in medieval times the involvement of the supernatural did not detract from the validity of a prediction, which may be compared in status to today's political forecasts. The prediction would be judged not by abstract theological beliefs, but by the quality of scriptural interpretation on which it was based.[19]

It can be said with certainty that Abarbanel had not the slightest shadow of a doubt when he wrote that the Messiah would arrive seven years from the time of writing. Had he fostered any doubts concerning the matter, Abarbanel would not have taken the risk. The disillusionment and potential damage involved in a wrong prediction – the more so a prediction made by the leader of the exile himself – obviously outweighs the short-term gains (only seven years' worth) of the prediction itself. Indeed, the obvious risks involved led the sages to take an antagonistic stance against making messianic calculations: "The spirit of those who compute the End-time should fail" (*Sanhedrin* 97b). The sinister threat is codified by Maimonides (*Hilchot Melachim* 12:2); Abarbanel, surely aware of the potential consequences, took the risk.

Together with interpretational and mystical computations, a significant factor that convinced Abarbanel to make the prediction was the urgency of the political scene that confronted him, and its correlation with his eschatological scheme. Constantinople had fallen to the expansionist campaign of the Turkish Empire, and Rome, the Christian capital of Europe, was militarily weak and vulnerable to a number of potential invaders. Surely, these momentous upheavals were not purposeless; surely, Rome would finally be made to pay for her iniquity; surely, the End was nigh.

And yet, Abarbanel was mistaken. The year 1503 went by, and the Messiah did not arrive. The script has been repeated countless times. Scriptural interpretation, the more so with regard to End-time affairs, is not clear-cut, and even the most honest scholar cannot help being swayed by the world in which he lives. The cases of Ibn Yechieh and Sir Isaac Newton, who predicted the coming of the Messiah hundreds of years after their own lifetimes, are pronounced rarities.

Most of this book has dwelt on the past. The following section, which looks toward the future, should be read with this cautionary note in mind.

---

19. See B. Netanyahu, *Don Isaac Abravanel: Statesman and Philosopher* (The Jewish Society of Publication, 1982), p. 219.

GOG AND MAGOG – THE GREAT ASSAULT

It is difficult to apply the details of prophetic revelations in the Midrash and other sources to the present day.[20] Furthermore, the precise nature of the prophesied wars – the countries and regions involved, the site of future battles, and the final outcome – are not specified by the midrashic sources. There is one great war, however, which is documented by Scripture in vivid detail, and which classical Jewish commentators explicitly link to the eschatological wars of Ishmael.[21] This is the multinational confrontation commonly known as the "War of Gog and Magog."[22]

In fact, the verses clearly indicate that Gog refers to an individual

---

20. Although their significance remains great, an inherent distinction must be made between eschatological Biblical prophecies, and the writings of the sages and rabbis. The Oral Tradition, which is based mainly on interpretations of Scriptural sources, may present only one aspect or theme of a particular epoch. Furthermore, any details revealed by the sages may represent a possibility of how Biblical prophecy will be manifested, and not a definitive description of what will take place. The Talmud itself mentions several dates for the coming of the Messiah (several dates are mentioned in Talmud, *Avodah Zarah*), all of which have already expired. Such dates never meant to express a definitive time, but are years in which the Messiah could potentially have come, had the particular generation been worthy enough (see *Zohar* 1:63b). A similar principle may apply to End-time predictions found in the teachings of the sages, which refer to details that can only be clarified by the final events. Furthermore, certain details are the subject of disputes among the sages of the Mishnah and the Talmud. According to the traditional view, both opinions of such disputes represent a facet of the truth, each one expressing a different angle of the same general theme. Only the final event, however, will clarify how these variant and sometimes conflicting aspects will combine.

21. Abarbanel, for instance, discusses three distinct phases of the Gog War, which he correlates to the three wars that Ishmael are destined to wage, as predicted by the previously mentioned midrashic source (see Commentary of Abarbanel to Ezekiel 38). Malbim also places special emphasis on the war being fought predominantly between the forces of Edom and Ishmael, as the Midrash predicts of the End-time.

22. Principally depicted in Ezekiel, chaps. 38–39, and Zechariah, Chap. 14. It is also mentioned in several other books of the prophets, such as Joel, chaps. 3–4, and Obadiah, Chap. 1.

leader, whereas Magog refers to a place: the Land of Magog (Ezekiel 38:2). In the opinion of several commentators, including Rabbi Shlomo Yitzchaki (Rashi),[23] Gog is the leader of the Land of Magog; it would accordingly be more correct to name the event "War of Gog *of* Magog." The Talmud (*Berachot* 7a), however, together with many later sources, refers to the *War of Gog and Magog*, which seems to imply that Gog is not king of Magog. The text of the verse itself, which reads, "Gog, the Land of Magog" (Ezekiel 28:2), is somewhat ambiguous. For simplicity, we will refer to the war as the "Gog War."

Ezekiel's prophecy describes the Gog War as a terrible invasion by an alliance of nations, predominantly from the north, who are destined to wage war against a flourishing Israel:

A land of open cities . . . tranquil people dwelling securely, all of them living without a [protective] wall . . . a people gathered from the nations, which possesses livestock and property, dwelling upon the navel of the earth. (13:11–12)

At the "End of Days" (38:16), a vast horde of warriors, led by the mighty Gog, is destined to advance upon Israel from the north (15–16). Then the anger of God will flare against the invaders (18–19), and they will perish in a series of supernatural plagues, including earthquakes, pestilence and blood, torrential rain and hailstones, fire and sulfur (19–22). Additionally, the invaders will die by the sword, when "each man's sword will be against his brother" (v. 21). Ultimately, God will be exalted and sanctified: "[A]nd I will make Myself known before the eyes of many nations; then they will know that I am the Lord" (v. 23). The next chapter of Ezekiel adds further details of the fate that will befall Gog and his cohorts, by which God will be sanctified through His people, Israel (39:28).

The opening verses of chapter 38 list a number of nations that will participate in the monumental clash:

The word of the Lord came to me, saying, "Son of Man, direct your face toward Gog, the Land of Magog, the chief prince of Meshech and Tubal, and prophesy concerning him: 'Behold, I am against you, Gog, the chief prince of Meshech and Tubal. I will lead you astray, and I will place hooks into your

---

23. Commentary to Ezekiel 38:2.

cheeks and bring you out with your entire army. . . . Persia, Cush, and Put
will be with them. . . . Gomer and all her cohorts, the house of Togarma in
the uttermost parts of the north, and all its cohorts – many peoples will be
with you.'"

A noteworthy feature of the prophecy is that Israel's traditional Biblical
enemies are not mentioned, and do not figure in the account. Syrians,
Assyrians, Babylonians, Moabites, Ammonites, Egyptians, Philistines,
Amalekites, Midianites, and Amorites – classical foes who feature as
Israel's main combatants during various Biblical periods, will be replaced by nations hitherto unknown, flocking from afar to wage war
against the ingathered people.

In itself, this indicates that the conflict foreseen by Ezekiel has to
do with issues different from and broader than those which have concerned Israel in the past. The situation is not, as formerly, Israel versus
her neighbor tribes and peoples, but Israel versus a global gathering.
Consequently, the status of Israel is also different. As Albert O. Hudson
wrote in 1968, "The battle is not against the Israel that conquered
Canaan under the leadership of Joshua, but a greater and more dedicated nation, which has gathered into a more extensive Holy Land
under the headship of God."[24]

THE LAND OF MAGOG

There is clearly no point in trying to identify Gog, himself. For all we
know, the word may be the name of a certain individual, or a title of
leadership, ancient or present. Until the time that he arises, his identity
will remain unknown.

The first land to be mentioned, however, may offer us an important
indication concerning the region from which the invaders will descend.
In fact, Magog is the *only definitive land* that is listed by the verses.
The other given names may be references to *nationalities*, which are
susceptible to change of location over lengthy periods of time, rather

---

24. From the first chapter of *Jacob's Trouble*, reprinted in *Beauties of the Truth*,
volume 12, no. 4, November 2001.

than geographical *lands*. The *Land of Magog*, however, is clearly a location, and therefore offers the strongest claim for accurately tracing the Gog War.

Attempts to define the Land of Magog have mainly been unconvincing, and based on weak linguistic connections rather than historical evidence.[25] Perhaps the most authoritative classical suggestion is provided by the Jewish historian Flavius Josephus, who wrote, "Magog founded the Magogians, thus named after him, but who are called Scythians by the Greeks."[26] Accordingly, scholars have linked the name Magog with Gagaia of the Tel el Amarna letters, which, in the fourteenth century BCE, was said to be a land of barbarians in the far north.[27] Today, this general region is generally inhabited by the former Soviet republics of Kazakhstan, Kyrgyzstan, Uzbekistan, Turkmenistan, and Tajikistan.

The identification by Josephus, however, is vulnerable to the same logical flaw that precludes a scientific identification of the other nations of the conflict. He refers specifically to *the nation of Magog*, and not to *the Land of Magog*. The original personality Magog was the son of Japheth, and grandson of Noah (Genesis 10:2). Although the Scythians may be the descendants of the Biblical Magog, the location of the Land of Magog at the time of the Great Flood (around 2100 BCE) may be relatively far from the areas that the Scythians later occupied.

Turning our eye to traditional Jewish sources, we find several identifications for the Land of Magog, grandson of Noah. The Midrash identifies the Land of Magog as Girmanya, a name that is also found in the ancient Biblical *targum* (translation) of Yonatan ben Uziel, which dates back to the Tannaic era.[28] In the Talmud, Magog is identified as Kandia (*Yoma* 10a), but older manuscripts suggest that this name has

25. Online, see Wikipedia (http://en.wikipedia.org/wiki/Gog), accessed February 22, 2009) for a rich array of interpretations concerning the identity of Magog.

26. Flavius Josephus, *Antiquities of the Jews*, 1.6.1.

27. See Keith W. Carley, *The Book of the Prophet Ezekiel* (Cambridge Bible for Schools and Colleges), p. 299.

28. Yonatan ben Uziel lived several years before the destruction of the Second Temple, a little after the beginning of the Common Era. Depending on variant manuscripts, Magog is rendered Germania, Germaya, or Gitya.

been mutated due to a copier's error, and that the original name is closer to Gytnia.[29] The name finds an echo in the Jerusalem Talmud (which was sealed before the Babylonian Talmud), which identifies Magog as Gytia.[30]

Long before Iran became the global threat it forms today (and well before the Province became commonly known as Iran), Yechiel Zvi Hirschenzon (Lichtenstein)[31] dedicated a section of his *Sheva Chochmot* ("Seven Wisdoms") to the identification of the lands occupied by Noah's descendants. Concerning Germamia or Germania,[32] he asserts that the reference is to Kerman or Kermania, which is the second-largest province in modern Iran, and whose main city is called Kermān to this day.[33]

Although Hirschenzon based his identification on the interchangeability of the letters G and K in the Hebrew alphabet, historical documents show that ancient Kermania was also known as Germania, precisely matching the talmudic name.[34] *Sheva Chochmot* also notes that the Greek historian Herodotus referred to the land as Germania of Persia: "*Persicus Germanus*" (p. 18). Rabbi Dr. Avraham Harcabi, in *Me'assef Nidachim* (a collection of writings from old Hebrew publications), reaches a conclusion identical to that of Rabbi Hirschenzon.[35]

The identification of Germania as the Kermān province is helpful in locating the talmudic Gytia, which presumably refers to the same or a

---

29. This is based on the Oxford and London manuscripts. In other manuscripts, the name appears as Gyntia, Kunta, and Kyntia.

30. Talmud, *Megillah*, chap 1, mishnah 9 (p. 10a).

31. Lichtenstein was a scholarly Jew, who later converted to Christianity, and was even active in missionary activities. For a fairly detailed article on his life, see Shmuel Leib Zitron, "Yechiel Zvi Hirschenson-Lichtenstein," in *Behind the Screen: Apostates, Traitors, Denyers* [Hebrew: *Me'achorei HaPargod: Mumarim, Bogdim, Mitkachshim*] (Vilna: 1925); the article is available online at http://benyehuda.org/zitron/hershenzon.html.

32. This should not be confused with the European Germany. In talmudic writing, Germany is referred to as "Germania of Edom."

33. Hirschenzon, *Sheva Chochmot* (Lemberg: 1883), part I, pp. 16–17.

34. See http://en.wikipedia.org/wiki/Kermān_Province, accessed February 22, 2009.

35. *Me'assef Nidachim* (Kedem Publishers, Jerusalem: 1970), p. 145.

similar region. Ancient historical sources – predominantly records of the wars of the Persian King Darius I the Great (522–486 BCE) – mention a country or region called Satta-Gydia, or Satta-Gytia.[36] The location of ancient Satta-Gydia is not entirely clear, and has been the matter of some scholarly debate. Livius's *Articles on Ancient History* places Satta-Gydia in the mountainous region between Iran and Pakistan, or the plain immediately beyond it, whereas others have suggested that its location is in Afghanistan rather than Pakistan.[37]

Assuming that the word *satta* is a prefix meaning "settlement" or "power,"[38] this identification would place the talmudic Gytia in close proximity to the midrashic Germania. In fact, Hirschenzon's *Sheva Chochmot* mentions the region of Baluchistan (Balochistan) in connection to the province of Kermān (pp. 16–17). Although the largest province in Iran carries the name "Sistān and Balūchestān," the entire region of Baluchistan includes both parts of Afghanistan and Pakistan, as well as the southeastern Iranian province. It is possible that the original name of this region was Satta-Gytia, and that this is the Land of Magog identified by the sages.[39]

In view of recent political shifts, the prospect of the land of Magog being modern Iran (or a part of it) is tantalizing – though, as noted below with regard to Russia, the Bible student must be wary of the temptation to follow current political trends in interpreting ancient texts. Following its establishment in 1979, the Islamic Republic of Iran has taken a radically hostile stance toward the Jewish State of Israel. This stance has been exacerbated by the leadership of Iranian President Mahmud Ahmadinejad, who declared in a 2005 speech that Israel

---

36. The earliest mention is in Section 21 of the *Behistun Inscription*. It is also mentioned in the inscription on Darius' tomb at Naqš-i Rustam, and in the Daiva inscription of King Xerxes.

37. For a scholarly analysis of the location of Sattagydia, see D. Fleming, "Achaemenid Sattagydia and the Geography of Vivana's Campaign," in *Journal of the Royal Asiatic Society of Great Britain and Ireland London*, 1982, no. 2, pp. 102–112.

38. In certain dialects of Indian, the word "*satta*" still means "power."

39. See http://hashemi.net/?p=360#gitya2, where this theory is proposed. An English translation is available at http://hashemi.net/?p=361 (accessed 5.6.12).

should be "wiped off the map";[40] his rhetoric since that time has not mellowed and history will judge whether his current successor will truly be any different.

The Islamic Republic of Iran likewise provides financial and technical support to Hezbollah, a Lebanese terrorist organization dedicated to the destruction of Israel (which the Lebanese government has been unable or unwilling to quash),[41] through which Iran could be allowed direct access to Israeli territory. Iran also sponsors other terrorist groups operating in the region.[42] To match the fanatical tone of its anti-Zionism and anti-Americanism, Iran has continued its traditional national policy of investing billions of petro-dollars in the acquisition of state-of-the-art weapons. The concept of a nuclear Iran, which is being brought ever closer by the assistance of several nuclear powers around the globe, brings dread to the heart of many an Israeli citizen. At the same time, the hands of the West are tied, and sanctions have not thus far been entirely effective in preventing Iran from continuing their programs for developing the Bomb.

---

40. In a May 14, 2008 speech in Gorgan, northern Iran, Ahmadinejad stated that "Israel's days are numbered," that "the peoples of the region would not miss the narrowest opportunity to annihilate this false regime," and that "the nations of the region despise this false and criminal regime." This is one of hundreds of similar declarations that the Iranian leader has made against Israel. "With God's grace," he stated at a conference marking the nineteenth anniversary of the death of Ayatollah Rohullah Khomeini, "your wish will soon be realized, and this germ of corruption will be wiped off the face of the world." Of course, this is hyperbole aimed at various audiences; and yet, the threat remains quite concrete.

41. The thirty-day war between Israel and the Hezbollah in the summer of 2006 demonstrated that the terrorist organization is a force to be reckoned with. Doubtless, any war with Iran would be coupled by the opening of a second front by the Hezbollah. With the recent instability of the Syrian regime, the danger of lethal weapons falling into the hands of Hezbollah has become a major fear for Israel and western powers.

42. Ties between Iran and Hamas, the popular terrorist organization that operates against Israeli civilian targets from within the "occupied territories" of Palestine, have long been alleged. Apart from obvious closeness on theological issues, these claims have not been clearly substantiated, although Iran did call for financial support to Hamas after its victory in the 2006 Palestinian Authority elections.

Time will tell whether the talmudic identification of Magog with Gytia or Germania means to include Pakistan, Afghanistan, or both, in the axis destined to launch its massive assault against Israel.

OTHER NATIONS OF THE GOG WAR

Gog is described by the verses as being the political leader, or Prince of Meshech and Tubal. Although these names refer to nations, and are therefore not necessarily accurate indications of geographical locations, their identity is fairly easy to decipher by reference to ancient Assyrian inscriptions.

These records describe the wars of Sennacherib, and later those of his son Esarhaddon, who led Assyrian armies to war against a northern Scythian onslaught, which was ultimately driven back. The invaders were called the Mushku, the Tabalu, the Gimirrai and the Tilgarimmu; the corresponding Bible names are Meshech, Tubal, Gomer and the House of Togarmah, all of which are mentioned as factions under the leadership of Gog.[43]

In fact, Meshech and Tubal are known historically as Scythian tribes that waged wars against Assyria in the twelfth century BCE, and whose locations, respectively, are central and eastern Asia Minor.[44] Tilgarimmu was a city-state in Eastern Anatolia, or the southeastern part of Turkey, near the Syrian border; this corresponds with Ezekiel's description of the House of Togarmah as being "from the remote parts of the north" (Ezekiel 38:6), far north of Israel. Gimirrai, whose people are also

---

43. The suggestion that Meshech and Tubal refer to the Russian cities of Moscow and Tobolsk, which has been mentioned by the notes to Ezekiel 38:2 in *The Scofield Study Bible* (and by other scholars and authors), is apparently erroneous. Apart from this interpretation having no foundation on which to stand (other than the weak linguistic association), we find Meshech and Tubal mentioned in Ezekiel 27 as trading partners with ancient Tyre. Such northern regions as Moscow and Tobolsk are hardly likely trading partners for Tyre, which corresponds geographically to modern Syria.

44. The location of Meshech and Tubal in Turkey or Southern Russia has been suggested by Thomas Ice and Timothy Demy, *Fast Facts on Bible Prophecy* (Harvest House Publishers 1997), p. 126.

194 / PROPHECIES & PROVIDENCE

known as the Cimmerians, was in north central Asia Minor, also a part of modern Turkey. The mention of these people under the leadership of Gog suggests an involvement of modern-day Turkey in the Gog War.

Whereas the previously mentioned nations have been the subject of ongoing speculation, no such debate rages concerning the identity of Persia, Kush, and Put. Persia cannot be other than Iran, which correlates well with the identification of Magog as an Iranian province. Put is traditionally identified as Libya, though it may be extended to the entire region of North Africa (except Egypt). Kush usually refers to the land in the south of Egypt, historically known as Ethiopia; yet, the identification of Kush with Sudan is also valid, and the Biblical Kush may be understood further to be present-day Iraq and the Arabian Peninsula. Although care must be taken to avoid basing Biblical interpretations on shifts in current affairs – which are susceptible to rapid upheavals – it is at least possible to understand the expression "Kush and Put" as indicating the modern Arab states.

It is important to note that although some Arab and Islamic states, such as Turkey, Egypt, and Saudi Arabia, are not considered to be "radical" Islamic provinces, this does not detract from the intensity of hatred that the populace feels toward Israel and the West, or from the political volatility that such countries can display. Egypt provides a clear example. Despite the peace treaty with Israel, Egypt has rarely ceased its vociferous opposition to Israel in virtually every area, and it never tires of spreading anti-Israeli rhetoric and disinformation, blaming Israel and the Jews for any evil that Egypt and the world may suffer. This has naturally bred a generation of fanatic Israel-haters; the fact that Egypt is classified as "moderate" does not alter any of these facts.[45] Indeed, Turkey's reaction to Israel's recent campaign in Gaza shows that vis-à-vis Israel, the title "friendly" can hardly be conferred on any Muslim state, and the "flotilla" event of 2010 has brought relations between the countries to an all-time low.[46] Jordan's participation in the 1967 Arab

---

45. An insider's account of the hatred felt by most Egyptians toward the West, and particularly toward Israel and the Jews, can be read in Nonie Darwish, *Now They Call Me Infidel.*

46. For the meantime, there is little sign of recovery in Israel-Turkey relations.

war against Israel is a prime example of how quickly Arab nations are willing to join the fray in a united front against Israel, and we cannot know when such a scenario might repeat itself on a far larger scale.

In recapitulation, the Gog axis depicted in the verses certainly points at an Islamic alliance, based primarily on the Arab or Muslim states in the Middle East, North Africa, Iran, Turkey, and possibly Pakistan and Afghanistan, which will set out with great force to destroy Israel. We cannot foresee the timescale of this event; it may come within months, years, decades, or even centuries. But the outcome is clearly described in the Biblical account: God will smite Gog and his great armies (Ezekiel 39:1–4); Magog will burn in flames (ibid., 39:6 – a reference to the volcanic activity of the Kermān province?); and the name of God will be forever sanctified (39:7).

ROSH – RUSSIA?

Some Biblical commentators have claimed that the Hebrew word Rosh implies a further nation under the command of Gog. Although we have mentioned the classical translation of *Nasi Rosh* as "Chief Prince,"[47] this combination of words is grammatically anomalous, and occurs exclusively in connection to Gog. The anomaly may be explained with the suggestion that the word Rosh should not be translated as an adjective, meaning a head or leader (as in *Rosh Hashanah*, the Head of the Year), but rather as a noun. Extending his domain past Meshech and Tubal, Gog would also be the prince of Rosh. Thus, the Hebrew scholars C. F. Keil and Wilhelm Gesenius both stated that *Rosh* of Ezekiel 38 is the name of a geographical location. Gesenius, moreover, left no doubt as to the identity of the location, which he wrote was "undoubtedly the Russians, who are mentioned by the Byzantine writers of the tenth century under the name Ros, dwelling to the north of Taurus . . . as

---

For a detailed overview of the flotilla event, see http://en.wikipedia.org/wiki/Gaza_flotilla_raid (6.6.12).

47. This is the translation of the *Targum*, and of all classical Jewish commentators.

dwelling on the River Rha [Wolga]."[48] Although the emphasis by the verses of Ezekiel on the northern source of the invasion fits well with the Russian province, it is also easily rebutted: Ezekiel could naturally have been referring to the northernmost areas known to him and to his civilization, which we identified earlier as areas of Turkey.

The appeal of an explicit reference to Russia in Ezekiel's list of Central Asian countries is understandable. Russia's military prowess is great, and in February 2007, then-Defense Minister Ivanov announced a five-year program of military modernization, which includes new nuclear submarines, aircraft carriers, a fleet of Tu-160 supersonic strategic bombers, and the development of a fifth-generation fighter jet. Politically, Russia is actively seeking to reassert its position as a global superpower to rival the United States, and a short analysis of contemporary Russian rhetoric reveals motivations that resemble the Soviet agenda before President Mikhail Gorbachev's *Perestroika* (restructuring) and *Glasnost* (openness). The continual obsession with the United States as its "principal adversary" has guided Russian foreign policy into alliance with the Muslim anti-American world, and in particular, with Iran and Syria, with which Russia has signed large-scale weapons contracts. The fact

---

48. C. E. Keil, "Ezekiel, Daniel" in *Commentary to the Old Testament*, trans. James Martin (reprint, Eerdmans Publishing Co., Grand Rapids, Mich.: 1982), 9:159; Wilheim Gesenius, *Gesenius' Hebrew-Chaldee Lexicon to the Old Testament*, trans. Samuel Prideaux Tregelles (Eerdmans Publishing Co., Grand Rapids, Mich.: 1949), p. 752. See also Tim Lahaye and Ed Hindson, general eds., *The Popular Bible Prophecy Commentary* (Harvest House Publishers, Eugene, Oregon: 2006), p. 191, which quotes from Clyde Billington, *The Rosh People in History and Prophecy*, pp. 59–61, who also concludes that "Historical, ethnological, and archaeological evidence all favor the conclusion that the Rosh people of Ezekiel 38–39 were the ancestors of the Rus/Ros people of Europe and Asia. . . . The Rosh people who are mentioned in Ezekiel 38–39 were well-known to ancient and medieval writers by a variety of names which all derived from the names of Tiras and Rosh. . . . Those Rosh people who lived to the north of the Black Sea in ancient and medieval times were called the Rus/Ros/Rox/Aorsi from very early times. . . . From this mixture with Slavs and with the Varangian Rus in the ninth century, the Rosh people of the area north of the Black Sea formed the people known today as Russians." Other Christian authors, such as Grant Jeffrey, Joel Rosenberg, Richard W. DeHaan, David Egner, Arno C. Gaebelein, and others, have also followed this identification.

that Russia, and particularly the former Soviet Union, was officially atheistic, made the theory even more appealing in the eyes of many authors.[49]

Yet, however attractive the sparkle of current affairs may be, to base Biblical interpretation on contemporary political trends is a well-trodden path to error. The linguistic comparison of "Rosh" to "Ros" or "Ras" is somewhat flawed, because of the slight, yet possibly significant difference in the "s" sound.[50] Even were there a solid linguistic link, the term "Ros" and the modern name "Russia" did not exist in ancient times, but both date rather from the tenth or eleventh centuries CE, making the comparison between the ancient Semitic word and the modern equivalent fundamentally meaningless.[51]

An additional weakness is the complete lack of historical record concerning ancient Rosh (or Ros, or Ras), in contrast to the convincing evidence that has been found with regard to Meshech and Tubal. Furthermore, we find elsewhere that Ezekiel refers to Meshech and Tubal, but makes no mention of Rosh (Ezekiel 32:26). It therefore appears more prudent to revert to the interpretation of classical Jewish commentators, who translate Rosh as an adjective of leadership, and not as a geographic location. The places and nations mentioned by Ezekiel thus remain strictly Islamic.

THE TIME OF THE END

Taken in its most literal sense, the Biblical verse that describes the death of Ishmael concludes with the words, "over all his brothers he fell" (Genesis 25:19). The next verse of the Bible begins, "And these

---

49. See Arno Clemens Gaebelein, *The Conflict of the Ages: The Mystery of Lawlessness: Its Origin, Historic Development and Coming Defeat* (Publication Office "Our Hope," New York: 1933). See also Fred G. Zaspel, *The Nations of Ezekiel 38–39* (available online at http://www.biblicalstudies.com/bstudy/eschato logy/ezekiel.htm, accessed 5.6.12), and sources cited therein.

50. Although vowels often differ between varying cultures and periods, consonants should not significantly differ from the original word, apart from known variations within language groups.

51. For a sound article explaining the fallacy of defining Rosh as Russia, see Fred G. Zaspel, *The Nations of Ezekiel 38–39*.

are the descendants of Isaac son of Abraham" (25:20). *Baal Haturim* (a fourteenth-century commentary) points out the significance of this juxtaposition: When Ishmael shall fall, the descendants of Isaac will arise.[52]

As we will see in the next chapter, there is some discussion over whether the Messiah will come in advance of the Gog War, or whether the War will usher in the Messianic Age. Whatever the case, there is no doubt that the descendants of Ishmael – the Arab people in a genealogical sense, and the Muslim people in what has become the ideological sense – will be heavily involved in the time of the End.

As based on the prophecies recorded in Scripture, our knowledge of the War and its aftermath remains, at best, sketchy. Obadiah forecasts the downfall of Edom (Chap. 1), while Daniel mentions an initial assault of the united armies *against* Babylon (Iraq) and Persia (Iran).[53] Joel prophesies natural wonders that will accompany the onset of the war,[54] and Zechariah (14:1–7) adds fantastic details: The inhabitants of Jerusalem will be exiled, the assailing armies will fall before the might of God, and the Mount of Olives will be split into two beneath the "legs of God." And there will come a day on which the light will be neither bright nor dim, neither day nor night – but toward the evening there will be light.

Time will unveil the meaning of these revelations; the day approaches, but when it will come, we cannot know. All we can do is believe, pray,[55] and anticipate.

---

52. *Commentary of Baal Haturim to the Torah*, by Rabbi Yaakov ben Asher (1269–1343).

53. Daniel 11:44, based on interpretations of Ibn Ezra and *Metzudot David*; see also Talmud, *Yoma* 10a, which discusses the future war of Persia and Rome, stating (at the end of the passage) that the Messiah will not come until Rome has taken control over the world for nine months.

54. Joel Chaps. 3–4.

55. The significance of prayer, in a world that follows the predestined plan of God, is explained in Appendix A.

Chapter 9

THE MESSIANIC AGE

THE COMING OF THE MESSIAH

The coming of a Messiah and the era he is destined to usher in are concepts shared by the Jewish and Christian faiths.[1] Strikingly, however, the very messianic concept common to both religions provides the issue around which the fiercest conflict between the two religions revolves. The distinctions between the Jewish messianic vision and the Christian concept will assist us in outlining the messianic doctrine from the perspective of Biblical prophecy and the commentary of Jewish sources.

Concerning the *future* advent of the Messiah, Isaiah appears to leave us with little doubt:

Behold My servant, whom I shall uphold; My chosen one, whom My soul desired; I have placed My spirit upon him so he can bring forth justice to the nations. He will not shout nor raise his voice, or make his voice heard in the street . . . But he will administer justice in truth. . . . I have long kept silent, I have been still . . . I will cry like a woman in childbirth . . . I will lead the blind on a way they never knew; I will have them walk on paths they did not know; I will turn darkness into light before them, and make the crooked places straight. (Isaiah 42:1–3, 42:14–17)

---

1. The concept of an Islamic Messiah, or Mahdi, does not occur in the Koran or in any reliable Hadiths, causing Sunni theologians to question the Mahdist beliefs generally upheld by Shiite sects. The lack of a clear messianic tradition sets Islam apart from Judaism and Christianity.

Jeremiah is no less explicit:

Behold, days are coming – the word of the Lord – when I will establish a righteous sprout from David; a king will reign and prosper and he will administer justice and righteousness in the land. In his days Judah will be saved and Israel will dwell securely. This is the name people will call him: the Lord is our righteous. (Jeremiah 23:5–6)

The verses continue to promise days of glory no lesser than those of the original redemption from Egypt. In these days, no longer will Israel refer to the God Who took them out of Egypt, but rather to the God who brought them "from the land of the North, and from all the lands wherein He had dispersed them" (23:8).

Ten chapters later, Jeremiah repeats the message:

Behold, days are coming – the word of the Lord – when I will fulfill the favorable matter [lit. "good word"][2] that I spoke concerning the House of Israel and the House of Judah. In those days, at that time, I will cause a sprout of righteousness to sprout forth for David, and he will administer justice and righteousness in the land. In those days, Judah will be saved and Jerusalem will dwell in security. (33:14–16)

Clearly, these prophecies are yet to be fulfilled. In order to accommodate such predictions together with their acceptance of Jesus as Messiah, many Christian theologians expect a Second Coming. In the Jewish faith, there is only one Coming – a coming the Jewish People have awaited since the destruction of the First Commonwealth,[3] and which they continue to anticipate.

LIVING FOR THE MESSIANIC AGE

The Jewish Messiah is in essence a man – a human, mortal man. "Do not think," writes Maimonides, "that the King Messiah must perform wonders in the world, or resurrect the dead, or anything of the sort"

---

2. Christians are familiar with the expression "the good word," which is an alternative translation for the Hebrew words *hadavar hatov*.

3. The period of the first Jewish kingdom in the Holy Land.

(*Hilchot Melachim*, 11:3.). The laws of the Torah, he continues, are eternally unchanging; and they will continue to form the central ideology of Jewish life, even during the Messianic Age. Indeed, among the basic criteria enumerated by Maimonides for recognizing the Messiah are his careful observance of the Law and his compelling the return of the people en masse to its precepts (ibid., 11:4).

In the Jewish tradition, the world of the Messianic Age will reflect the human character of its King. True, it will be an era of happiness, a utopian existence in which both material and spiritual aspects of life will reach perfection. Yet, the natural order of the world will be preserved. After introducing the basic premise of unchanging laws of nature, Maimonides depicts life in the Messianic Age:

In that time there will be no hunger, nor war, nor jealousy and competition – for then, goodness will be plentiful, and delights will be as bountiful as dust. And the entire world will be occupied solely with the knowledge of God. (Ibid., 12:5)

It is fitting that Maimonides should conclude his *magnum opus* of Jewish Law with these words. Just as the Law is a *thing of this world*, instructing human beings in the living of human lives, so the Messiah, as well as the Age he ushers in, is a *thing of this world*. The Messianic Age, as we will see below, is the climax of the Law.

A wide cleavage separates the messianic concept described by Maimonides and the Christian messianic vision. Whereas Jews search the future for the Messiah, Christians find him in the past, in a figure that lived, suffered, and ultimately died a death of martyrdom. While various sects of Christianity interpret the consequences of his life and death in different ways, all concur that the era he ushered in cannot be physically discerned from its predecessors. What is more, the forces of evil have clearly continued to rear their ugly heads, contaminating all things pure and holy with corruption. Human pain and suffering remain prevalent, and the promised redemption by faith and good works is patently limited to the domain of the spirit.

In Christian theology, the impression made by the Messiah is closely related to his Divine stature,[4] a definition that presents a sharp depar-

---

4. See John 10:30, 14:9b. Although the concept of the Trinity has been subject

ture from the Jewish messianic tradition of a *human* figure. Like the constant guidance of God over His world, the impact of the Christian Messiah was made *behind the scenes*. His suffering and death, according to one of the most central Christian doctrines, served to atone for the sins of all humanity, and exempted the world from *the curse of the Law*.[5] His teachings, or his very appearance upon earth, direct the course of mankind toward the great Day of Judgment[6] and the world beyond.

It thus emerges that although the messianic concept is the cornerstone of Christian faith, it has little practical bearing on contemporary life. With the exclusion of millennial theology, which incorporates concepts borrowed from the Jewish messianic tradition into the promised Second Coming,[7] the Christian messianic doctrine may be likened to quantum mechanics: of central importance in theory, yet hard to apply to the tangible reality of the world.

For the Jew, the Messianic Age is far more than a theoretical doctrine underlying existence on a hidden plane. The purpose of Jewish life, a mode of living by which every aspect of human living is elevated as part of a relationship with the Divine, is explicit in the verse, "This nation I have fashioned for Myself, that they should declare My glory" (Isaiah 43:21). The fulfillment of this purpose will be realized in the Messianic Age.

Though the fundamental condition of nature will remain unchanged, the time of Messiah will witness deep human appreciation of God's creation of the universe, and of His continual guidance of the course of history. Unified under a single banner of God, all the nations will recognize the unique place of Israel in the Divine scheme, and will

---

to different interpretations by various sects of Christianity, and has been rejected outright by others, the essentially Divine nature of the Messiah King remains widely accepted by all Christians. Only the most daring of Christians, including such radical (and, indeed, heretical) theologians as Sir Isaac Newton, relegated the status of Jesus to that of an ordinary human prophet.

5. The words are of Paul; see Galatians 3:10–13.

6. Although there is little agreement over its details, virtually all Christian denominations agree on the concept of the Last Judgment, in which men and women will be judged according to their faith in Jesus.

7. Millennial beliefs have never been accepted by the Catholic Church.

send their gifts to the rebuilt Temple in Jerusalem (ibid., 66:20, 18:7). Throughout his life, a Jew dedicates his actions toward this glorious destiny: "To perfect the world in the sovereignty of God."[8]

In Christian theology, the Messiah lived, suffered, and died for the sake of humanity. In the Jewish sense, it can be said that humanity – and in particular Israel – lives, suffers, and dies for the revelations of the Messianic Age.[9]

HUMAN PROGRESSION

There are thus two ways in which the Jewish messianic vision looks to the future. Together with the fact that the Jewish Messiah has not yet come, Judaism sees the world as moving forward, as progressing toward redemption. Even with regard to the foundation of the rival monotheistic religions, whose violent antipathy toward Judaism was already well-established, Maimonides finds the world heading toward redemption:

All these matters relating to Jesus of Nazareth and the Ishmaelite [Muhhamad] who came after him only served to clear the way for King Messiah, to prepare the whole world to worship God with one accord, as it is written, "For then will I turn to the peoples a pure language, that they all call upon the name of God to serve Him with one consent" [Zephaniah 3:9].[10]

In Christianity, the world is not going forward toward messianic salvation; on the contrary, the plague of human failing forever widens the gap between man and his God. When God finally grants the gift of

---

8. From the *Aleinu* prayer, recited thrice daily at the end of services.

9. The central place of the Messianic concept in Jewish theology is evidenced by its presence in Maimonides' *Thirteen Principles of Faith*. The Rambam terms these principles "foundations," reflecting their status as ideas on which the entire edifice of religious observance stands. Together with God, the Torah, and prophecy, belief in the coming of the Messiah – however long he may delay – comprises one of the thirteen fundamental beliefs enumerated by the Rambam. It is a "foundation" of Judaism.

10. *Mishneh Torah, Hilchot Melachim* 11:4.

salvation, it comes not as the climax of a progression, but as the Divine rescue of humanity from its spiraling course of disaster.

In the book of Romans, we find Paul arguing that on account of the "original sin" that infected all of humanity, "all have sinned and fall short of the glory of God" (Romans, 3:23). This human flaw renders men incapable of achieving redemption on their own merits. Salvation depends not on "human will or exertion, but on God who shows mercy" (ibid., 9:16). The task of Jesus, who took the form of man in order to save humanity, is to redeem humankind from the eternal perdition it deserves: "For God so loved the world that He gave his only Son, that whoever believes in Him should not perish but have eternal life" (John, 3:16).

The essential divinity of the Christian Messiah thus goes beyond the personal sphere, negating the Jewish concept of a messianic progression. In Christian scripture and doctrine, the messianic idea describes the salvation of a world utterly unable to save itself. Although different factions of Christianity have long debated the nature and meaning of salvation, this central tenet is common to all. In a joint statement issued in 1998 by Evangelicals and Catholics Together, a group that includes some of America's most influential Catholic and Evangelical theologians, the theological belief was clearly articulated:

God created us to manifest his glory and to give us eternal life in fellowship with himself, but our disobedience intervened and brought us under condemnation. As members of the fallen human race, we come into the world estranged from God and in a state of rebellion. This original sin is compounded by our personal acts of sinfulness. The catastrophic consequences of sin are such that we are powerless to restore the ruptured bonds of union with God. Only in the light of what God has done to restore our fellowship with him do we see the full enormity of our loss. . . . The restoration of communion with God is absolutely dependent upon Jesus Christ, true God and true man . . . and "there is no other name under heaven given among men by which we must be saved" [Acts 4:12].[11]

---

11. "The Gift of Salvation," *First Things* (January 1998), pp. 20–23.

Nothing could be more different from the Jewish concept of the messianic process and the role of humanity in the scheme of all things. In the Jewish model, redemption is the culmination of a long path; moreover, the path is paved with stones of human action, deeds that invite the coming of the savior. Although opinions vary as to just how far the concept of "messianic activism" can be taken (see below), the words of the verse leave no doubt as to the central place of human works:

And it shall come to pass, when all these things have come upon you, the blessing and the curse, which I have put before you, and you shall have a turn of heart while still among all the nations. . . . And you shall return to the Lord your God and shall obey Him. . . . Then the Lord your God will turn your captivity, and have compassion upon you, and gather you from among all the nations, to which the Lord, your God, has scattered you. (Deuteronomy 30:1–3)

In chapter 2 of this book, we mentioned the talmudic debate over whether or not the redemption is contingent on the prior repentance of the people (*Sanhedrin* 97b). At this stage it is fitting to note that even Rabbi Yehoshua, who maintains that the redemption will come even in a sinful state, concedes that the nation *will repent* in advance of the redemption. The debate is only over whether there is a guaranteed date by which the Jews will certainly repent – motivated, if required, by God – or not. In the words of Maimonides, "The Torah has already assured us that Israel will finally repent at the end of its exile and immediately be redeemed" (*Laws of RepentanceHilchot Teshuvah* 7:5).

Fittingly, the climax of the Jewish prayer,[12] the act that so forcefully expresses the place of humanity in the Divine scheme, is the coming of the Son of David.[13] Prayer, the paradigm of human works, reaches its zenith together with the coming of Messiah. The Messiah is not a Divine gift given *in spite of human deed*, but rather, a Divine gift

---

12. The *Amidah* prayer, which is the central component of all Jewish prayer services.

13. See Talmud, *Megillah* 17b; the penultimate blessing of the central chapter of the *Amidah* relates to the coming of the Messiah; the last blessing relates to the acceptance of prayer itself.

206 / PROPHECIES & PROVIDENCE

procured by means of human deed. Rabbi Meir Soloveichik has expressed the difference with eloquence:

While Paul saw humanity forever cursed by the sins of its ancestor Adam, the messiah of Hebrew Scripture symbolizes the ability of man to defy his own past, and to bring about his own redemption.[14]

THE LAW OF THE MESSIAH.

The divergence of theological attitudes concerning the Law – a concept so vital to Judaism and so derided by Christianity – follows on from the differences in outlook outlined above. For a doomed humanity that necessarily falls short of the glory of God, the law is surely a curse. But if humanity *is* able to know and connect with God, then the law of God – by which we not only learn of God, but even emulate His ways in human deeds – is the greatest blessing on earth. Prophecy tells that this blessing will not end with the coming of the Messiah; on the contrary, it will arrive at its zenith.

We have already seen that the Messiah will spread knowledge of God throughout the world, so that "all flesh together will see that the mouth of the Lord has spoken" (Isaiah 40:5). Together with the rejuvenated faith he is fated to instill, Jeremiah reveals that the Messiah is destined to preside over a renewed sacrificial service:

And for the Priests, the Levites, there will never be cut off a man from before Me who offers elevation-offerings and burnt meal-offerings and performs feast-offerings all the days. . . . If you could annul My covenant with the day and My covenant with the night, and day and night would not come in their proper times, so, too, could My covenant be annulled with David, My servant, that he would not have a descendant reigning on his throne, and with the Levites and the Priests, My attendants. (Jeremiah 33:18–21)

In the context of this chapter, the significance of sacrifices in the Messianic Age is that they form an integral part of the Law. Scripture

---

14. Meir Soloveitchik, "Redemption and the Power of Man," in *Azure*, Winter 2004 (16), pp. 51–77, 61.

indicates the continuing importance of the Law even in the age of the Messiah:

I will gather you from the peoples, and assemble you out of the countries where you have been scattered, and I will give you the Land of Israel. . . . And I will give them one heart . . . and I will give them a heart of flesh, so that they may walk in My statutes, and observe My ordinances, and do them. (Ezekiel 11:17–20)

Apologetics by Christian scholars, in particular in recent times, have tried to tackle the problem of Law in the End-time. The chapters at the close of Ezekiel (chaps. 40–46), which describe at length the elaborate architecture, vessels, and ritual of the Messianic Temple, including the sacrificial order of the year, have provided a particularly thorny issue for the classical Christian stance.[15] Dwelling on this passage, Edmund P. Clowney has made the point quite clearly: "If there is a way back to the ceremonial law . . . then Paul labored in vain – more than that, Christ died in vain."[16]

Several approaches have been suggested by Christian scholars seeking to understand the surprising return of the Law.[17] For the believing Jew, however, the presence of the Law in the Messianic Age is perfectly natural.

---

15. The verses list 318 precise measurements for the Temple's design, including the outer court, the inner court, the Temple itself, the chambers of the outer court, and the inside of the Temple. Ezekiel is called to witness the return of the Shechinah (the Holy Spirit) to the Temple, and is instructed to record everything that had been revealed to him. Chapters 44–46 detail the regulations that concern the priests and their service. These chapters give details of the sacrificial system, including New Moons, Sabbaths, Sin Offerings, Burnt Offerings, the Passover, other festivals, and so on.

16. Edmund P. Clowney, *The Final Temple*, p. 85, quoted in Tim Lahaye and Ed Hindson, general eds., *The Popular Bible Prophesy Commentary*, p. 209.

17. See *The Popular Bible Prophesy Commentary*, p. 209.

TIMING AND ORDER

When will he come, this Jewish Messiah? More than any other theological investigation, this problem has gnawed at Jewish minds for over two thousand years. For time immemorial Jews have speculated on the time of his arrival, basing themselves on rational, mystical, and interpretational arguments. Perhaps in appreciation of the problems latent in such calculations, a great talmudic sage once exclaimed, "All the dates have passed; the matter depends only on repentance and good deeds" (*Sanhedrin* 97b).

The only definite messianic dating scheme mentioned by the Sages is an upper limit: The Messiah will undoubtedly come no later than six thousand years from the Creation, or 2240 CE. The Talmud teaches that the final 2,000 of these 6,000 years are *years of the Messiah* – meaning, according to Jewish tradition,[18] that they are years in which the Messiah can come (*Sanhedrin* 97a). Within this time span, there have been countless calculations that attempt to pin the event to some hoped-for time. So far, none has been realized; the long-awaited Messiah continues to tarry.

Indeed, the Talmud teaches that the timing of the Messiah's coming is inherently ambiguous. Dwelling on the ambivalent statement of Isaiah's concerning the time of redemption – "I am the Lord; in its time I will hasten it" (60:22) – the sages queried whether the redemption would come at an appointed time or whether the time depends on the repentance of the Jewish People. The conclusion reached by Rabbi Alexandri is that both are true: "If they are worthy, 'I will hasten it.' If not, [the redemption will come] 'in its time'" (*Sanhedrin* 98a). According to this interpretation, only the latest time for the coming of the Messiah can be fixed; depending upon human works, however, he may come at any earlier time.

Even the order of End-time events is markedly unclear. According

---

18. Some Christian scholars have interpreted the passage of the Talmud to mean literal years of the Messiah – years during which the Messiah (Jesus) has already come. This interpretation was rejected by Jewish scholars, and the point was often brought up in medieval debates between Jews and Christians.

to a midrashic source, the Gog War will pre-empt the coming of the Messiah (*Vayikra Rabba* 9:6). This is also implied by the order of blessings of the *Amidah* prayer: We first pray for the reinstitution of the Judges, who are destined to execute judgment on Gog.[19] Only after this does the prayer move on to the rebuilding of Jerusalem (including the Messianic Temple), and to the coming of the Messiah.[20]

Maimonides, however, places the coming of the Messiah *before* the Gog War:

> From the simple interpretation of the prophets, it would appear that the war of Gog and Magog will take place at the beginning of the Messianic Age. (*Hilchot Melachim* 12:2)

This conclusion is apparent from a passage of the Talmud, in which Gentiles are drawn to convert to Judaism by the glory of the Messianic Era, but are dissuaded by the powerful invasion of Gog, quickly betraying their new-found faith by joining his ranks in the war against Israel.[21]

A third opinion maintains that the Gog War will commence before the coming of the Messiah, but will only be concluded after his coming.[22] Some maintain that Messiah ben Joseph, a figure who is destined (according to Talmudic, Midrashic, and in particular Kabbalistic tradition) to pave the way for the coming of Messiah ben David (of the Davidic dynasty), will precede the Gog War, whereas Messiah ben David will follow the war.[23] Although sources differ as to the particulars of Messiah ben Joseph's life and death, all agree that he will be killed in battle, just as Saul (of the tribe of Benjamin, Joseph's only full brother) was killed prior to the ascension of David.

Only time will reveal which of the different opinions will dominate the historical outcome.

---

19. See Talmud, *Megillah* 17b.

20. Commentary of Yefei Toar on the Midrash.

21. Talmud, *Avodah Zarah* 3b; see also Radak, Zechariah 12:2, and Ezekiel 38:7, who likewise maintain that the war of Gog and Magog will take place after the redemption. See also the *Responsa of Chatam Sofer*, vol. 6, no. 98.

22. Commentary of Maharsha on Talmud, *Sukkah*, p. 52a.

23. See Talmud, *Sukkah* 52a, b.

A NECESSARILY HAZY PICTURE

So fundamental is the ambiguity that shrouds the coming of the Messiah that it is codified by Maimonides:

All of these matters, and those similar to them, will remain unknown to all men until they will come to pass, for the matters are sealed in [the words of] the prophets, and the wise have no tradition concerning them, other than interpretation of the verses, which is the cause of differences of opinion in the matters. (*Hilchot Melachim* 12:2)

The vagueness associated with the coming of the Messiah is not a matter of chance. In visions that relate to the final redemption, Daniel is told repeatedly to *seal the vision*,[24] for it pertains to the End of Days. On occasion, Daniel himself admits that he did not comprehend the eschatological visions he was shown.[25] The visions were intentionally blurred at source.

Scripture presents a coherent, yet misty picture of the End-time, comparable perhaps to an Impressionist painting, or an out-of-focus photograph. The general picture can be discerned, but the details are hazy. In the case of the Messiah, both the manner and timing of his coming, and the nature of the era over which he will preside, are *necessarily hazy*. "If somebody tells you when the Son of David will come," writes the Midrash, "do not believe him, for the heart has not been revealed to the mouth."[26]

The messianic trail plots the course of the world's destiny, relating directly to the inner purpose for which God created the world. The rudimentary axioms of this purpose are revealed and provide us with an elemental dichotomy. The world was created, as the verse states, for the sake of God's glory (Isaiah 43:7). Simultaneously, and without implying any contradiction, the universe was fashioned for the exclusive benefit of humankind.[27]

---

24. See Daniel 8:26, 12:4, 12:6.
25. See Daniel 8:27, 12:8.
26. *Midrash Sochar Tov* (Psalms), Chap. 9.
27. See Job 35:6–7.

The same elemental keywords apply to the Messiah. On the one hand, God "brings a Redeemer . . . for His Name's sake." Yet on the other, the very same statement concludes that the messianic coming will be "with love."[28] The purpose of the Messiah is to sanctify the Name of God – yet his coming will be the ultimate expression of love for God's people. It is only out of His infinite love that God allows men the privilege of having His Name revealed among them.

Apart from these essential principles, and the basic conditions of future times that we have outlined, we know very little. The remainder – the intricate details of the Divine masterpiece – remain concealed. They will be revealed to us as the plan unfolds.

TOWARD SUNRISE

"Unfolds" is quite the right word for describing the messianic process. The Talmud (*Sanhedrin* 98a) teaches that there are two contradictory versions of the manner in which the Messiah may come: "If they merit it, [he will come] 'with the clouds of the sky' (Daniel 7:13); if they do not merit it, [he will come as] 'a pauper riding a donkey' (Zechariah 9:9)." The first manner describes a miraculous coming, a messianic advent that will rock the world to its foundations. The second describes the coming of the Messiah as an integrated process, in harmony with the natural course of the world. We appear to be witnessing the second possibility.

Following a historical track that does not interfere with the harmony of the natural world, the messianic route, like most great historical processes, is winding and protracted. Although the final result might be "born on one day"(Isaiah 66:8), the process that brings it about can be long and arduous – much like the pregnancy that leads up to the birth.

This is not to say that there will not be miracles. Scripture promises that "As the days of your coming forth from Egypt, I shall show you wonders" (Micah 7:15). The Talmud teaches further that the incredible miracles of the Exodus from Egypt, including such wonders as the midnight death of Egyptian firstborns, the splitting of the sea before the

---

28. From the conclusion of the first blessing of the *Amidah* prayer.

fleeing Israelites, and so on, are destined to be eclipsed by the miracles of the final redemption (*Berachot* 12b–13a).[29] Yet, Maimonides writes that the Messiah will not have to perform any sign or wonder to confirm the truth of his identity, proving the point from the great Rabbi Akiva, who believed that Ben-Kozeva (Bar Kochva) was the Messiah – until the latter was killed in battle.[30] It is therefore clear that the initial stages of the Messianic Era may come through natural processes; ultimately, however, the miracles of the End will astonish the world even more that those of Egypt.[31]

The Midrash[32] confirms that the coming of the Messiah will be a gradual process:

The redemption of this nation does not come in one instant, but rather bit by bit . . . for they are presently engulfed by great troubles, and if the redemption will come in one instant, they would be unable to bear so great a salvation . . . therefore it comes bit by bit, and gradually gains momentum. Therefore, the redemption is compared to dawn, as the verse states, "then your light will burst out like the dawn" [Isaiah 59:9] . . . for there is no time during the night which is darker than the instant before the morn, and if the sun would rise at that time, all the creatures of the world would be ensnared.[33] Rather, the break of dawn rises, giving the world the first glimpse of light, after which the sun rises to shine upon the world . . . as it says, "The path of the righteous is like the glow of sunlight, growing brighter until high noon" [Proverbs 4:18].

Gradually, like the emergence of daylight from the darkness of night, the redemption will shine its light upon the world. Using a variety of similes, the same idea is conveyed by numerous midrashic and talmudic sources,[34] as well as by the *Zohar* (1:170a). Rabbi Yissachar

---

29. The Talmud extracts this teaching from Scriptural sources.

30. *Yad Hachazakah, Hilchot Melachim* 11:3.

31. See also Dr. Chaim Zimmerman, *Torah and Existence* (Jerusalem-N.Y.: 1986), pp. 44–67, who explains at length why the messianic process does not necessitate miracles.

32. *Midrash Sochar Tov* (Psalms), Chap. 18.

33. They would be unable to bear the transition between the darkest point of the night and the brilliant radiance of sunlight.

34. See Jerusalem Talmud, *Yoma* Chap. 3, Halachah 2; ibid. *Berachot* Chap. 1,

Shlomo Teichtel (*Eim Habanim Semeichah*, p. 101), after quoting several sources, suggests that this is the reason why Scripture terms the Messiah *tzemach*[35] – literally, a plant. So slowly does the plant grow, that its growth is indiscernible to the human observer – yet grow it does, until full stature is achieved. Such, too, is the way of the messianic process.

The darkest point of the night, assigned by the Midrash to the time just before dawn, can possibly be associated with the Holocaust – the blackest period of the long night of Jewish exile. Perhaps in anticipation of this terrible time, we find certain talmudic sages exclaiming, "Let him [the Messiah] come, but I should not see [the troubles that will precede his coming]" (*Sanhedrin* 98b). "A time to weep, and a time to laugh" writes Ecclesiastes (3:4). Following the time of weeping, explains the *Zohar*,[36] will come the time of joy – the time of the Messiah.

After the indescribable terror of the Holocaust, the world began the journey toward light. As we have outlined in chapter 4, the period initiated after the Holocaust is termed *Evening-Morning*: a time that heads toward dawn.[37] The final revelation, however, will be sudden, like the dazzling moment of sunrise: "Behold, I am sending My messenger, and he will clear a path before Me; suddenly, the Lord Whom you seek will come to His sanctuary" (Malachi 3:1). Until that instant, we must bear the journey – a trail that has already proved arduous, and which may prove more difficult still. The direction, however, in which we slowly but constantly progress, is toward sunrise.

ACTIVE MESSIANISM

Although the great majority of Jews, both observant and secular, believe in the future coming of the Messiah (in some form or other), there is something of a divide as to the role of humankind in the messianic process. Although all accept that human works are critical in the process,

---

Halachah 1; *Song of Songs Rabba* 6:10; *Midrash Tanchuma* Deuteronomy 1.

35. Zechariah 3:8, Zechariah 6:12, Jeremiah 23:5; the expression is also used in Jewish prayers, including the *Amidah* prayer.

36. *Tikkunei Zohar Chadash* p. 80b.

37. See above, p. 80.

the nature of those works is disputed. As we have already detailed in chapter three, awaiting the Messiah has generally been a predominantly passive notion. The redemption was a constant prayer, a perpetual dream, but not a cause for positive action that went past the realm of the spiritual.

While the historical reason for this is clearly pragmatic – over the long centuries of exile, Jews had little opportunity to hasten the redemption by returning en masse to the Holy Land, or by any other worldly means – many rabbinic authorities made a theological principle of it. Even given the opportunity, it is not the part of humankind to take practical steps toward initiating the messianic era. Whenever the time was ripe, God would gather his people "on the wings of eagles" (Exodus 19:4), bringing the redeemed people to a euphoric reunion with the Messiah King. One of the most forceful arguments articulated in rejection of the Zionist movement consisted of this principle. According to the Munkaczer Rebbe (some of whose words we have already quoted in chapter three), any effort to settle the Holy Land with human hands involves an abandonment of "faith in miraculous redemption from heaven."[38] Like many other Haredi figures who reacted with hostility to the Zionist vision, the Munkaczer asserted that "One may not rely on any natural effort or on material salvation by human labor. One should not expect redemption from any source other than God."[39]

Rabbi Moshe Sofer (d. 1839), the leader of Hungarian Jewry and one of the most authoritative *halachic* (legal) decisors of his time, addressed the issue with the following words:

There may have been times in the past when we could have been partially redeemed [or given peace with the nations under whose shadow we live] or even granted such redemption as [were our forebears] is the days of the Second Commonwealth. . . . But it would have been pointless, for even had we compromised and accepted that sort of redemption for ourselves, our holy ancestors could never have reconciled themselves to anything less than full redemption. Thus, it is worthwhile for the people of Israel to suffer prolonged exile in order to attain such redemption in the end. (*Torat Moshe* 1:36)

---

38. *Chaim Veshalom* 1:42, 70, 77–78, among other sources.
39. *Chaim Veshalom* 1:41, 71, 2:58, 88, 98–99, among other sources.

Notwithstanding Rabbi Sofer's sensitivity for the Jewish plight, he espouses a course of leadership by which the Jewish People will settle for
nothing but the utopia of full redemption. Given the choice between
actively seeking a step toward redemption, and passively awaiting the
full redemption, the decisive authority of Rabbi Sofer falls clearly in
favor of the latter.

The disciples of the Vilna Gaon (early nineteenth century), who
were the first to actively seek the resettlement of the Land by political
means, adopted a radically different theological stance. In their view, it
is incumbent on individuals to do everything in their power to catalyze
the redemption process. In accordance with numerous sources,[40] settlement of the Land is a prerequisite for the coming of the Messiah; to
achieve it is thus a holy obligation on a national scale.[41]

A central issue around which the debate has raged is the interpretation of the verse in Psalms:"If the Lord will not build the house, in
vain do its builders labor on it" (127:1). Those who embrace passive
expectation point to the verse as proof of their argument: A movement
that is not set in motion by God is doomed to fail. Active messianists,
however, believe that the process must be initiated specifically by human
action – as, indeed, was the house that King Solomon built. Its success,
however, and its ultimate completion, depend upon Divine assistance.

Indeed, whereas the Talmud teaches that God, Himself, is destined
to build the Third Temple (*Bava Kama* 60b), the *Zohar* writes that the
Divine construction will descend upon an already standing edifice.[42]
When the Messiah will come, adds a midrashic source, he will stand
upon the rooftop of the Temple[43] – implying that the Temple will have
already been built prior to the Messiah's revelation. A Tosefta (an early
Tannaic source) reads: "It has been given over to the hands of Israel to

---

40. See chapter two of this book; see also Commentary of Radak to Isaiah 9:6.

41. This is apart from the mitzvah (obligation/command) of settling the Land,
which, according to the majority of authorities, applies universally – for every Jew
at all times. Whereas there are circumstances in which the "ordinary" mitzvah
does not apply, the messianic ideology raises the concept of settling the Land
beyond the conventional boundaries of *yishuv Eretz Yisrael*.

42. *Tikkunei Zohar, tikkun* 21, p. 60b.

43. *Pesikta*; *Yalkut Shimoni*, Isaiah Chap. 60, no. 499.

build the Temple."[44] The first step toward building the Temple is to settle the Land with inhabitants willing to build it.

A further part of the argument is the role of foreign nations. We have already seen that the first stage of the final return will come by the grace of foreign nations – much as the First Return from Babylon took place by the grace of Cyrus.[45] Were there no desire to return on the part of Jews, consent of foreign powers would do little for the sake of the redemption. "Rebuild Your House," we pray in the festival prayers, "as it was at first, and establish Your Sanctuary on its prepared site." The expression "as it was at first" implies a man-made construction. After the work of man is complete, we ask for the second stage: "Establish Your Sanctuary on its prepared site; show us its rebuilding, and gladden us in its perfection."

The debate over the messianic process continues to rage, albeit not with the fury of generations past. Yet, while men debated the theological dilemmas involved, the fulfillment of the word of God did not slow. Over the course of a century, the resettlement of the Land evolved from distant dream to concrete fact. Although the process remains incomplete, the Land is settled: its fertile soil is blooming and its cities are teeming with human activity, including much that is characteristically Jewish.

Without a doubt, this has been achieved by the grace of God – to this day, the success of Israel's early military campaigns continues to dazzle analysts. For those who have investigated Israel's military history, the word "miraculous" is hardly an exaggeration.[46] Yet, it has been achieved by a close partnership with man: Israel has been built by human initiative, human resourcefulness, and, above all, by the dedication of the great human spirit.

As we have already mentioned, the definition of the State of Israel in terms of the messianic time line is an issue that divides Orthodox Jewry,

---

44. *Tosefta, Pesachim* 8:2; several authorities have also ruled that granted the technical means of doing so, there is an obligation to build the Temple.
45. See above, p. 59.
46. See, however, p. 200.

and there is no reason for us to enter the debate. A process, however – a progression of return and rebuilding – is surely underway.

SHALOM

There is one aspect of the Messianic Age that we are able to describe by contrasting with its familiar opposite. It will be a time of enduring, absolute peace:

He will judge among the nations, and will settle the arguments of many peoples. They shall beat their swords into plowshares and their spears into pruning hooks; nation will not lift sword against nation, neither will they learn war any more. (Isaiah 2:4)

We have discussed something of the religious significance of the Messiah and the Messianic Age. For the Jews of exile, living through centuries of hardship and persecution, the human aspect of the Messianic Age was surely that with which they most identified. In its redemptive function, the Messianic Age will see the Jewish People relieved of their exilic condition, freed of the yoke of the nations, and initiated into a state of peace and harmony. Moreover, this condition will extend to embrace the entire world.

Without meaning to belittle the considerable good it harbors, our world continues to accommodate intense hatred, great suffering, widespread discrimination, ethnic cleansing, war, terrorism, and all things evil and malicious. We have come to see these failures as a part of life, inevitable aspects of a flawed human existence. The Messianic Age will reveal that this melancholy presumption is a fallacy. The word *Shalom*, Peace, is based on the root *shalem*, which means *complete*. The time of the Messiah will reveal a world of completion – a world whose citizens will dwell in the same harmony as that displayed by the cycles of nature.

Although to the eye of a human observer, the path may seem convoluted, the world is heading toward an era of universal peace, tranquility, and harmony. The most important components of Jewish liturgy, such as the *Amidah* prayer, *Birkat Hakohanim*, and *Birkat Hamazon*,[47]

---

47. The Priestly Blessing, and Grace after Meals, respectively.

conclude with a mention of *Shalom*.[48] Shalom is the true destiny of the world, the pinnacle of human endeavor.

While the Jewish messianic vision does not relinquish the concept of nationalism,[49] the peace it envisages is universal. From a world of discord, a world of patriotic egoism and nationalistic ambition, a new world will emerge that knows only harmony and tranquility.

Yet, unlike some visions of universal peace,[50] unity among nations will not imply their demise. Peace will not come through the dissipation of national and individual identities, not by the abolishment of religion, and not by the annulment of a rigorous judicial system. Rather, the world, *with all its diversity*, will be unified under a single banner, a single purpose that will bind all of humanity in a bond of peace.

Like the *Amidah* prayer and the Blessing of the Priests, we end this book with *Shalom*.

---

48. See *Midrash Rabba, Bamidbar* 21:1.

49. This demonstrates a further difference between the Christian vision and the Jewish counterpart. In the Jewish version, the nation of Israel remains a separate entity, even during the Messianic Era. In the Christian view, the universalism of the Messiah will abolish national distinctions.

50. The famous sixties (or early seventies, to be precise) song "Imagine" is a good example of such a vision; for a discussion thereof, see Ze'ev Maghen, "Imagine: On Love and Lennon," *Azure* 7 (1999).

◈ Appendix A

THE PURPOSE OF PRAYER

One of the recurring themes of this book is the concept of prayer. In particular, we have returned a number of times to the daily Jewish prayer – the *Amidah*. This prayer, which was compiled by the Men of the Great Assembly[1] – a body of Jewish leaders that included a number of prophets[2] – was intended to replace the sacrificial order of the Temple in times of Destruction.[3] Appropriately, it has become the cornerstone of Jewish religious service throughout the long centuries of the present exile.

Our ordinary perception of prayer is closely related to human desire and ambition. Indeed, the sages make clear that prayer is an integral component of human achievement. The Talmud offers practical advice for those who wish to attain a variety of material gains: One who wishes to gain wisdom should dedicate his time to studying the Torah, and one who wishes to become wealthy should conduct his business dealings in good faith. "Surely many have done so," questions the Talmud, "but have not succeeded? Rather," concludes the Talmud, "they should

---

1. Talmud, *Berachot* 33a.

2. These include Ezra and Zerubbabel. The foremost members of the Great Assembly returned from their Babylonian exile together with Zerubbabel; see Ezra 2:2.

3. Talmud, *Berachot* 26b.

beseech Him that wisdom (or wealth) is His, *for one [practical measures] without the other [prayer] cannot succeed*" (*Niddah* 70b).

Yet, the content of the daily Jewish prayer suggests a deeper layer of meaning than the simple achievement of human aims. Thrice daily, the range of blessings recited far exceeds our immediate requirements and desires. Moreover, as the Talmud points out (*Megillah* 17b), the blessings form a chronological order, culminating in the establishment of the Messianic Dynasty. What is the purpose of prayer in this sense? The fate of history is surely a matter of Divine guidance, beyond the reach of human prayer – is it not?

To understand the significance of the prayer, and, indeed, the importance of prayer in a general sense, is to understand the fundamental purpose of human service of God. Our basic conception of God is that He is an omniscient, omnipotent, and eternal being; He does not need the deeds of man, nor require his lip service. Job's friends summed it up eloquently: "If you have sinned, how do you affect Him? And if your transgressions are multiplied, what do you do to Him? If you are righteous, what do you give Him – or what does He receive from your hand?" (Job 35:6–7).

What, then, is the need for human service of God – the service that reached its climax in the sacrificial order of the Temple, and that continues today in the form of prayer?

In Jewish thought, this question is far from new. It has been pondered by numerous thinkers, by Jewish philosophers of medieval times, and later by Kabbalistic authorities. I will present only a short overview of the matter, insofar as I deem necessary to complement the content of this book. Rather than directly quoting ancient or later authorities, the following explanation is my own understanding, as based upon the teachings of my mentors.

An essential introduction to the question of human purpose is the dichotomy of God's control over the world. On the one hand, God guides the world as He sees fit; He moves the world purposely forward, toward its pre-ordained destiny, and nothing that any human being does can affect or prevent this perpetual guidance from taking effect. Looking back on the course of history, all will know that "I . . . am He, and there is no god with Me: I kill, and I make alive; I have wounded, and I heal; and there is none that can deliver out of My hand" (Deuteronomy 32:39).

On the other hand, God *responds* to human deeds: Righteousness is rewarded, and iniquity is punished. That is not to say that we can always perceive the recompense given to the righteous or the castigation of the wicked. The ways of God, which include such concepts as the refinement of souls and the rectification of spiritual worlds, are far beyond the reach of human consciousness.

Nevertheless, the centrality of Reward and Punishment is well chronicled throughout Scripture: Abraham was chosen by God to father the Chosen Nation because of his deeds;[4] of the twelve spies that Moses sent into Canaan, only Joshua and Caleb, by virtue of their faithfulness to God, were spared the harsh fate of their comrades. Moreover, the Admonitions of Leviticus and Deuteronomy leave no room to doubt the far-reaching consequences of misdeed. These consequences are vividly demonstrated by the narratives of the Book of Kings, in which the Nation of Israel quickly falls from grace due to its spiritual failings.[5]

How these two distinct layers of Divine guidance converge – the layer of God's all-encompassing master plan on the one hand, and the layer of Divine justice[6] on the other – is not for us to ponder. The matter is closely related to the famous question posited by Maimonides: If God's knowledge is infinite, how does room remain for man's independent free will?[7] – but it is not the subject of our current discussion.

What *is* important for the current argument is that we, as human beings, are entirely subjugated to the layer of Divine justice. The idea that we may do as we please, founded on the assumption that whatever we succeed in doing is undoubtedly the will of God, is a grave heresy in Jewish law and thought.

The progress of the world along the track of fate is thus a matter of

---

4. See Genesis 22:16.

5. Commentators point out further that the Destruction of the First and Second Temples were fulfilments of the Admonitions of Leviticus and Deuteronomy, respectively (see Nachmanides' Commentary to Torah on Leviticus 26:16).

6. This is the term used by Rabbi Moshe Chayim Luzzato (Ramchal), whose *Daat Tevunot* expounds on the two layers of God's guidance over the world.

7. *Hilchot Teshuvah* (Laws of Repentance), Chap. 5, no. 5.

partnership: It is the doing of God, but it is catalyzed by human deed. When God created the world, the verse relates that although plant life had already been formed,[8] it did not grow beyond the crust of the earth until the first rain fell. The fall of rain, in turn, awaited the creation of Adam. Rashi explains the need for this delay: Only after Adam would realize the need for it, and pray to God accordingly, could rain descend upon earth.[9] Rain, the quintessential symbol of Divine blessing, could only come in the wake of human prayer.

The verse states that God did not cause rain to fall upon the earth, because "there was no man to till the soil" (Genesis 2:5). The scriptural simile for man's service of God is working the earth. Like the action of plowing the field, our spiritual labors prepare the earth for receiving Heavenly blessing. The paradigm of this spiritual labor is the act of prayer.[10] In articulating our total reliance on God, the act of prayer establishes the relationship between God and humankind.

Prayer personalizes the give-and-take connection between God and humankind. Rather than a survival contract, in which man requests and is subsequently granted the requirements of his human frailty, the arrangement takes on the structure of an interpersonal relationship. God *gives* – not an automated handout, but an act of giving laden with the desire of those who serve Him. And man *receives*, obtaining his sustenance not from an impersonal cosmic force, but from a loving God, Whose primary interest is the welfare of His children.[11]

In this arrangement, humankind is elevated beyond the status of a passive receiver, to that of an active partner in the Divine plan. Throughout history, as the Divine will unfolds before human eyes, we are set the task of partnering God by means of human deeds – and first

---

8. On the third day of the Creation.

9. Commentary of Rashi (Rabbi Shlomo Yitzchaki) on Genesis 2:5.

10. This is also true of personal supplications. The Divine blessing required to fulfill our needs is prepared in advance; only through prayer, however, is the blessing "activated."

11. When the three Hebrew letters of the word *Adam* are spelled out in full (aleph, dalet, mem), the extra letters (apart from the first constituent letters) spell the word *mitpalel* – "one who prays." The underlying purpose of man is fulfilled though his relationship with God – by means of prayer.

and foremost, through the act of prayer. God wishes to reveal Himself to us not as a unilateral act, but as part of the relationship established through prayer.

Thus, even when prophecy has revealed a future event in advance of its coming to pass, it remains incumbent on man to pray for its fulfillment. Daniel, for instance, having deciphered Jeremiah's prophecy of the impending return from Babylon, immediately prayed for its fulfillment.[12]

On the day that King Solomon consecrated the great Temple he constructed, he prayed on behalf of the future prayers of humanity – firstly for those of his nation Israel, and even for those of foreign nations:

Even concerning the stranger, who is not of Your people, Israel . . . for they shall hear of Your great name, and of Your mighty hand . . . when he shall come and pray toward this house; You shall hear, Heaven, Your dwelling-place, and do according to all that the stranger calls You for – so that all the peoples of the earth may know Your name. (I Kings 8:41–43)

Even today, the thrice-daily *Amidah* is recited facing Jerusalem, toward the site on which Solomon constructed the Temple. As the time of its promised rebuilding draws closer, the obligation to play a part in the process takes on special urgency: to pray for the glory of God that is hidden, for the Jewish People, and for all humanity.

---

12. As Nachmanides mentions (in his commentary to Leviticus 26:16), Daniel's confession fulfilled the instruction of Leviticus 26:40, which states that the return from exile will come together with a national confession of sin. The prayer, however, which Daniel added to his confession of national sin, indicates the importance of human prayer in spite of an explicit prophecy.

✍ Appendix B

THE RESURRECTION

Following the coming of the Messiah, there is a further stage of Jewish eschatology, which is not dealt with in the main body of this work: the Resurrection.

The first reason for its exclusion is that although the Resurrection comprises a fundamental facet of our faith, enumerated as the last of Maimonides' "Thirteen Principles of Faith," Scripture makes scant, if any, mention of it. Although the Talmud suggests several scriptural sources for the Resurrection (Sanhedrin 90b ff), it cannot, in the strictest sense, be considered a scriptural prophecy.

In addition, as we will presently explain, the Resurrection is somehow tangential to the theme of Divine Providence that this work has attempted to highlight. Although the world leads toward the Resurrection, it does so by a pathway that cannot be discerned by human observers. The path is not merely hidden, as can be said of the Messianic destiny, but insofar as the human conscience is concerned, it cannot be called a path at all. The *Amidah*, which describes a chronological progression,[1] ends with the rebuilding of Jerusalem and the coming of the Messianic Age; no prayer is offered for the Resurrection.[2]

---

1. See Talmud, *Megillah* 17b; see also Appendix A.

2. The awakening of the dead is mentioned in the beginning of the *Amidah* as a praise of God. In contrast to the Messianic Age, however, there is no prayer for the coming of the Resurrection.

Our grasp of God's guidance over the world is necessarily worldly; our appreciation is innately limited by the finite boundaries of the human psyche. The Resurrection, however, represents a time in which the world, together with its human inhabitants, will shed much of its materialistic nature. The path of our world toward the Resurrection is like the path of the finite toward the infinite. Just as the infinite is beyond our mental grasp, so the path toward it exists in a dimension that we cannot sense.

It is perhaps for this reason that we find no explicit prophecy in Scripture concerning the Resurrection. For someone born blind, the promise of future sight is incomprehensible, and is largely without meaning. The anticipation of something essentially beyond human consciousness cannot inspire; the prophecy thereof is of little value.

Nevertheless, the Resurrection *is* an integral part of the Jewish faith system. Its meaning, moreover, is of far greater significance than the simple "coming alive of the dead." The Resurrection is a time in which the world will be elevated to a totally new mode of existence, shedding the familiar ways of nature for new standards that we are today incapable even of imagining.

A clue as to the new natural order of the Resurrection is found in the Talmud. The Romans, the Talmud records (*Sanhedrin* 90b), once asked Rabbi Yehoshua ben Chananya to prove two basic precepts of Judaic faith: that God is destined to resurrect the dead, and that He knows the future in advance of its coming to pass. Rabbi Yehoshua answered with a single verse: "The Lord said to Moses: Behold, you are about to lie with your fathers, and rise up" (Deuteronomy 31:16).

The Romans were quick to express their reservations concerning the scriptural source. The words "and rise up," or the Hebrew single word *vekam*, ostensibly refers not to Moses but to the Israelite People: "This nation will rise up, and go astray after the foreign gods of the land" (ibid.). Rabbi Yehoshua conceded that the proof of the Resurrection can be questioned, but asserted that the verse remains a proof of God's foreknowledge of the future. Yet, immediately following this passage of the Talmud, Rabbi Yochanan, in the name of Rabbi Shimon bar Yochai, is quoted as basing both the Resurrection and God's infinite knowledge on the same markedly debatable source.

There are, in fact, far clearer scriptural references to the Resurrection. One such verse, which is quoted in the Talmud (*Sanhedrin* 92a), is the concluding verse of the Book of Daniel: "But you go your way until the end be, and you shall rest, and rise to your lot at the end of days" (Daniel 12:13). Another (also cited by the Talmud) is found earlier in the same chapter: "And many of those who sleep in the dust of the earth shall awaken, some to everlasting life, and some to reproaches and everlasting abhorrence" (12:2).

Rabbi Yehoshua and Rabbi Shimon bar Yochai, however, chose to base the Resurrection on the more ambiguous source mentioned above. The reason for this, it would appear, is that both the Resurrection and the omniscience of God are thus revealed in the same verse.

The two concepts are closely interrelated. The knowledge of God is not limited by time: The infinite *presence* of God implies the breakdown of such worldly barriers as past, present, and future. In the time of the Resurrection, the entire world will experience the eradication of these barriers. Rather than the simple awakening of the dead, the Resurrection implies *the awakening of the past*. Past, present, and future will converge to a single, unified present. From the current human perspective, such a state of affairs is not only unfamiliar. It is impossible.

The Resurrection is thus excluded from the prayer service. We cannot pray for that which we cannot fathom. Its explicit mention is similarly omitted by prophecy. Scripture cannot convey a concept that is entirely beyond human experience. Nevertheless, the Resurrection is alluded to in Scripture, and it is an integral part of the Jewish faith. Whenever a Jew comes across Jewish graves, he offers a blessing to the One "Who revives the dead."[3]

How will the Resurrection come about, and who will be included in it? In accordance with the nature of the subject, the material that the sages have bequeathed us concerning these questions is scant, to say the least.

The single teaching of the Mishnah concerning the Resurrection reveals the importance of belief: Those who do not believe in the Resurrection will be excluded from it (*Sanhedrin* 90b). One cannot hope to be part of a process without believing in it. One midrashic source states

---

3. See Talmud, *Berachot* 58b.

that animals will not take part in the Resurrection;[4] the implication is that all of humanity, including the nations, will participate. Another source states that whereas the generation of the Flood is excluded from the Resurrection, the nations of the world are included.[5] The Talmud, however, implies that the role of the nations in the Resurrection will be secondary to that of the Jewish People (*Sanhedrin* 91b).[6]

As to *how* events will take place, classical sources divulge virtually no information. Kabbalistic sources reveal that the Resurrection will take place forty years after the final ingathering of the Nation;[7] we learn further that the entire population of the world will die,[8] so that all the evil that remains should perish before they are brought back to life.[9] One opinion maintains that depending on their righteousness, different individuals may experience the Resurrection at different times (*Zohar* 1:140a, in the name of Rav Nachman); others maintain that the Resurrection will occur at the same time for all (ibid., Rav Yosi), although the process may take up to 214 years (ibid.).

These details, in the context of a world that humankind cannot begin to fathom, are meaningful only in a theoretical or academic sense. In a practical sense, the Resurrection is beyond; it is unknown, and will remain so until it comes.

The message of the Resurrection, however, is monumental. It is our faith that no element of God's creation goes to waste; that somehow, every second that passed and "died" is destined to live once more. Our duty, for the time being, is to live the present; a time will come when we will live even the past.

---

4. *Midrash Tehillim (Sochar Tov)* (Psalms), Chap. 19.
5. *Pirkei Derabbi Eliezer*, Chap. 33.
6. See also *Taanit* 7a.
7. See *Zohar* 1:136b, 139a, 140a; 2:10a; this is corroborated by one opinion in the Talmud, which states that the Messianic Age will last forty years (Talmud, *Sanhedrin* 99a).
8. This, however, will not be a natural death, such as that to which we are accustomed, and which is perpetrated by the Angel of Death, but rather death at the hands of God Himself, solely for the sake of immediate resuscitation. See Talmud, *Shabbat*, 152b.
9. See *Zohar* 2:108b.

RETURN OF THE LOST TRIBES

The tale of the Lost Tribes began with the fateful split of Israel into two sets of tribes: Ten tribes,[1] the large majority of the nation, broke away from the remainder and formed an independent Northern Kingdom, known as the *Kingdom of Israel*.[2] The Tribe of Judah (which had absorbed the Tribe of Simeon) and the Tribe of Benjamin remained in the southern part of Eretz Yisrael, under the rule of the Davidic dynasty:

Ahijah grabbed hold of the new garment that was upon him, and he tore it into twelve pieces. He said to Jeroboam, "Take ten pieces for yourself, for the Lord, God of Israel said, 'I am taking away from the hand of Solomon and I shall give the ten tribes to you . . . [This is] because they have forsaken Me.'" (I Kings 11:30–31)

For the sake of David, however, God delayed the decree until after the death of Solomon. Only in the days of Rehoboam, Solomon's heir, would the kingdom split into two. Yet, unbeknownst to the great Solomon, the road to disaster had been initiated.

If the Tribe of Judah was considered to have forsaken God, as God informed Jeroboam, the Ten Tribes, under a long succession of wicked

---

1. Because the Tribe of Levi had no territory, they were not included in the tally.

2. Henceforth, the Northern Kingdom.

leaders, would do much worse. Despite the courageous efforts of prophets such as Elijah to bring them to repent,[3] their continued iniquity sealed their fate and they were exiled from the Land.

The Book of Chronicles reveals that the first to suffer the fate of exile were the tribes that dwelt on the east of the Jordan: Reuben, Gad, and half of Manasseh (I Chronicles 5:26). Having exiled these tribes, Tiglat-Pileser of Assyria turned his attention to the Land of Israel. It was not long before the Tribe of Naphtali was cut off from its heritage:

In the days of Pekah king of Judah, Tiglat-Pileser king of Assyria came and took . . . Hazor, Gilead, and the Galilee – all of the land of Naphtali – and he exiled them to Assyria. (I Kings 15:29)

The rest of Israel – the remaining six and a half of the Ten Tribes – were soon to follow. After Shalmaneser, King of Assyria, discovered that the King of Israel had betrayed him, he invaded the entire territory of the Northern Kingdom and exiled its people.

The Bible reveals the places to which the Tribes were exiled: Halah; Habor, by the River Gozan; and the cities of Media. Although the Talmud does identify these locations, we cannot be sure of their precise whereabouts. Wherever they may be, the connection between the Ten Tribes and the Tribes of Judah and Benjamin was severed. The Ten Tribes became the Lost Tribes of Israel.

Several verses leave little doubt as to the fate of the Lost Tribes: They are destined to return to the fold:[4]

---

3. See I Kings, Chap. 18.

4. Rabbi Akiva, in one of the most surprising statements recorded by the Mishnah, maintains that "the Ten Tribes are not destined to return" (Talmud, *Sanhedrin* 110a). In order to resolve this statement with numerous explicit verses, commentaries have suggested four possible explanations. The most commonly upheld of them is that Rabbi Akiva was referring to the first generation of the Ten Tribes that were exiled; "The Ten Tribes are not destined to return" means that they have no portion in the World to Come (*Rashi, Radvaz, Rabbeinu David,* and *Tosafot Yom-Tov,* among others).

In those days the House of Judah will walk with the House of Israel, and they will come together from the land of the North to the land that I have given as a possession to your fathers. (Jeremiah 3:18)[5]

The verses, moreover, reveal a significant difference between the gathering of the Lost Tribes, and the gathering of Judah:

He will raise a banner for the nations and assemble the castaways of Israel; and He will gather in the dispersed ones of Judah from the four corners of the earth. (Isaiah 11:12)

The Vilna Gaon, in his annotations to Isaiah, points out the distinction between the *assembly* of Israel and the *gathering* of Judah. Over the centuries of their exile, the Jews have, indeed, been scattered to the four corners of the earth. In the current return, Jews from over one hundred countries have been gathered in to the Holy Land.

The Tribes of Israel, however, in contrast with the concept of world Jewry associated with Judah, will not require a *gathering* per se; they will be *assembled*, taken from their place of residence and transferred to the Land of Israel. This suggests that the Lost Tribes will return to the Land as a unified body, a people who did not split into thousands of communities and ethnic groups, but remained united throughout the centuries.[6]

The phraseology used in an additional verse reveals a further quality of the Lost Tribes: They are, indeed, lost, in the deepest sense of the word:

It shall be on that day that a great horn will be blown, and those who are lost in the land of Assyria and those cast away in the land of Egypt will come, and they will prostrate themselves to the Lord on the holy mount in Jerusalem. (Isaiah 27:13)

---

5. See also Jeremiah 30, 31, among many verses.

6. The distinction between the Tribes of Judah and the Tribes of Israel has already been made by Nachmanides (*Commentary to Song of Songs*, 8:13). Nachmanides states further that the assembly of the Ten Tribes will precede the gathering of Judah. Rabbi Moshe Chayim Luzzato (Ramchal), however, writes that the gathering of Judah will precede the coming of the Ten Tribes (*Maamar Hageulah*).

The implication of "those who are lost in the land of Assyria" is that the exiles do not even know of their own identity, or, at the very least, that their self-identity has been clouded by the passage of time. This, together with the first indication of a large ethnic concentration living in one location, is well applied to the Pathans of Afghanistan and Pakistan.[7] Although nothing can be said with certainty about the identification of the Lost Tribes, the Pathans are among the likeliest candidates.

Dwelling in close proximity to the border between the two countries, the Pathans number some 8–9 million Afghans, and some 10–11 million Pakistanis. The ethnic origin of this group has long been a topic of conversation, for their Semitic countenance resembles none of the known ethnic groups present in the region: the Indian-Iranian, the Turkish, the Mongolian, or the Persian. Many researchers have therefore concluded that their origin is Israelite.

This has been corroborated by a great deal of suggestive, if insufficiently conclusive evidence. The names of the tribes to which the Pathans belong clearly indicate an Israelite descent: Ruveini (Reuben), Shinuri (Simon), Leveni (Levi), Daftani (Naphtali), Gagi (Gad), Ashuri (Asher), Yusuf (Joseph), and so on. According to the royal family of Afghanistan, they are descended from the Tribe of Benjamin.[8]

Eyewitness accounts have testified that Pathans have a tradition of male circumcision on the eighth day, which follows the Torah law. Their customary separation from women during menstruation also corresponds closely to that ordained by the Torah; they have traditions of levirate marriage, of abstention from forbidden foods, and of observing the Sabbath, all of which correspond to Torah law. This is only a sampling of dozens of similarities that observers have noted; in addition,

---

7. The U.S. screening of a television documentary by Simcha Jacobovici in the spring of 2000 did much to spread awareness of the Pathans and their possible Israelite origins.

8. According to the tradition, King Saul, who was descended from the Tribe of Benjamin, had a son named Yirmiyah, who had a son named Afghanah. Afghanah grew up on the knees of King David, and remained in the kingdom until the exile of Nebuchadnezzar. At this time, Afghanah's descendants fled to what is today central Afghanistan, where they settled permanently. They were converted to Islam by Mohammed in the year 662.

232 / PROPHECIES & PROVIDENCE

there are several eyewitness accounts of finding amulets containing an inscription of the Hebrew words *Shema Yisrael*.[9]

There is much to be said concerning the ongoing attempts to locate Lost Tribes: There are also many Jewish sources, both ancient and more modern, which make reference to the Jewish kingdoms on the *other side of the Sambatyon* – the river that would cease to flow on the Sabbath. In connection with our current work, however, we would like to make an altogether different point.

If we consider the marginal role of the Jews in world history from the Destruction until the twentieth century, the extent to which the fate of the Lost Tribes has captured the imagination of the Western mind is truly remarkable. Tudor Parfitt fittingly opens his book on the subject with the following words: "The quest for the Lost Tribes of Israel . . . is one of the enduring motifs underlying Western views of the wider world."[10]

Israelite origin, as Parfitt continues to document, has been bestowed on virtually every part of the "new world" that European travelers have gradually uncovered. To this day, "Lost Tribes mythology" forms a part of the national culture in such far-reaching locations as China, Japan, India, the United States, New Zealand, parts of Africa, and so on. No romantic theme is so ancient, durable, and widespread as the history and destiny of the Lost Tribes.

How much of this Israelite origin is pure fiction, and how much may have grains of truth, is not the central question.[11] The point, rather, is that the medium of the Lost Tribes has ensured that the global conscience should never forget the exiled state of the Jews, and their undying hope of redemption. Whenever that redemption will finally arrive, it will come as the culmination of a long tradition, the conclusion of an epic trail in the psyche of the Western and global mind.

---

9. For more details on the Pathans, and on other tribes that may be of Israelite origin, see Rabbi Eliyahu Avichail, *Shivtei Yisrael* (Hebrew), Jerusalem, 1999.

10. Tudor Parfitt, *The Lost Tribes of Israel: The History of a Myth* (Phoenix, 2003), p. 1.

11. Parfitt, himself, in common with most of the academic world, is quite skeptical of virtually all claims to Lost Israelite identity.

In particular, the establishment of the State of Israel and its Law of Return has catalyzed renewed interest in the Israelite tribes. The universal awareness of a distant past, manifest in the Lost Tribes of Israel, has taken on practical connotations in the twentieth and twenty-first centuries, in bringing such groups as Ethiopian Jews "home."

Like the messianic process described in chapter nine of this book, the discovery and ultimate return of the Lost Tribes is also emerging as a gradual progression. Finally, the words of Ezekiel will be fulfilled:

Behold, I am taking the Children of Israel from among the nations to which they have gone; I will gather them from all around and I will bring them to their soil; I will make them into one nation in the land, upon the mountains of Israel, and they will no longer be divided into two kingdoms, ever again. . . . They will dwell on the land that I gave to My servant Jacob, within which your fathers dwelled; they and their children and their children's children will dwell upon it forever; and My servant David will be a leader for them forever. . . . I will be a God to them and they will be a people to Me. Then the nations will know that I am the Lord, Who sanctifies Israel, when My sanctuary will be among them forever. (Ezekiel 37:20–28)

Some Israelis, aware of Lost Tribe theology and its current manifestations, have expressed concern over the possibility of mass immigration of Indians,[12] to name one example, into their westernized society. When the prophecy will be fulfilled, however, ethnic and cultural differences will be set aside, and the Jewish People, split apart for close to three thousand years, will no longer know division.

---

12. The Shinlung of Mizoram (on the India-Burma frontier), who call themselves the Benei Menashe, are strong candidates for receiving "official" Lost Tribe status.

Appendix D

THE THREE OATHS

Although this book opened with a declaration of its non-political nature, a particular issue, while often cited in the context of political polemic, is of special religious significance. Because of the centrality of the argument in anti-Zionist expositions, and because of its theological importance, we have dedicated this appendix to a short summary of the issue.

It should be made clear from the outset that the anti-Zionist argument based on the issue of the Oaths, which relates to the possible violation of a well-known talmudic dictum, has no bearing on the general content of this book. This work has attempted to investigate and chronicle the workings of Divine Providence in recent Jewish history. The adherence of the human participants in this history to talmudic dicta may have great religious significance; in respect of destiny, it remains of little relevance.[1]

The issue we wish to consider concerns the proscriptions commonly referred to as the Three Oaths. Commenting on three verses found in Song of Songs, all of which mention an oath imposed upon the daughters of Jerusalem to the effect that they may not *awaken or arouse the love, until it is desired*,[2] the Talmud quotes the following teaching:

---

1. See chapter three of this book, where we have made this point at greater length.

2. Song of Songs 2:7, 3:5, 8:4.

Rabbi Yosi in the name of Rabbi Hanina taught: What are these three oaths? One that Israel shall not ascend [to *Eretz Yisrael*] the wall [by force]; one that God adjured Israel not to rebel against the nations of the world; and one that God adjured the nations of the world not to oppress Israel overmuch. (*Ketubot* 111a)

The first two Oaths convey similar messages: Israel is forbidden to throw off the yoke of the nations, and is likewise forbidden to use force to make an ascent to the Holy Land. These Oaths have often been invoked in order to invalidate the idea of hastening the redemption by political or military means. The restrictions have thus served as ready ammunition for those who have taken a religious stance against the Zionist movement, whose basic principles clearly violate the Oaths.

Rabbi Yehudah Loewe – the renowned Maharal – writes that the law of the Three Oaths is so stringent that it applies "even in a generation of sin, when the Gentiles kill us with terrible torture."[3] Rabbi Yoel Teitelbaum's treatise, *Vayoel Moshe*, which is dedicated to the study and promulgation of the Oaths and to their violation on the part of the Zionists, explains why the prohibition invokes special stringency. Breaking them, Rabbi Teitelbaum reasons, is tantamount to heresy, in declaring that the fate of the Jews is determined by their own hands, and not by God.[4] Even Rabbi Zvi Hirsch Kalischer (d. 1875), who, in the mid-nineteenth century, advocated immigration en masse to the Holy Land (and whose vigorous campaign in favor of the settlement was instrumental in laying the foundations for modern Zionism), was wary of violating the Oaths by employing force or political means to establish a Jewish government.[5] The entire vision of settling the Land was limited to peaceful means, with the consent of nations.

Yet, although the Oaths are mentioned by many prominent authorities,[6] they have not been universally accepted as binding. Maimonides,

---

3. *Netzach Yisrael*, Chap. 24. Although Maharal interprets the oaths allegorically in his commentary to the Aggadic sections of the Talmud, this does not detract from the actual prohibition they imply.

4. *Vayoel Moshe*, pp. 92–93.

5. *The Writings of Rabbi Kalischer* (Jerusalem: 1947), p. 230.

6. Examples of such authorities include Rabbi Yitzchak bar Sheshet (*Rivash*,

the foremost codifier of Jewish Law, does mention the Oaths in a letter to the Jews of Yemen, yet his omission of the Oaths from *Mishneh Torah* – his *magnum opus* of talmudic Law – has proved a thorny problem for those who uphold the Oaths as a full-scale prohibition, and indicates that the Paths belong to the genre of *aggadah* (non-legal) rather than *halachah* (legal).[7] What is more, Rabbi Chayim Vital, the great disciple of Rabbi Yitzchak Luria, writes that the Oaths expired after the termination of the first millennium of the two thousand *years of Messiah*.[8]

A possible qualification of the injunction of the Oaths emerges from a short statement of the Vilna Gaon. Quoting the proscription they imply, the Vilna Gaon makes specific mention of *going out to rebuild the Temple*.[9] This could be construed as implying that the prohibition of re-settling the Land by force is limited to the building of the Temple – a position that would explain the political activism of the Gaon's disciples who immigrated to the Holy Land.[10] A century later, a similar idea found practical expression in the writings of Rabbi Zvi Hirsch Kalischer. Dwelling on the injunction against "forcing the end," Rabbi Kalischer

---

Responsum no. 101); Rabbi Shlomo bar Shimshon (*Rashbash*, Responsum no. 2); Rabbi Abraham Burnstein (*Avnei Nezer*, Responsa no. 454–6 – although Rabbi Burnstein states that with the permission of nations, the prohibition of the Oaths does not apply); Rabbi Shmuel Salant (see *Tzefunot*, year 3, issue 1, p. 46); Rabbi Yechiel Michl Epstein (*Aruch Hashulchan, Choshen Mishpat* 2:1). Nachmanides (end of *Maamar Hageulah*, p. 274 in the Mossad Harav Kook edition) implies that the prohibition of the Oaths applies even when permission of the nations has been granted.

7. This assertion has been postulated by a number of authorities; see Rabbi Abraham Burnstein (*Avnei Nezer* 544); *Penei Yehoshua, Ketubot* 112a.

8. Introduction to *Shaar Hakdamot*; concerning the two thousand years of Messiah, see chapter nine of this book.

9. *Tikkun* 26, p. 70a, cited in *Siddur Hagra* (Jerusalem: 1971), p. 48.

10. Much research concerning the political ambition of the disciples of the Gaon has been conducted by Arie Morgenstern. See Arie Morgenstern, *Natural Redemption: The disciples of the Gra in Israel 1800–1840* [Hebrew] (Maor, Jerusalem: 1997); Arie Morgenstern, *The Return to Jerusalem: The Renewal of the Settlement in Jerusalem at the Beginning of the Nineteenth Century* [Hebrew] (Shalem Press, Jerusalem: 2006). For an overview in English, see Arie Morgenstern, *Hastening Redemption: Messianism and the Resettlement of the Land of Israel* (Oxford, 2006).

wrote that the proscription was not in conflict with the program of settling the Land. The injunction, in his view, refers only to forcing the actual End, a destiny whose achievement must remain solely in the hands of God. Concerning the beginning, the path of settling the Land that leads "little by little" toward the End, there is no proscription – on the contrary, doing so is a religious obligation.

Rabbi Aviezer of Tiktin, one of the disciples of the Vilna Gaon who immigrated to the Holy Land in the beginning of the nineteenth century, adopted a somewhat different stance in confronting the issue of the Oaths. Obviously inspired by his own experiences, he writes that the prohibitions do not apply to "extraordinary times" in which the coming of the Messiah may be hastened by human action.[11] Rabbi Israel of Shklov, who was one of the leaders of the original settlers, contended that because the Gentiles had not kept their part of the Oaths [namely, not to "overly" persecute the Jewish People], the Jews were absolved of theirs.[12]

Specifically with regard to the Oath not to "ascend the wall," Rabbi Yehudah Alkalai (d. 1878), one of the pre-Zionist rabbis who favored the settlement of the Land, offered a particularly creative solution. The injunction, he explained, prohibits only collective ascending in a sudden, revolutionary thrust, encouraging the settlement of the Land in a gradual manner: "The Holy One, blessed be He, wishes the redemption to take place in a dignified and orderly way; therefore, He adjured us not to all go up together, not to be scattered about the face of the field like tent dwellers, but [to go] little by little, until our land is rebuilt and established."[13]

Paradoxically, the Oath is therefore supportive of the move toward settling the Land of Israel: Israel is adjured not to "ascend the wall" (meaning, by force), but is obligated to ascend! Specifically with regard to the Zionist settlement of the twentieth century, a number of leading

11. *Shaarei Tzedek* (Jerusalem: 1843), p. 46b.

12. Abraham Yaari, Letters from the Land of Israel, p. 352; cited by Morgenstern, *Natural Redemption: The Disciples of the Gra in Israel 1800–1840*, p. 9.

13. Rabbi Yehudah Alkalai, *Kitvei Harav Yehudah Alkalai*, ed. Yitzchak Werfel (Jerusalem: 1944), pp. 202, 240, 302.

halachic authorities wrote that the settlement was not considered "ascending the wall" because it was done with the permission of the nations[14] – though this position is not unanimous.[15]

Today, the discussion concerning the Oaths is largely academic. Indeed, with regard to the secular Zionist movement, it was always academic. The founding of the State of Israel did not take place because of halachic permission, for which founding Zionist leaders cared little. The armed struggle against the British, which gained momentum after the Second World War and included large-scale illegal immigration, can perhaps be labeled "ascending the wall" – though the boundaries of the concept remain ambiguous and elusive. To my knowledge, no halachic authority was consulted before action was taken. As for the post-State period, Rabbi Dr. Chaim Zimmerman has pointed out that the prohibition of the Oaths is confined to *ascending to* the Holy Land by force. For Jews already present in the Holy Land, no prohibition applies.[16]

We would like to conclude with one additional point. The Midrash teaches that the purpose of the Oaths is to maintain the integrity of Israel's exilic status: The Jews are adjured not to "press the end" by means of force, whereas Gentiles are adjured not to overly oppress the Jews, which would also force a premature redemption (*Song of Songs Rabba* 2:20).

Addressing the injunction against the excessive oppression of the Jews, the term *overly* can only be defined by first defining a standard

---

14. Notable examples are Rabbi Meir Simcha of Dvinsk (*Or Sameach*) and Rabbi Avraham Bornsztain (*Avnei Nezer*).

15. See above, note 47.

16. Dr. Chaim Zimmerman, *Torah and Existence* (Jerusalem-New York: 1986), pp. 67–75. Rabbi Zimmerman thus defends the military actions of the original Zionists, who only combated the indigenous Arabs after a broad Jewish settlement had been established. Rabbi Zimmerman bases his theory on the wording of the Talmud, which asserts that Israel was adjured not to *ascend*, an expression that implies entry into the Land of Israel from without. Additionally, he quotes an explicit Midrash (*Song of Songs Rabba* 2:2) that refers to "ascending the wall from the Diaspora," which confirms that the proscription is limited to advancing by force from outside the Holy Land.

for what is *normal*. Using history as the benchmark for "normal" oppression of the Jews in their exilic condition, the Holocaust, as Rabbi Kalonymous Kalman Shapiro (the Piaseczna Rebbe and Rabbi of the Warsaw Ghetto) noted, undoubtedly constituted an instance of their being *overly* oppressed.[17]

Assuming the accuracy of this analysis, it is remarkable that the "violation" of the Oaths at the hands of the Gentiles was followed almost immediately by a second "violation" on the part of the Jews. It seems as if the grotesque killings of the Holocaust precipitated a new era, in which the Oaths no longer bound the Jewish nation to their traditional course of exilic passivity, permitting the establishment of a Jewish autonomy for the first time in more than two thousand years.[18]

Even dedicated adversaries of Zionism appreciated that the establishment of the State of Israel involved the hand of God. Rabbi Yitzchak Zev HaLevi Soloveichik, for instance, who was among the staunchest

---

17. In his weekly sermons, Rabbi Shapiro had initially placed the atrocities of the Germans in the context of previous anti-Semitic assaults on the Jewish nation. Later, however, after the commencement of the Great Deportation in 1942, he acknowledged that there was no historical precedent for what was happening: "Only persecutions such as those inflicted until the end of 5702 [fall 1941] had earlier precedent. The grotesque persecutions, however, and the terrible, grotesque deaths that the unnatural wicked murderers created for us, the House of Israel, since the end of 5702 – according to my knowledge of the word of our sages of blessed memory and the histories of the Jews in general, there has never been anything like this. May God have mercy upon us and rescue us from their hands in the blink of an eye" (Henry Abramson, "Deciphering the Ancestral Paradigm: A Hasidic Court in the Warsaw Ghetto," unpublished paper, United States Holocaust Memorial Museum Symposium: *The Ghettos of the Holocaust, New Research and Perspectives on Definition, Daily Life, and Survival.* Cited in Kassow, *Who Will Write our History*, p. 461).

18. See *Shulchan Aruch, Yoreh De'ah* 236:6, concerning two people who swore oaths to one another; the *Shulchan Aruch* rules that if one person transgresses his oath, the other is automatically absolved of his corresponding oath. This ruling has been cited by a number of authorities in explaining why the Three Oaths no longer apply: See Rabbi Shalom Adler, *Rav Shalom* (Munkacs 5662), p. 140; Rabbi Shlomo Kluger of Brodi, *Maaseh Yedei Yotzer.*

opponents of Zionism, stated that the UN vote in favor of partition was "a smile from Heaven; but the [secular] leaders of the State ruined it."[19]

To what degree the Zionists ruined the Divine smile is debatable. As far as the Oaths are concerned, however, the luxury of hindsight induces a thought no less attractive than it is provable: Perhaps the time of "until it is desired," which releases Israel from their Oaths, had finally come.

---

19. Quoted in Rabbi Shlomo Wolbe, *Bein Sheshet LeAsor* (*Olam HaYedidut*), p. 146.